Moral Psychology

This is the first philosophy textbook in moral psychology, introducing students to a range of philosophical topics and debates such as What is moral motivation? Do reasons for action always depend on desires? Is emotion or reason at the heart of moral judgment? Under what conditions are people morally responsible? Are there self-interested reasons for people to be moral? *Moral Psychology: A Contemporary Introduction* presents research by philosophers and psychologists on these topics, and addresses the overarching question of how empirical research is (or is not) relevant to philosophical inquiry.

Valerie Tiberius is Professor of Philosophy at the University of Minnesota.

Routledge Contemporary Introductions to Philosophy
Series editor: Paul K Moser, Loyola University of Chicago

This innovative, well-structured series is for students who have already done an introductory course in philosophy. Each book introduces a core general subject in contemporary philosophy and offers students an accessible but substantial transition from introductory to higher-level college work in that subject. The series is accessible to non-specialists and each book clearly motivates and expounds the problems and positions introduced. An orientating chapter briefly introduces its topic and reminds readers of any crucial material they need to have retained from a typical introductory course. Considerable attention is given to explaining the central philosophical problems of a subject and the main competing solutions and arguments for those solutions. The primary aim is to educate students in the main problems, positions and arguments of contemporary philosophy rather than to convince students of a single position.

Ancient Philosophy
Christopher Shields

Classical Modern Philosophy
Jeffrey Tlumak

Continental Philosophy
Andrew Cutrofello

Epistemology
3rd Edition
Robert Audi

Ethics
2nd Edition
Harry J. Gensler

Metaphysics
3rd Edition
Michael J. Loux

Moral Psychology
Valerie Tiberius

Philosophy of Art
Noël Carroll

Philosophy of Biology
Alex Rosenberg and Daniel W. McShea

Philosophy of Economics
Julian Reiss

Philosophy of Language
2nd Edition
Willam G. Lycan

Philosophy of Mathematics
2nd Edition
James Robert Brown

Philosophy of Mind
3rd Edition
John Heil

Philosophy of Perception
William Fish

Philosophy of Psychology
José Luis Bermudez

Philosophy of Religion
Keith E. Yandell

Philosophy of Science
3rd Edition
Alex Rosenberg

Philosophy of Social Science
Mark Risjord

Social and Political Philosophy
John Christman

Forthcoming:

Free Will
Michael McKenna

Metaethics
Mark van Roojen

Philosophy of Literature
John Gibson

Moral Psychology

A Contemporary Introduction

Valerie Tiberius

 Routledge
Taylor & Francis Group

NEW YORK AND LONDON

First published 2015
by Routledge
711 Third Avenue, New York, NY 10017

and by Routledge
2 Park Square, Milton Park, Abingdon, Oxon, OX14 4RN

Routledge is an imprint of the Taylor & Francis Group, an informa business

Library of Congress Cataloging-in-Publication Data
CIP data applied for

ISBN: 978-0-415-52968-6 (hbk)
ISBN: 978-0-415-52969-3 (pbk)
ISBN: 978-0-203-11756-9 (ebk)

Typeset in Garamond Pro and (
by Apex CoVantage, LLC

MIX
Paper from responsible sources
FSC
www.fsc.org FSC® C013604

Printed and bound by CPI Group (UK) Ltd, Croydon, CR0 4YY

Contents

Preface

When I was asked to write a textbook on moral psychology that included both traditional philosophical and new interdisciplinary approaches, I was excited, but also daunted. The field seems to me one of the most interesting and valuable areas of research in philosophy and the social sciences today, but it is also large and growing. No introduction could cover all the interesting work in one discipline, never mind more than one. Moreover, practitioners of philosophical and interdisciplinary moral psychology do not have the same conception of what the subject matter of moral psychology is, which makes it tricky to bring the two into conversation with each other. I think it is important, therefore, that the subtitle of the book is "A Contemporary Introduction." It is just that: *an* introduction, not *the* introduction. It is, furthermore, an opinionated introduction, like many of the other volumes in the Routledge Contemporary Introductions to Philosophy series. The way I have chosen to introduce the subject reflects my own interests and philosophical views. This would not, perhaps, be appropriate for a book that is a basic introduction, but I think it is the right approach for a book such as this one that is designed for advanced undergraduates, beginning graduate students and other academics with an interest in philosophy. A basic introduction that simply describes arguments without engaging in them would bore this intended audience.

One way in which the text reflects my own interests is that it includes a fair amount of meta-ethics. In part, this is because I think that psychological research has potentially important implications for meta-ethics. (I'm certainly not alone in this—some of the best known "new moral psychologists" work at the boundary between meta-ethics and empirical psychology.) I also wanted to write a textbook for an upper-level contemporary ethics course, where the philosophy instructor is interested in teaching moral psychology but for whom there doesn't yet exist an appropriate "moral psychology" course. I think this book is well suited for that purpose.

Another feature of the book is that is that it covers a wide range of topics and has therefore at times prioritized breadth over depth. In part, I made this choice because I want the book to be useful to people with a range of needs and interests. It seemed to me that since there is no other philosophy textbook on moral psychology at the moment, and since many philosophy departments do not offer a specialized moral psychology course, it makes sense to try to give an overview of the field that shows how it's connected to other topics in moral philosophy. I've also chosen to include some topics because of the way they catch people's attention (in the classroom and in the media), even where these topics might not be the ones analytic philosophers would deem most important. I think it's important to cover these topics and to encourage clear thinking about them, so that we don't get carried away by exaggerated pronouncements about what we know now about moral psychology. There is another motivation for breadth here, too, which is that when I learn about a new field I find the most difficult thing to do is to get "the big picture." To my mind, putting together a big picture is a useful task that can be performed by a textbook. My hope is that readers who want to delve into the details of a particular debate will find the big picture painted here to be good preparation for doing so. The lists of suggested readings at the ends of the chapters, and the cited works within the text, are a good place to start.

Though it is an opinionated introduction, I have tried to explain views with which I disagree carefully and charitably, and to consider how people with different views might take the debate forward. In my view, the virtue of charity in philosophical interpretation and argument is a crucial one that is under-rewarded in undergraduate philosophy (and elsewhere). The questions considered in this book are complex and difficult; it isn't going to be easy to answer them, and we are likely to do a better job if we are open to various perspectives and sources of information. I hope I have succeeded well enough in demonstrating open-mindedness and charitable interpretation that the textbook can serve as an example of these virtues, but, if not, then I hope students will be inspired by the magnitude of the issues to do better.

Many people helped me at various stages of writing this textbook. I would like to thank Michael Bishop, Fiery Cushman, Colin DeYoung, John Martin Fischer, Jesse Graham, Josh Greene, Claire Horisk, Eranda Jayawickreme, Victor Kumar, Joshua Knobe, Bob Kruger, Jimmy Lenman, Ron Mallon, Christian Miller, Eddy Nahmias, Shaun Nichols, Alexandra Plakias, Jesse Prinz, Connie Rosati, Adina Roskies, Chandra Sripada, Nina Strominger, Simine Vazire, Walter Sinnott-Armstrong, Stephen Stich, Karen Stohr, Liane Young, the Department of Philosophy at the University of Buffalo, the Moral Psychology Research Group and my Twin Cities Reading Group (Melanie Bowman, Jim Dawes, Michael Furstein, Daniel Groll, Stephanie Hake, Melissa Koenig and Jason Marsh). I am very grateful to the National Endowment for the Humanities for a fellowship that supported me while I worked on this project. Thanks also to my editor, Andy Beck, in particular for having the idea that it was time for a textbook like this.

John Doris deserves special thanks. Had he not invited and encouraged me to join the Moral Psychology Research Group, I would not have been able to write this book and would not have met many of the inspiring researchers whose work is discussed here. I am especially grateful to Tim Schroeder for his painstaking and constructive comments on the first draft of the manuscript. Finally, as with all of my philosophical work, writing this book would not have been possible without the unflagging emotional and intellectual support of my husband, J. D. Walker.

Part I

Moral Psychology and Moral Philosophy

1 What Is Moral Psychology?

- **Distinguishing the Questions**
- **Distinguishing Psychological States**
- **Structure and Aims of the Book**
- **Summary**
- **Study Questions**
- **Notes**
- **Further Readings**

Think about the last time you did a good thing. Maybe you helped an elderly person across the street, helped a friend move, or took in a stray cat. What made you do it? Did you do it because you wanted to or because you thought you should? Are you just a good person? Did you think about a duty to help those in need? Were you thinking that you might want to ask your friend to help you move some day? Did the sad look on the cat's little face pull on your heart strings? Now think about the last time you did something bad. Perhaps you were in a hurry so you pretended not to hear the elderly person ask for your help, or you broke your promise to help your friend move, or you yelled at the poor cat to get out of your way. Why did you do that? Are you just selfish? Were you overwhelmed by anger? These are basic questions about moral psychology. They are questions about the psychological aspects of moral (or not so moral) actions. Questions about why we sometimes do the right thing quickly lead to other questions in moral psychology: Is there a difference between doing something good and acting morally? Does it matter if we do something good but for the wrong reasons? Are only certain kinds of good deeds really praiseworthy? If so, which ones—actions done from duty, from virtue, or from sympathy? Are we really responsible for what we do? In the most general terms, moral psychology is the study of the psychological aspects of morality.

There are some ways of answering these questions that call on the expertise of scientists. If we want to know what was going on in your brain or your body when you yelled at the cat, we should ask a neuroscientist or a psychologist, not a philosopher. But there other ways of understanding these questions that explain philosophers' interest in them. Some of these questions involve concepts that philosophers study. For example, the question "Did you do it because you wanted to or because you think you should?" presupposes that *wanting* is different from *thinking you should*, and not all philosophers accept that this is true. And some of these questions are really not empirical questions at all. The question of whether only certain forms of moral motivation are good or praiseworthy is really a moral question, not an empirical one. Moreover, how these questions are answered has important implications for what philosophers say about other topics in moral philosophy.

In moral philosophy there are normative questions, which are questions about what ought to be or what is good (such as the question of whether you only get any moral credit for what you do if you do it out of duty). There are conceptual or theoretical questions about what it makes the most sense to say about a given concept (such as the concept GOOD in the previous sentence[1]). And there are empirical questions about how to accurately describe the world that can be investigated by science, such as the question of what circumstances make people more likely to help strangers.[2] These questions are often all mixed up together. For example, consider this question: "Are people motivated to do what they morally ought to do?" To answer this question we need to know what it means to say that a person *ought* to do something (a conceptual or theoretical question). Once we know this, we also need to know something about what people ought to do (a normative question) in order to investigate what motivations people have to do it (an empirical question). From this example we can see that moral psychology and moral philosophy are profoundly intertwined.

Before we move on, it will be useful to clear up something about the terminology we will be using. In philosophy, since moral psychology has been recognized as a subfield (in the last sixty years or so), moral psychology has not been thought to include empirical questions and methods. The way philosophers have thought about what moral psychology is has focused on normative and conceptual questions and left the empirical questions for psychologists. I think this is unfortunate (and, fortunately, now changing), in part because these three types of questions (normative, conceptual/theoretical and empirical) are so intertwined that it is very difficult to make progress on one set without making some assumptions about another. The way I understand *moral psychology* in this book does not exclude empirical questions and methods. Indeed, a major theme of the book will be to explore how these three kinds of questions are related and how answering one can help answer another. Of course, this is a book written by a philosopher primarily for students of philosophy, so our focus will be on moral psychology as it relates to philosophical questions and research.

Distinguishing the Questions

I said above that research in moral psychology is relevant to other parts of moral philosophy. To understand this, it will help to have a better sense of what moral philosophy is. Briefly, moral philosophy is the study of morality, but this isn't very helpful! There are many different kinds of questions about morality we could ask. One question is about what is or is not moral (right, wrong, good, bad, and so on). This is a normative question, which means that it is a question about what ought to be as opposed to what is. If you want to know whether it is morally wrong to eat animals, for example, you are not asking whether most people *think* it's right; you are asking whether it *is* right. Many philosophers would put the point in terms of reasons, like so: normative questions are questions about what we have reason to do, and questions about what's morally right are questions about what we have moral reason to do.

A quick detour on the word *reason* is needed here, since this is a word we're going to see a lot of in this book. A reason is a consideration in favor of doing or believing something. In this book, almost all of the discussion of reasons is about *practical reasons*, or reasons for action, as opposed to *theoretical reasons*, or reasons to believe. (If I mean to refer to theoretical reasons, I'll say so explicitly.) Practical reasons are considerations in favor of doing something no matter what else philosophers want to say about them, but (as we'll see) philosophers have many different views about what makes a consideration a reason. It's worth mentioning one possible source of confusion here, which is that *reason* is also used to refer to our rational capacities or our *ability to reason*. To help avoid confusion, I will refer to the capacity as *reasoning* or sometimes as *Reason* with a capital "R." When I use the word *reason* I will be talking about a consideration in favor of an action (or, in the case of motivating reasons, as we'll see, a factor that explains an action). Reasons and reasoning are related, insofar as we use our reasoning capacity to figure out what our reasons are.

Moral philosophers interested in normative questions (typically) aim to develop theories that explain which actions are morally right and wrong. In other words, they aim to develop theories that systematize and explain our moral reasons. They proceed by reflecting carefully on the implications of various possible principles or positions and refining their ideas until they arrive at a comprehensive and useful theory. Each moral theory has a different position on what kinds of considerations count as moral reasons and why. For example, questions about whether we have a moral reason not to eat animals or whether we have a moral reason always to tell the truth can be answered in a variety of ways. Utilitarians think that to answer such questions we should appeal to facts about pleasure and pain. Kantians think that we should appeal to considerations about rationality and respect. Virtue ethicists think we should appeal to the notion of human flourishing and the virtues that are necessary for it.

Another type of question we might ask is about the status of the answers to our moral questions and of our moral theories themselves. Let's say someone tells you, "It's wrong to eat animals because animals are sentient beings." Is this a factual statement, like the statement "Animals feel pain"? Or is it an expression of an emotion, like "Grrr! Don't eat animals!" Are moral statements such as "It's wrong to eat animals" the kinds of things that can be true or false? Are moral theories objective and universal? Such questions about meaning, truth conditions and objectivity are *metaethical* questions. These metaethical questions are often thought to be conceptual. In the last century of analytic philosophy, conceptual analysis dominated the field and many analytic philosophers believed that philosophy is just the analysis of concepts. Typically, conceptual analysis proceeded by suggesting necessary and sufficient conditions for the application of a concept until a definition was reached that covered all the intuitive cases. Conceptual analysis has come under some fire recently. The analysis of concepts from the armchair (that is, without any empirical investigation) risks producing analyses that are idiosyncratic. Philosophers in their offices might not use concepts (such as OUGHT) in just the same way that everyone else does. If our goal is to characterize the concept as it is used by people in general, then the armchair method might not be a good one. Fortunately, the grip of the idea that "pure" conceptual analysis is all there is to philosophy has loosened recently. Now philosophers recognize that other methods and approaches are legitimate and can work together. Still, philosophers do have a special contribution to make when it comes to understanding concepts, because we are trained to think analytically and to clarify important distinctions between different concepts.

The view I will take in this book is that what I will call "theoretical analysis" is an important philosophical method. Theoretical analysis might employ standard philosophical methods like conceptual analysis, counterexampling and thought experiments, but it also includes attention to larger theoretical goals and to what we know from science. We can think of this method as the method of figuring out what makes the most sense to say about some complex topic (such as virtue, responsibility or happiness) given the relevant background information, the kinds of judgments we make about it and how it is different from other things. The method of theoretical analysis is useful for answering normative and conceptual questions such as the ones that come up in ethics and metaethics.

Notice that this kind of theoretical thinking is not only useful for philosophers. In psychology, *construct validity* refers to the extent to which the way you have operationalized something so that you can measure it actually measures the very thing that you're interested in, given the theory that you start with. For example, let's say you're a psychologist who wants to know whether rich people are happier than poor people. First, you need something you can measure. You devise a scale with some questions to ask people. To keep things simple, let's imagine that your scale just has one question: "How happy are you?" Then you get a random sample of people from the population, find out about their wealth, ask them your question, correlate the two variables—and voila! Now you know! Or do you? The measure you have used has some serious construct validity problems. When we want to know how happy people are, do we really just want to know how they would answer this question? Probably not. We might want to know whether rich people are better off than poor people in some other way than just how they feel. (Do they get more of what they want? Do their lives have more rewarding or fulfilling experiences?). Or, even if we are just interested in how they feel, we might think that people's self-reports do not track how they actually feel very accurately. Before a psychologist does her research, she needs to ask what she is really interested in: how people say they feel, how people really feel, or something else altogether? In other words, she needs to define her concepts carefully before she moves on to empirical (scientific) investigation.

Now that we have distinguished normative and metaethical questions and the methods that are designed to answer them, we can ask about the third category: empirical (or scientific) questions and methods. Do empirical methods and findings answer these normative or metaethical questions? When it comes to normative questions, the answer is no, at least not directly.[3] Normative questions are questions about what ought to be, not questions about what people think or feel is the case. We could discover everything there is to discover about the psychology of our moral judgments about animal pain—what happens in the brain when we witness cruelty to animals; what sentiments, desires or beliefs are involved in making the judgment that people ought not to eat meat; and so on—and we would not have discovered whether it is actually wrong to eat animals. But this does not mean that psychology is irrelevant to questions about what we have reason to do. How it might be indirectly relevant is a theme that will be explored throughout this book. For now, consider this example: Many moral philosophers hold the principle "ought implies can," which means that it can't be true that you *ought* to do something if you're completely unable to do it. If this is right, then our psychologies do at least constrain what we ought to do. For instance, if "ought implies can" and if we are, in fact, only capable of acting for the sake of our own selfish interests, then it cannot be the case that we ought to act altruistically as some moral theories demand (more about this in Chapter 3).

Is empirical psychology relevant to metaethical questions? The answer here depends on what metaethical question is being asked. First, consider the question of whether the "ought implies can" principle is true. This is a question about the concept OUGHT, and it cannot be answered by the methods of science alone. The question about whether moral reasons necessarily motivate people, which we will consider in Chapter 4, is also a conceptual question. But other questions are mixed. For a second example, consider the question of whether moral reasons apply to everyone universally. This might be a mixed question, depending on what view you have about what moral reasons are. If you think that as a matter of the concept, moral reasons have to motivate people, then whether they apply to everyone depends on what motivations people actually have, which is an empirical matter. If, on the other hand, you think that moral reasons are not necessarily motivating, then you will probably think that the question of whether they apply to everyone universally is also a conceptual or theoretical question. Third, some metaethical questions might just be empirical questions about our psychology, even though this hasn't been acknowledged. For example, the question about the role of emotions in moral motivation—do emotions help or hinder us in acting morally?—is an empirical question that philosophers have discussed for millennia (though we do have to make some normative assumptions in order to answer it).

What I've said is that there are three kinds of questions that are involved in moral philosophy: normative, conceptual (or theoretical) and scientific (or narrowly empirical). These questions are often closely related in such a way that you must presuppose an answer to one in order to answer another, and you must answer more than one type in order to answer the big questions in ethics and metaethics. Of course, I've made things considerably more complicated than they were in the opening paragraph. We began by asking "Why do we act morally?" and "Why do we sometimes fail to act morally?" Let's return to one of these basic questions to see where we are. Why did you take in that stray cat? Notice that in taking this to be a question about moral action, we are assuming that taking in the stray cat was a morally good thing to do. This is a normative assumption that can be supported by a normative theory. Once that assumption is granted, we can propose some hypotheses for investigation about why you did it. Here are four:

- You wanted to.
- You felt sorry for the cat.
- You are a good person.
- You made the judgment that you have a duty to help suffering creatures when you can.

Thinking that these are four *competing* explanations assumes that these explanations are incompatible with each other. For example, it assumes that if you did it because you wanted to, then you did not do it because you felt sorry for the cat. It assumes that judgments about our moral duties are distinct from desires and feelings. It assumes that being a good person is different from wanting to help. I hope reading this introduction will have encouraged a tiny bit of skepticism about these assumptions (and that reading the entire book will encourage more). The idea that these explanations are mutually incompatible depends on particular theoretical views about what desires, feelings, virtues and judgments are like. Understanding the explanation of moral action, then, requires engaging with normative, conceptual and empirical questions, and using all the methods at our disposal.

Distinguishing Psychological States

As we've just seen, distinguishing different hypotheses about what motivates people to act morally requires distinguishing different psychological states. In the four bullet points above, I have assumed that we can distinguish between desires, emotions (e.g., pity), character traits and judgments or beliefs. It is worth saying a little something about how we do this.

Philosophers and psychologists have often divided mental states (or mental systems) into affective, conative and cognitive states or systems. Very roughly, affective mental states are feelings (e.g., emotions and moods), conative mental states are drives that propel us to action (e.g., goals and desires) and cognitive mental states are thoughts (e.g., beliefs, understanding and reasoning). Affective states tend to have associated bodily experiences and cognitive states tend to be ones over which we have more control, but these generalizations are not true of every state that counts as affective or cognitive. Moreover, affect, conation and cognition work together in many ways: how we feel can influence what we think and what our goals are, and what we plan to do can influence how we feel. In this book, I will often use this terminology to refer to the kinds of states just listed because it is a convenient way to refer to a general type of mental state, but it should be noted that we do not have exact definitions for these three kinds of states and the distinctions may not carve nature at its joints. This is okay for our purposes. What we need to be able to do is distinguish particular mental states (particular affective responses or cognitive processes) from one another; except for convenience, the labels *affective, conative* and *cognitive* are not that important.

You might think that the way to distinguish different kinds of mental states is by their contents. All of the mental states discussed in the previous paragraph have intentional content, that is, they are about or directed at something.[4] This is an important feature of the mental states we will be discussing in this book, and we should keep in mind that any theory about what these states are must explain this feature. But content, or "about-ness," is not what distinguishes affect (emotions) from cognition (beliefs), because both kinds of mental states are about something. This is easy to see with beliefs: the belief that there is a spider in the sink is about that spider. It is also true of many affective states. Emotions like fear are not just raw experiences like a tingle or an itch; they also reach out from the mind to represent something about the world (in the case of fear, a danger). The belief that the spider is in the sink is different from the fear of the spider, though they are both directed at (or about) the same spider.

The best way for us to distinguish between different psychological states (like emotions and beliefs) is in terms of their functions. To do this, we do not have to understand exactly how these states can represent aspects of the world (a profound and difficult question in the philosophy of mind and language). It is enough for us to know that mental states can be about the same thing yet be distinct because of the role they play in our mental economies. According to this way of thinking, known as functionalism in the philosophy of mind, a desire is a desire, a belief is a belief, and an emotion is an emotion because of the role each of these states plays in the mental system to which they belong. For example, let's say you're experiencing an attitude toward coffee. What makes this attitude a desire? Well, if the attitude that you have causes you to head for a Starbucks and if it goes away after you've had your cappuccino, then it's a desire. On the other hand, if the attitude was caused by your reading an article about the caffeine content of coffee and disposes you to report to your friend that Starbucks's coffee has more caffeine than other brands, then it's a belief. Emotions such as fear seem to be identified in part by how they feel, but also by their role in alerting us to features of our environment (danger, in the case of fear) and disposing us to respond in an appropriate way (fleeing or fighting).

Distinguishing mental states by their functions is a useful way for us to think about mental states for two reasons. First, it gives us a way of understanding the ordinary psychological concepts that are at issue in moral psychology. Many of the questions in moral psychology are questions about these ordinary psychological concepts: Are people motivated by the emotion of sympathy or the desire for their own pleasure? Is moral judgment a kind of belief or an emotional response? Does happiness consist in getting what we want? Distinguishing mental states on the basis of their function allows us to use the same ordinary concepts we use in normal conversations about our mental lives, while leaving a lot of room for a variety of views one might have about the physical structures that underlie mental states. We do not have to know exactly how things work (biologically or neurologically) to be able to talk about what makes a belief different from a desire.

Second, this way of defining mental states comports with the way many psychologists understand the mental states that they study. Psychologists who study the relationship between emotions and moral judgment, for example, must start with some idea about what an emotion is so that they can invoke it and see its effects. Consider an experiment in which half the participants are put into disgusting surroundings, the other half are in clean surroundings, and everyone is asked some questions about a scenario. The experiment showed that people who are experiencing disgust tend to make harsher moral judgments. We will talk about this experiment in more detail in Chapter 5; the point that's important for us now is that the psychologists conducting the study had to have a conception of disgust and a conception of moral judgment to work with at the outset, and functionalism helps with this. Disgust is the emotion, induced by dirt, germs and old food, that makes us wrinkle our noses and shun the offending objects. Moral judgments are attitudes about actions that have to do with our treatment of other people; they incline us to make public declarations, and negative moral judgments tend to give rise to feelings of indignation or guilt. To be clear, these are not definitions of disgust and moral judgment. I am merely suggesting some rough and ready ways of picking out these two states. My point is that distinguishing different mental states from each other based on their functional relationships to other mental states, behavior and features of the world is compatible with how psychologists who make use of folk psychological concepts in their research proceed.

Structure and Aims of the Book

"What is moral action?," "Why do we act morally?" and "Why do we sometimes fail?" are deceptively simple questions. Indeed, one of the main aims of this book is to show you how complex these questions really are, and how much trying to answer them requires different methods of investigation and charitable interpretation of others' views. Philosophers have not always acknowledged that empirical research is relevant to their questions, and psychologists have not always acknowledged that normative and conceptual research is relevant to theirs. This is beginning to change and the field of moral psychology is becoming more interdisciplinary and collaborative, but we are in the early days of this transformation. Another aim of the book, then, is to illustrate the potential benefits of acknowledging the mutual importance of the theoretical and empirical methods of inquiry. In the next chapter (Chapter 2), I'll say more about the difference between psychology and philosophy and how they both figure into the study of moral psychology. Finally, the book aims to introduce key topics in moral psychology as practiced by philosophers for anyone who wants to understand what philosophers have said about these topics.

Part II of the book covers some basic answers to our complex questions about moral action. We begin in Chapter 3 with a discussion of the various views about what moral action is. Sometimes (frequently in empirical research) it is assumed that moral action is "pro-social" action, that is, that moral action is the same as action with good consequences for other creatures. But this assumption eliminates many philosophical views from the debate at the outset, so we will not start this way. Instead, we will start with a full deck of philosophical positions to explore in subsequent chapters. We will also consider a major challenge to many of these views: psychological egoism. According to many traditional ideas about morality, motivation does not count as moral at all if it is self-interested. If all action is motivated purely by self-interest, as psychological egoism has it, then these traditional moral theories imply that moral motivation is psychologically impossible for us. There just wouldn't be any moral motivation according to Kant or Aristotle, for example, if psychological egoism were true.

Chapter 4 focuses on the thought that our desires are what explain why we sometimes act well and sometimes act badly. Here I will introduce the Humean Theory of Motivation (according to which desire is necessary for motivation and no belief can motivate us to do anything by itself) and the Humean Theory of Reasons (according to which having a desire to do something is a necessary condition for having a reason to do it). We will consider what kinds of questions these theories are supposed to answer and what the implications of these theories are for what moral reasons we have.

Part III considers three views about how moral motivation might be something special and distinctive. Chapters 5 and 6 consider the possibility that moral judgments themselves are motivating, that is, that in judging something to be wrong we are *thereby* motivated to avoid doing it. This view takes two forms. In one, moral judgments are essentially emotional and, since emotions motivate us, making a moral judgment motivates us by itself. We consider this view in Chapter 5 on emotion and moral judgment. This theory is called sentimentalism and, if it is true, then one traditional view about the emotions must be wrong. Historically, some philosophers have thought that the reason we act badly is because we are drawn away from the good and rational course of action by unruly and disruptive emotions. As we'll see in this chapter, however, once we understand what emotions are and what their role is in morality, we can't take seriously the blanket condemnation of emotions.

The other form of the view that moral judgments are themselves motivating takes moral judgments to be rational judgments that motivate us to act morally insofar as we are rational beings. We consider this type of rationalism in Chapter 6. In the discussion of moral judgment in this chapter we will raise some problems for the idea that moral judgment is based entirely on sentiment, and we will consider what is at stake in the debate about whether moral judgments are based on sentiments or Reason.

Chapter 7 considers the idea that we act well or badly depending on whether we are virtuous or vicious people. Here we will consider the debate about whether people actually have virtues and vices in the way that would be necessary to explain our behavior. As we'll see, the literature on virtues provides an excellent opportunity to look at the way in which empirical evidence is relevant to the assumptions made by moral philosophers.

Why people do what they do is relevant to another important set of questions in moral psychology. These are questions about praise, blame and responsibility, the focus of Part IV. In Chapter 8, we will consider what is distinctive about responsible agency: What is it about certain kinds of beings that makes it appropriate to hold them responsible for some of their actions? After a brief overview of the methodology that is used in debates about free will and responsibility, we consider two basic positions. Some theories say that we are responsible to the degree to which our actions resulted from our "real self"—the self we identify with, the one we want to be. According to this way of thinking, we are not responsible when our actions are caused by external forces or by parts of us that we disavow. According to other theories, people are responsible for their actions to the extent that they are responsive to the reasons that there are for acting one way or another. Both of these theories are compatibilist theories, which means that they hold that people could be responsible even if determinism were true.

Chapter 9 takes a step back and considers the debate about determinism and moral responsibility more broadly. We survey various arguments against compatibilism and see how compatibilists have responded to these challenges.

This will lead us to investigate the methodology behind the free will debate in more detail and to ask what experimental philosophy has contributed to it. We will also consider the claim that some neuroscientists have made: that they have shown there is no free will by investigating the brain.

In the final section of the book, Part V, we will take an ever broader point of view and consider some of the implications of research in moral psychology for three big questions in moral philosophy. Chapter 10 considers the question "Why be moral?" Here we'll survey theories of well-being and look at the evidence for thinking that acting morally is actually good for the person who does it. Chapter 11 takes up the epistemological question "How do we know what's morally right?" Typically, moral philosophers have used a method called reflective equilibrium, which justifies beliefs about morality by bringing our intuitions about particular cases and our principles into a coherent whole. Research that shows that our intuitions about cases are biased, or that "we" don't have unified intuitions, seems to cause some problems for this methodology. Finally, Chapter 12 explores answers to the question "Can you get an ought from an is?" In this chapter we'll draw on the preceding chapters to illustrate the various ways in which the descriptive (is) and the normative (ought) are related.

Summary

- Moral psychology is the study of the psychological aspects of morality. The two most basic questions of moral psychology are, Why do we act morally? and Why do we sometimes fail? Answering these questions requires that we first figure out what counts as moral motivation for action. Another central question is, Under what conditions are we morally responsible for our actions?
- Moral philosophy in the broadest sense includes moral psychology, normative ethics and metaethics.
- There are three different types of questions in moral philosophy: normative, conceptual/theoretical and scientific/empirical.
- Theoretical analysis is particularly useful for answering normative and conceptual questions. It is a method of careful reflection that aims to make sense of some concept in light of how it is used, what we use it for and what other distinct concepts are available.
- Scientific methods employed mainly by psychologists are useful for answering (narrowly) empirical questions. Scientific methods must begin by defining the object of study, which means that theoretical methods are needed in psychology too. In psychology when an operationalized definition matches the theoretical construct, the definition has *construct validity*.
- Often, these different kinds of questions are related such that you can't answer one without assuming some answers to the others.

Study Questions

1. As you begin reading this book, what questions about the psychological aspects of morality would you like to have answered? What "psychological aspects of morality" do you think are particularly important or interesting?
2. If you wanted to figure out whether a political candidate is a good person, how would you go about it? What kinds of questions would you need to ask? Would these questions be normative, conceptual or empirical—or some combination?
3. If you wanted to conduct a study of moral behavior with the ultimate goal of producing more of it in your community, how would you start?

Notes

1. It's a philosophical convention to use small caps when you want to talk about a concept, rather than the thing to which the concept refers. I'll follow that convention.
2. For many philosophers, all questions are ultimately empirical in some sense. I will use the word *empirical* in a narrower sense that comports with the way philosophers often use it. *Empirical questions* are questions that can be answered by science.
3. There are many different ways in which normative questions may be settled by science *indirectly*. For instance, you might have a conclusive philosophical defense of a metaethical theory according to which normative questions are just empirical questions. I don't mean to rule this out.
4. The term *intentional content* can confuse people, because it sounds like it must have something to do with our conscious intentions. It does not. Your belief that there is a spider in the sink has intentional content—that the spider is in the sink—but this does not mean that you have any intention that is related to this belief (you need not have any intention to kill the spider, photograph the spider, and so on). I will try to remind readers of this possibility of confusion when I use the term.

Further Readings

Anscombe, G. E. M. 1958. "Modern Moral Philosophy." *Philosophy* 33 (124): 1–19.
Doris, J., and the Moral Psychology Research Group, eds. 2010. *The Moral Psychology Handbook*. Oxford University Press.
Nadelhoffer, T., E. Nahmias, and S. Nichols. 2010. *Moral Psychology: Historical and Contemporary Readings*. Wiley-Blackwell.
Sinnott-Armstrong, W. 2008–2014. *Moral Psychology. Vol. 1–4*. MIT Press.
Wallace, R. J. 2005. "Moral Psychology." In *The Oxford Handbook of Contemporary Philosophy*, F. Jackson and M. Smith (eds), 86–114. Oxford University Press.

2 What Are Philosophers Doing Here?

- **Moral Agents or Blobs of Flesh?**
- **Moral Realism and the Challenge from Evolution**
- **Responses to the Challenge**
- **Moral Psychology and Moral Philosophy**
- **Summary**
- **Study Questions**
- **Notes**
- **Further Readings**

Some people, when I told them I was working on a moral psychology text-book, reacted with puzzlement. "Aren't you a philosopher? And you're writing a psychology textbook?" Moral psychology has been a branch of moral philosophy since before psychologists were interested in morality, but this puzzlement raises legitimate questions about the role of philosophy. Philosophers used to do everything, after all, but as science makes progress in a field of inquiry, philosophers tend to hand that field over to the scientists. Aristotle (a philosopher) had a lot to say about biology, but no philosopher today would presume to do biology research unless that philosopher also had scientific training and a lab. Why isn't it the same way with morality? Even if the science of moral psychology isn't quite up to the task yet, why not think that eventually—and probably fairly soon—what used to be moral philosophy will be a field of science that philosophers have no business monkeying around in?

Anyone who read the introduction to this book should see that there's some room for good philosophical thinking even when it comes to doing science, because there are some conceptual questions that need to be answered in order to ask the right questions for empirical investigation. But this doesn't make the subject matter philosophical; it just means that scientists who investigate moral psychology need to think clearly about their concepts, which is true in any endeavor.

The deeper challenge to moral philosophy comes from the idea that the science of moral psychology makes the philosophical questions (particularly the normative ones about values and oughts) irrelevant. The worry is that science by itself answers all of our normative questions in a way that makes moral evaluation and moral deliberation—and hence moral philosophy—pointless. Once we see that there is a science of morality, in other words, we don't need anything else. In my experience teaching moral psychology, I have noticed that a number of people assume this is true (though few of the philosophers and psychologists I know believe it). For those who don't share this assumption, I'll need to explain what the problem is that others think they see. In a nutshell, the thought is this: to take moral questions seriously we must assume that we are autonomous, rational beings living in a world that is infused with moral significance to which we can respond appropriately or not. But science proves that we are not like this, so moral questions cannot be taken seriously and moral philosophy has no point.

This way of thinking about morality and moral philosophy is tempting but, in my view, mistaken. In this chapter I will first explain in moral detail what the worry is and why it seems compelling. I'll then outline some alternative ways of looking at things that clear the way for the rest of this book.

Moral Agents or Blobs of Flesh?

Here's one way of seeing the problem. We can see ourselves as the scientist does: as blobs of flesh acted on by causal laws, responding to other blobs in the environment, all of which are made of the same physical stuff. Or, we can see ourselves from a spiritual, religious or humanistic point of view, according to which we have special powers of reasoning and choice that we use to respond not just to the physical world, but also to the world of value and moral principles. These two ways of thinking about us seem incompatible. If we are just physical blobs in a physical universe, then we are not beings with special powers in a rationally structured universe, and vice versa. For people who are particularly taken with science or who have lost their confidence that we are more than physical blobs in a universe that can only be described in scientific terms, it starts to look like morality must just be about our blobby flesh and our psychology, because there isn't anything else for it to be about.

There are many ways of making this basic concern more specific. One has to do with free will and responsibility, which we will consider only very briefly here since it is a topic that we will discuss in detail in Part IV. Another has to do with evolution and moral realism, and this we'll ponder in more detail in this chapter.

You might think that the scientific perspective on morality makes moral philosophy irrelevant because moral philosophy assumes that we can choose how to behave, that we can decide to act for moral reasons, and that we are responsible for these choices and decisions, while the scientific perspective proves that these assumptions are false. This challenge raises a whole bunch of question about what it means to say that someone freely chose to do something, what moral responsibility is, and whether free choices and responsibility are compatible with causal determinism. We will address these questions in detail later in the book, but for now I'll just point out that even if you think you are entirely determined to do what you do by everything that has come before, this doesn't really get you out of the problem of having to decide what to do. Since you don't know what you are causally determined to do (if you are so determined) and since your mental processing (deliberating, considering various reasons and alternative options) is surely part of the causal stream that produces your actions, it's not clear how believing you are determined really changes things. If we are causally determined to do what we do, then some of us are causally determined to engage in moral philosophy and nothing about determinism *per se* proves that the thoughts we arrive at when we philosophize could not be ones that are part of the causal stream that makes us act. To put the point another way, if you are a causally determined blob of flesh, then you are a causally determined blob of flesh who has been caused to think about what to do, how to live your life, what it is to be a decent person and so on. Being causally determined doesn't get you out of thinking about what you should do.

One might have a more specific worry, though, about moral responsibility and determinism. You might think that if the scientific perspective is correct and we are just blobs of flesh behaving in accordance with the same causal laws that govern rocks and rubber plants, then we aren't really morally responsible for what we do. If anything is responsible, the causal laws are responsible, but this isn't relevant in the context of moral evaluation (we're not going to put the universe on trial for causing Smith to murder Jones). One might worry that moral judgments about who should be blamed or punished, praised or rewarded, make no sense in a deterministic world. People decide what to do, sure, but since their decisions are determined by powers beyond their control, they cannot be held responsible for them. This too is a topic we will cover in much more detail later, and it is important to note that many, many philosophers think moral responsibility is *compatible* with our actions being causally determined. But for now, notice that, even if you think that we can't really hold people morally responsible, this doesn't mean that science answers all of our moral questions. Even if we think people aren't fundamentally responsible, we will still make evaluations and will want to know what the basis is for them. For example, we still need to make decisions about how to respond to people who are destructive and dangerous. This means we have to make evaluations about who is dangerous or harmful, which means that we will have to think about what things are worth protecting from harm. This is moral thinking—and no purely scientific study about the causes of our behavior is going to tell us what is ultimately worth worrying about, whether or not we are fundamentally morally responsible.

Moral Realism and the Challenge from Evolution

A different kind of scientific challenge to moral philosophy arises from thinking about the way in which our capacities for moral judgment, evaluation and sentiment evolved. The basic idea is this: you grow up thinking there are real moral facts, divinely given or somehow woven into the fabric of the universe, and that these real moral facts provide standards for how we should live our lives. But then you read about human evolution, and you realize that we just evolved to think that there are real moral standards for how to live so that we wouldn't kill each other off. The fact that we think there are such moral facts doesn't give us any real reason to believe in them—the whole thing could just be a big evolutionary hoax!

Philosophers have elaborated this basic idea into what have come to be called evolutionary debunking arguments against moral realism.[1] According to one form of this argument, because evolutionary pressures have shaped our moral judgments, we would make the moral judgments that we make even if there weren't any moral facts (Joyce 2006). For example, even if there were no moral fact that it is wrong to steal from your neighbors, we would have evolved to make this judgment because it was adaptive (stealing from your neighbors would have been a good way to get yourself killed). The fact that we would make the judgments that we make whether or not there were facts to make them true means that our judgments don't give us any reason to believe that there are such facts. This is an argument for skepticism; it doesn't prove that there are no moral facts, but it undermines our evidence for believing that there are.

According to a different form of the argument, defended by Sharon Street, the moral realist faces a dilemma. To understand Street's argument, we first need to see what she means by a moral fact. Moral facts (such as the fact that you shouldn't steal someone's wallet) are real, according to Street, if they exist completely independently of our evaluative attitudes.[2] To say that there are real moral facts is to say that there are some truths about how we ought to behave, morally speaking, that do not depend in any way on our wanting people to behave that way, liking that kind of behavior, being angry at people who fail to behave in this way or having any other kind of attitude toward the behavior in question. Street argues that if we think about how evolution has likely shaped what kinds of moral judgments we make, it becomes very difficult to take this kind of moral realism seriously (Street 2006).

Street's argument presents a dilemma for the moral realist. Either the moral realist must say that the evolutionary influences on our moral judgments are irrelevant, that is, that there is no relationship between how we have evolved and what the moral facts are, or he must say that they are related and explain how. Either way, there is trouble for the moral realist. If, on the one hand, the realist says that evolutionary pressures have nothing to do with moral facts whatsoever, then these pressures could just as easily have led us to false conclusions as to true ones, and it starts to seem very likely that most of our moral judgments could just be totally off base. Think of an analogy to tasty food. Evolution seems to have shaped our taste so that we judge food to be tasty when it is high in sugar and fat. This is (probably) because in the environment in which we evolved, high-calorie foods were rare and we needed calories to keep going. We did not evolve to find carrot sticks and bran flakes particularly exciting, because evolution was not responsive to the kind of diet that would keep us alive into our eighties in a fast-food culture; as far as evolution goes, we only need to be healthy enough for long enough to have kids and raise them to the point at which they can have more kids; we do not need to avoid obesity, heart disease, diabetes and arthritis when we're middle aged and older. Assuming most of us do want to avoid these things, and given this evolutionary history, what tastes good to us isn't necessarily what's good for us, and our sense of taste is (often) pretty far off track when it comes to a diet that will let us avoid cancer and heart disease for decades after we've ceased being terribly useful. This is easy to accept (though a pain to live with) in the case of food, but in the case of morals it's much harder to accept the idea that there are truths about morality but most of our moral judgments get them wrong. When it comes to food we can just say, well, there's tasty food and there's healthy food and they don't necessarily overlap! But when it comes to morals, the thought that our convictions about the wrongness of stealing, lying, raping and torturing might just be totally misguided is a very disturbing thought.

If, on the other hand, the realist says that evolutionary pressures *are* related to the moral facts, then he needs to provide an explanation for how this works. The most obvious explanation is that it works the way lots of other kinds of judgments work: we evolved to make the moral judgments that we do because it was evolutionarily advantageous for us to track the truth about morality. Similarly, we evolved to make accurate judgments about whether a vicious beast is charging us because it was adaptive for our judgment to track the truth about charging beasts. Now you'll notice that the realist is putting forward a scientific hypothesis, namely, that the best explanation for why we make the moral judgments we make is that there are free-standing, attitude-independent moral facts that it was adaptive for us to get right in the same way that it was adaptive for us to get it right about lions. Street argues that this is not the most plausible hypothesis out there. In short, there is a much simpler and more obvious explanation available, which is that we evolved to cooperate and to engage in other moral behaviors because it was adaptive to do so and that is why we now think that cooperating is a good thing. The supposition that there are attitude-independent moral facts is entirely superfluous.

Responses to the Challenge

The question for us now is this: How can we take moral questions seriously given the arguments just discussed? There are many ways to respond to these arguments. We'll consider the main avenues of response here.

First of all, moral realists have defended themselves directly against these evolutionary debunking arguments. One line of defense goes this way: Recall Street's dilemma that either there is no relationship between evolutionary influences and mind-independent moral facts (which would make it a miracle if our moral judgments turned out to be correct, given that they are influenced by evolution) or there is a relation and the moral realist must explain what it is. Avoiding the first horn, the realist could point out that the critic (in this case, Street) has not yet provided us with anything like a full explanation of all of our moral judgments that makes reference to natural facts alone (Shafer-Landau 2012). Since this is so, the realist can maintain that moral facts are part of the explanation of why we make the moral judgments that we do, even if evolutionary pressures have also been partial causes.[3] Granted, realists do not have a complete explanation of exactly how this would work, but the debunkers also don't have a complete explanation.

If you don't accept the realist defense, there are still many different options for responding to these evolutionary debunking arguments. Richard Joyce, one defender of the evolutionary debunking argument, does not think we can do away with morality or moral philosophizing. He thinks that morality is a fiction, but a useful fiction, and one we should endeavor to maintain. According to this theory (called *fictionalism*), our moral beliefs are about categorical imperatives that command us to act in certain ways with overriding force and these beliefs are false. But this doesn't mean that there's no point to acting in the ways our moral beliefs lead us. In the long term, acting in accordance with our moral beliefs (say, about the wrongness of stealing, lying and hurting other people) will help us stay out of trouble and in the good graces of the people we care about. Moral beliefs can help us resist the temptation of short-term advantages that have serious long-term costs; they can keep us on track, even if they aren't true. If we accept fictionalism, then, we shouldn't abandon thinking about morality, and we do not need to abandon moral philosophy, which can help us think clearly about which fiction works best and for what purpose.[4]

Fictionalism is an option, then, but it's not the most popular option among philosophers. The more popular strategy of response is to argue that there are moral facts or true moral beliefs, though they are different from what is presupposed by these skeptical arguments.[5] To see how this works, let's consider Street's view. Street's argument leaves the door open for the existence of moral facts that aren't "real" moral facts as she defines them, and this opens the door to several different options. Recall that Street defines a "real moral fact" as one that exists completely independently of our evaluative attitudes. It is "out there," just like gravity or a charging beast. But there are other ways of thinking about moral facts.

You might think that moral facts are just facts about our attitudes. For example, you might think that moral facts are facts about what we would want if we were fully informed and thinking in the right way about things. This would make you a naturalist, who thinks that moral facts are a kind of natural fact, namely, facts about the desires we would have under certain ideal conditions (Railton 1986). These facts would not have any special force to compel us to do anything, they would not be categorically binding on all rational beings, but they do seem to be important facts that most of us would be interested in. Most of us would probably like to be guided in our actions by what we would want if we had better information and were thinking about things rationally. Moreover, this kind of naturalism has an easy explanation for how we evolved to make the moral judgments that we make. Our moral judgments track the moral facts fairly well (though not perfectly) because the moral facts just are facts about what judgments we would make under certain conditions.

An alternative view is that moral facts are facts about what members of the moral community would (or implicitly do) agree to. This position is called contract theory or *contractualism*. The basic idea is that if you were thinking rationally about how best to promote your own long-term self-interest, you would agree to rules that prohibit all the members of your community (including yourself) from interfering with each other (Hobbes 1994/1651; Gauthier 1986). You might also agree to rules that obligate members of your community to help people (including yourself) when they are down and out. The rules that you would agree to if you were thinking rationally are the moral rules that define what it is right and wrong to do. Contract theories that draw on other motivations besides self-interest have also been developed. T. M. Scanlon noticed that in addition to being motivated by self-interest, we are also motivated by a desire to be able to justify ourselves to each other: we care that what we do makes sense to the other members of our community. According to Scanlon, then, the right set of moral principles is the one that nobody has a legitimate complaint against as the basis for regulating how we treat each other (Scanlon 1998: 153). According to this theory, the facts about moral wrongness are facts about what kinds of actions would be disallowed by these acceptable principles, and our moral beliefs are true when the actions we think are wrong really are the ones that would be forbidden by principles that no one could reasonably reject. Contractualists like Scanlon think we *are* motivated to do the right thing, by and large, because we want to act in ways that we can justify to each other; we are motivated to act in accordance with moral principles by our desire to be able to look other people in the eye and know that we aren't just trying to get away with something sneaky. Moreover, contractualism can explain how we might have evolved to make the moral judgments that we do by appeal to the ways in which our interactions with others in our moral communities have shaped our moral thinking.

A third alternative is that moral facts are facts about what follows from a person's evaluative point of view. This position is called *constructivism* (Street 2010). According to this theory, our moral beliefs are true when they accurately reflect what is implied by our basic values. For example, a constructivist could argue that it follows from your valuing friendship that you should not lie to your friends about important subjects; in this case it is your basic evaluative attitude toward friendship that makes lying to your friends wrong. Again, it's not hard to see how this theory could explain how we evolved to make the moral judgments that we do. Basically, the idea is that our moral judgments track what we care about and insofar as we care about things that led to our survival—cooperating with one another, having close relationships with friends and family, and so on—we will have evolved to make moral judgments that contribute to these values. Constructivism explains why morality is important to people and why most of us do try to act in accordance with moral rules: most of us care about one another, about getting along, about living long, happy lives, and these values are the ones moral rules track.

There is much more to say about all of these arguments, but I hope to have said enough to convince you that it isn't *obvious* that science undermines moral philosophy. The skeptical arguments we have surveyed are controversial, and there are many questions one might ask about them. But even if they are correct, they only rule out a few positions. There are many other positions one can take about moral facts that do not make them incompatible with a scientific perspective on the world.

Moral Psychology and Moral Philosophy

There is room, then, for taking moral questions seriously (for moral reflection and philosophizing) even in a scientific worldview. Questions about what we should do, what kind of motivations we should cultivate, how we should treat other people and so on are vital questions for us, whatever science says about us. Furthermore, as I hope the rest of this book will demonstrate more clearly, even as the science of moral psychology advances, it's not clear how science could answer these moral questions by itself. We will return to this topic at the end of the book, but for now it's important to say what bearing all this has on moral psychology.

I believe that moral psychology and moral philosophy shouldn't be pulled too far apart. Of course, experts need to focus on their areas of expertise, and I would not advocate that philosophers and psychologists should do each other's jobs. We can learn from each other without doing each other's jobs, however, and conversation, collaboration and cooperation between the two fields would make for better investigations into the terribly important subject of morality. As I said in the introduction, and as we'll see demonstrated in subsequent chapters, many questions about moral psychology are mixed questions that require making normative or conceptual assumptions before empirical investigation can proceed. Moreover, though psychologists are (usually) careful not to make prescriptive judgments in their research, their work is often taken as the basis for normative moral conclusions by policymakers and journalists. So, too, many philosophical questions require making empirical assumptions in order to answer them. No matter how much philosophers might like to avoid the messy real world, they cannot do so entirely if their moral theories are supposed to apply to real people. Because of this, philosophy will be better if it is informed by an accurate picture of human psychology, and psychology will be better with an informed perspective on the normative domain.

To illustrate this point about the interaction between moral philosophy and moral psychology with an example, consider some recent discoveries in the science of moral psychology that have drawn a lot of attention. Jonathan Haidt's Social Intuitionist Model (SIM) of moral judgment has been an influential view in moral psychology, and we'll talk more about this theory in Chapter 6 (Haidt 2001; Haidt and Bjorkland 2008). For now it is enough to know that according to the SIM, emotion and Reason work together to produce a moral judgment, but intuitions (automatic, emotional responses) have a kind of primacy. (As we'll see, many philosophers agree that emotions or sentiments are of the utmost importance for making moral judgments.) Furthermore, different kinds of moral rules are associated with different moral sentiments. For example, norms of harm (such as "don't hit people") are associated with anger toward people who violate the norm (or with guilt, if the norm violator is oneself); norms of purity or sanctity ("don't do things that are unnatural") are associated with disgust. Thus our various sentiments carve out different domains of moral value.

In recent work on what he calls the "Moral Foundations Theory," Haidt and his colleagues propose that there are at least five moral domains or foundations:

1. **Care/harm:** This foundation is related to our long evolution as mammals with attachment systems and an ability to feel (and dislike) the pain of others. It underlies virtues of kindness, gentleness and nurturance.
2. **Fairness/cheating:** This foundation is related to the evolutionary process of reciprocal altruism. It generates ideas of justice, rights and autonomy.
3. **Loyalty/betrayal:** This foundation is related to our long history as tribal creatures able to form shifting coalitions. It underlies virtues of patriotism and self-sacrifice for the group. It is active anytime people feel that it's "one for all, and all for one."
4. **Authority/subversion:** This foundation was shaped by our long primate history of hierarchical social interactions. It underlies virtues of leadership and followership, including deference to legitimate authority and respect for traditions.
5. **Sanctity/degradation:** This foundation was shaped by the psychology of disgust and contamination. It underlies religious notions of striving to live in an elevated, less carnal, more noble way. It underlies the widespread idea that the body is a temple that can be desecrated by immoral activities and contaminants (an idea not unique to religious traditions).[6]

Studies of these moral domains have shown that different types of people tend to make judgments in different domains. In particular, Haidt and his colleagues argue that political conservatives recognize domains of moral value that political liberals do not tend to recognize (Haidt 2012). Liberals tend to make moral judgments based on norms of harm or respect. Conservatives do make moral judgments based on norms of harm and respect, but they also make moral judgments based on norms of authority or sanctity, which liberals tend not to do.

Though Haidt states that he is describing our morality rather than pre-scribing anything, he does suggest that the descriptive picture he paints will provide grounds for a more positive appraisal of moral frameworks that are different from our own (Haidt 2012). Certainly, some American conserva-tives have taken him to be saying that the fact they use more domains of morality is a good thing about political conservativism. As Haidt himself says in an interview about reactions to his book, "The reviews on the right say: 'Hey, conservatives, you should all read this book because it shows that we have more moral foundations than they do. Nah, nah, nah, nah, nah'" (Goldman 2012). But how do we get from the fact that some people rely on a broader range of sentiments in their moral judgment to the conclusion that such people are *better*? Think of this argument for a moral conclusion:

1. All of Smith's moral judgments are based on harm or respect norms.
2. Jones's moral judgments are based on harm, respect, authority or sanctity norms.
3. Jones relies on more norms to make his moral judgments.
4. Jones makes better moral judgments than Smith. (Alternatively, we should emulate Jones, not Smith.)

As anyone who has taken introductory logic will see, there's a premise missing in this argument, because "better" isn't mentioned in premises 1–3. What could this missing premise be? Here's a possibility:

5. More norms result in better judgments.

This would forge a connection between the premises and the conclusion, but is it true? I don't know. How would you go about showing that it is true? First, you'd need a criterion for what counts as "better." Where would such a criterion come from? How will we establish such a criterion without engaging in some reflective philosophical thinking about moral standards (otherwise known as moral philosophy)?

Maybe the missing piece is something like this: different moral norms draw on different moral sentiments, those who rely on more sentiments are more broad-minded, and being broad-minded is good. This would help close the gap between the premises and the conclusion, but these premises are not necessarily true. Do more sentiments always improve our judgment? No. Sometimes anger can lead us to blame people for things they didn't do, fear can lead us to make mistakes about how much risk there really is, and love can blind us to the faults of our loved ones. So as a blanket statement, "those who rely on more sentiments are more broad-minded and broad-mindedness is good" doesn't seem correct. We need to think about which sentiments and in what context. We also need to think about what constitutes better moral judgment, which depends on how we conceive of what we are judging; what counts as better moral judgment depends on what you think the moral facts are that we are talking about when we make moral judgments. Notice that if we are doing nothing more than reporting our sentiments when we make moral judgments, then there are no grounds for saying that *more* sentiments are better. If all we are doing when we make moral judgments is reporting our sentiments, then whatever sentiments we have should be good enough. There's no sense to the idea that more is better. If, on the other hand, when we make moral judgments we are talking about what is implied by our values, or what members of the moral community would agree on, or what we would want if we were fully informed, then it might be that some sentiments help us appreciate these facts better than others. But this is going to be a complex matter to figure out. To establish that more is better when it comes to sentiments would take a good deal of argument.

Haidt does, ultimately, make a normative argument for the importance of the moral domains that conservatives use more than liberals. Haidt argues that the sanctity foundation—the domain of morality associated with the sentiment of disgust—allows us to maintain a sense of what is sacred, which in turn "helps bind individuals into moral communities. When someone in a moral community desecrates one of the sacred pillars supporting the community [the kind of action that can evoke disgust, such as burning a national flag], the reaction is sure to be swift, emotional, collective and punitive" (Haidt 2012: 268). Haidt's argument does rely on a moral premise, namely, the premise that being bound to a moral community in this way is a *good* thing. This is a very plausible premise, though we might ask whether it's enough to get to the conclusion. To get to the conclusion that disgust is a basis for sound, moral judgments, the argument also needs to assume that this disgust-based binding is *worth* whatever costs it incurs, such as exclusion of people who are deemed disgusting due to their sexual orientation, class or ethnicity. Whatever you think of these premises, the point is that, in order to conclude that it's a good thing to trust moral judgments that employ sentiments such as disgust, we need some premises that are not purely a description of how things are.[7]

If there are moral lessons to be drawn from science, the arguments that support these lessons will have to include both scientific and normative premises. There is a need for moral philosophy, then, and room for philosophers in the study of moral psychology insofar as moral questions and questions about our psychology are intertwined.

Summary

- Some worry that once we know more about morality from a scientific perspective, normative questions will be answered or shown to be irrelevant.
- One source of this worry is the thought that science shows that we are not really free and responsible agents. This topic will be explored in Part IV.
- Another source of this worry is that there is no place for moral facts in the scientific view of the world. Some argue that we make the moral judgments that we make because we evolved to, not because of the existence of moral facts, and that this gives us a reason to be skeptical about moral facts; such arguments are called evolutionary debunking arguments.
- It is not obvious that evolutionary debunking arguments succeed in justifying skeptical conclusions, because debunkers have not provided any complete explanation of how we could have evolved to make the moral judgments that we make without the existence of moral facts.
- Evolutionary debunking arguments also assume that moral facts are a particular kind of thing: either they are facts that have a special categorical force that makes us do things, or they are facts that are "out there," completely independent of our attitudes.
- There are other positions one could take about moral facts that are not targeted by evolutionary debunking arguments.
- Normative questions are not answered by science, nor are these questions shown to be unanswerable. There is room and need in moral psychology for philosophical thinking about what matters.

Study Questions

1. Think about some of the things that you have (most likely) evolved to do: care about your future, care about your family members, find certain things cute (babies, puppies). Would it matter to you if you would not have these attitudes were it not for evolution?
2. Think about the moral theories with which you are familiar (perhaps Utilitarianism, Kantianism or Virtue Ethics—the "big three" generally taught in introduction to ethics classes). How might scientific research be relevant to the defense or application of these theories?
3. Could science prove that there are no moral facts or no moral standards? How would it go about doing so?
4. If we knew everything about the causes of our moral judgments (including how we evolved to make them and what sentiments are behind them), would we know what to care about?

Notes

1. As with so many philosophical terms, *moral realism* gets defined in different ways. For our purposes, think of it as the view that there are moral facts that are independent of our judgments of them.
2. One of Street's main targets is Russ Shafer-Landau (2003).
3. Realists might even get some help here from some scientifically minded moral psychologists who argue that specific evolutionary explanations of our moral capacities are very unlikely to be found (Machery and Mallon 2010).
4. For those who have studied some metaethics, you'll notice that fictionalism is a kind of error theory (see Mackie 1990).
5. For simplicity sake, I'm going to talk about *moral facts* and *true moral beliefs*. Not everyone likes these terms, and that will matter if you go on to read the literature about moral realism, but the nuances do not matter for our purposes here.
6. This list is from the Moral Foundations website: www.moralfoundations.org/. See also Haidt 2007.
7. For more discussion of morality and disgust, see Nussbaum (2009) and Kelly (2011).

Further Readings

Haidt, J. 2012. *The Righteous Mind: Why Good People Are Divided by Politics and Religion.* Penguin.
Joyce, R. 2006. *The Evolution of Morality.* MIT Press.
Shafer-Landau, R. 2012. "Evolutionary Debunking, Moral Realism and Moral Knowledge." *Journal of Ethics & Social Philosophy* 7: 1–37.
Street, S. 2006. "A Darwinian Dilemma for Realist Theories of Value." *Philosophical Studies* 127 (1): 109–166.

Part II

Motivation and Moral Motivation

The Basics

"What motivates us to be moral?" is a fundamental question of moral psychology that requires all three methods of investigation (theoretical, normative and empirical) to answer. In this part of the book we will be dipping into some deep philosophical waters and this will lead us to go beyond the basic question. A warning: some of these waters are not only deep but murky. If you find yourself getting lost, you can always return to the basic question about moral motivation (or one of your own basic questions about moral psychology if you thought of some at the end of Chapter 1) and ask what bearing the philosophical discussion has on this question.

It is worth noting that some philosophers use "moral motivation" to refer to a narrower set of issues than we will be covering in this book (namely, the issues that have to do with how our moral judgments motivate us, a topic we will take up in Chapters 5 and 6). Because this book aims to bring philosophy in touch with psychology, the broader sense of moral motivation is appropriate.

3 Moral Motivation

What It Is and Isn't

Harry and Susan have something very rare in common: both have donated a kidney to a total stranger. Here's Susan's explanation of her action: "I believe I should try to help people. This seems to be a perfect opportunity to help someone in a big way with minimal inconvenience to myself" (McCann 2012). And, yes, she does know that "minimal inconvenience" includes a 1 in 2,500 risk of death during surgery. Harry's most frequent response when he is asked why he did this is to say that "it was the right thing to do" (Steinberg 2003).

To understand moral motivation, we need to know what a moral action is. Altruistic donation provides a fairly clear case, because it is a case in which a person acts in a way that benefits others at some cost to herself for what look like morally good reasons. These are hallmarks of moral action. But are these necessary features of moral action? Does all moral action benefit others? Do all moral actions involve self-sacrifice? Is an action only moral if it's done for the right reasons? Not necessarily. According to some moral theories, moral action is not the same as action that produces beneficial consequences. According to some moral theories, the fact that an action is in your self-interest does not disqualify it as a moral action. And according to some moral theories, acting for the right reasons is not necessary for acting morally.

Moral Theories and Moral Motivation

For our purposes, we can divide moral theories into four types, each of which has distinct implications for what counts as moral motivation. Let's start with Utilitarianism. According to Utilitarianism, a consequentialist theory, the right action is the one that produces the greatest welfare or happiness for the greatest number in the long run. Typically, Utilitarians have not thought that it matters very much what motivates someone to produce happiness; producing the best consequences is the right thing to do no matter what your reasons for doing it. There are certainly consequentialists who care about motives, but they identify good motives in terms of their reliability at bringing about the best consequences (Driver 2001).[1]

Kantian moral theory takes quite a different position on the importance of motives. According to Kant, the only actions that are morally worthy are actions done from the motive of duty. The motive of duty is the motive of a good will, which is the kind of thing that is always good to have. It is, Kant thinks, unconditionally good:

> A good will is not good because of its effects or accomplishments, and not because of its adequacy to achieve any proposed end: it is good only by virtue of its willing—that is, it is good in itself. . . . if with even its utmost effort it still accomplished nothing so that only good will itself remained (not, of course, as a mere wish, but as the summoning of every means in our power), even then it would still, like a jewel, glisten in its own right, as something that has its full worth in itself.
>
> (Kant 2002/1785: 394/196)

When we act from duty, we act with the intention—not just an inclination, but the "summoning of every means"—to do the right thing, because it is the right thing, no matter what we feel like doing. A person who acts from the motive of duty does the right thing in virtue of her recognition that morality demands it and her background rational commitment to do what is morally required of her. The motive of duty is important not only because it is the only morally good motive, but also because morality only applies to beings who are capable of being motivated by duty (that is, according to Kant, rational beings).

Kant's position may sound rather extreme, but the insight that a morally admirable motive is one that will get you to do the right thing no matter how you happen to be feeling is a good one.[2] To see this, think of someone who gives money to charity simply because she feels sympathy for the victims of a natural disaster. It's not that she believes this is the right thing to do, nor that she is concerned to do the right thing—she is just, say, feeling sorry for the people she saw on television and responding from her gut. Certainly she isn't doing anything wrong, but is what she's doing admirable? Consider that her sympathetic motive might be quite fickle. When the television stops showing the suffering, she stops helping; when suffering people appear on TV who do not engage her sympathies (perhaps because they are from a different continent or follow a different religion from her), she doesn't help; when her sympathy is swamped by feeling annoyed at her boyfriend for forgetting her birthday, she doesn't help. The motive of duty is supposed to be much more dependable and consistent than this. The motive of duty can motivate us even when the going gets tough; because it is independent of our feelings and desires, duty can motivate us to do the right thing even when we're feeling lazy, or mean, or we want to do something else. Intuitively, this sounds like a motive that's worth praising.

Motives are important for Kantians. It can look like we never do anything right at all unless we act purely from the motive of moral duty. But this is probably not what Kant meant. There is room, in Kantian moral theory, for a distinction between right action and morally worthy action. The right action is one that conforms to the supreme moral principle, the categorical imperative, which tells us to treat others as unconditionally valuable ends in themselves, never merely as means to our ends. Morally worthy actions are right actions done from the motive of duty. On this interpretation, we can do the right thing from an unworthy motive. For example, if I keep my promise to meet you for dinner, I have treated you in the way you deserve as a rational being, and, according to the categorical imperative (the supreme moral principle), I have done the morally right thing. But I may not have been motivated by duty; instead, I might have kept my promise because I wanted to eat at that restaurant anyway. In this case, I will have done the right thing, but not from morally admirable or worthy motives. So, the Kantian is not stuck saying that in keeping my promise for the wrong reasons I did the wrong thing. Still, Kantian moral theory enjoins us to do the right thing *for the right reasons*, that is, from the motive of duty. The important point for our purposes is that, according to the Kantian view about moral motivation (where this means motivation that is worthy of admiration and not just whatever happens to get us to do the right thing), it must be possible for us to act independently of our inclinations. Notice that this makes the Kantian picture depend on a claim about human psychology, namely, that we are capable of acting against our inclinations. Whether this claim is tenable and just how much it matters for Kantianism will be considered in the next few chapters.

According to a third type of moral theory, contract theory, morally right action is defined in terms of a hypothetical contract between moral agents. There are many different versions of contract theory, but the one I want to focus on here is T. M. Scanlon's contractualism. According to Scanlon (1998), the right thing to do is the action that follows the principles that no one could reasonably reject as a basis for regulating our interactions with each other. In Scanlon's view a right action could be done for the wrong motive: if your action is in accordance with the principles, then it's morally right. But Scanlon thinks that any moral theory must explain why we should care about the imperatives that it offers; therefore, he pairs his theory with a view about moral motivation that fits together with it naturally. Scanlon believes that we desire to justify ourselves to others on grounds they could not reasonably reject and that this desire explains how we feel about certain aspects of morality. For example, Scanlon (1982) reports that his own feeling about not meeting his obligation to help suffering people in distant places (and what might motivate him do more) is not to feel bad out of genuine sympathy for those other people, but to feel like he couldn't really justify his lack of attention to the suffering people given how easy it would be for him to give more. In his experience, this desire for his actions to be justified to others is an important moral motive. Contractualism does not hold that this desire to justify ourselves to others is the only moral motive, but it is an important one because it provides a reason for us to care about the hypothetical contract.

Finally, virtue ethics takes moral motivation to be extremely important because being motivated in the right way is essential to being a good person who lives a flourishing life. (Much more will be said about virtue ethics in Chapters 7 and 10.) According to the most prevalent version of virtue ethics, the one influenced by Aristotle, the best life for a human being is the life of virtue, because virtues (such as courage, temperance, justice and wisdom) are the excellent exercise of our human capacities and the best life for human beings is the life spent exercising these capacities in the most excellent way. Importantly for our purposes, virtues are partly constituted by certain kinds of motivating states, like desires and emotions. For example, a truly generous person wants to give people things and feels pleasure in doing so, which motivates her to do it again. Some virtues are defined in terms of the right amount of emotion: a courageous person, for example, feels fear, but not too much or too little and not in the wrong circumstances. Moral motivation, according to virtue ethics, is virtuous motivation; it therefore requires desires and emotional dispositions that are appropriately tuned and governed by wisdom.

Different moral theories have different views about what kinds of motivation are good or praiseworthy, as well as about whether motivation matters to getting the action right in the first place. According to Kantianism, an action isn't a morally worthy action if it isn't done for the right reasons, and according to virtue ethics, right action is action that stems from virtuous motives. Contractualism assumes that we are motivated by a desire to justify ourselves to others and, while it is possible on this view to act rightly without being directly motivated by this desire, the theory is only a plausible moral theory (according to one of its main proponents) if we do indeed have this desire. In subsequent chapters we will want to see if these claims about our motivations are well founded. If they are not, we have some reason to abandon the theories that make them. It is surely a count against a moral theory if it makes implausible assumptions about moral motivation.

Now, you might think that we could make things easier for ourselves if we stick with Utilitarianism and investigate why people sometimes promote general happiness and sometimes do not. This does seem to be the starting assumption of a good deal of psychological research about moral motivation; much attention in psychology is devoted to investigating the causes of "pro-social behavior," which is behavior that produces good outcomes understood in basically utilitarian terms. If our sole interest were in promoting pro-social behavior or figuring out how to make people more helpful, this wouldn't be a bad strategy. In other words, if our interest in moral motivation were itself consequentialist (if we just want to know what motivates people to act in a certain way so that we can produce more of that kind of action), then assuming that consequentialism is the right moral theory makes sense. But, if consequentialism doesn't explain everything there is to explain about moral action, then we would miss something by assuming that it is true. If there are right actions that are right for non-consequentialist reasons, then there is a reason to be interested in moral motivation beyond the consequentialist desire to produce more good consequences.

More importantly, even if motives don't determine which actions are morally right, we care deeply about motives and it is worth thinking about which motives are relevant to the question of how to live. That is, once we distinguish rightness of actions from moral motivation, we can see that both are important. To see this, consider some examples. Picture a philosopher who goes to visit a very sick friend in the hospital, and the friend asks why she has come. The philosopher tells her friend that she thought perhaps her presence would remind him to pay back the five dollars he owes her. Or imagine the philosopher is on a sailboat with her boyfriend who falls overboard. She later reports that she saved him rather than the drowning stranger next to him because the demand to maximize expected happiness permitted her to save her own boyfriend; the boyfriend and the stranger were about the same age and she had no way of knowing which of them would contribute more during their lives to the greatest happiness.[3] In both cases, the philosopher did the right thing, but we probably wouldn't want her for a friend. There is something wrong with people who have these motives, rather than the motives of friendship, sympathy and love.

If we think about the kind of friends we want to have, or the kind of friend we want to be, *how* we are motivated to help seems just as important as whether we end up helping. A gift given by a friend out of the expectation of a gift in return is not as nice as a gift that your friend gives you because she thinks it will make you happy. A person who gives to others freely and with pleasure seems more admirable than one who gives grudgingly. And most people would rather raise children who are sympathetic, kind people who have good friends and at least enough of a sense of duty to keep their promises and vote in elections. I hope these cases are enough to motivate the thought that we need to look beyond the causes of pro-social behavior in order to understand moral motivation in its fullest sense.

Now one might think that all this deliberation about motives—which ones are praiseworthy, which ones we should seek in our friends, which ones we should cultivate in ourselves—is irrelevant because we are at the core selfish creatures who can only be motivated by the desire for our own good. If we are always selfish, then most of the theories we've discussed so far make false assumptions about how we can be motivated. If I always act for the sake of number one (me), then I cannot act for the sake of duty, or from a desire for someone else's good, or from a desire to justify my actions to others whose regard I esteem, or out of genuine virtuous compassion. It is therefore worth considering whether there is some truth to the idea that we are always selfish. This is the challenge we will consider in the remainder of the chapter.

The Challenge of Psychological Egoism

Psychological egoism (henceforth just *egoism*) is the view that all voluntary action is motivated by self-interest, or, to put it another way: we always act selfishly. The opposing view, psychological altruism, or what I will call *non-egoism*, is the view that *not all* voluntary actions are motivated by self-interest. You can see why egoism challenges some of the moral theories we just considered. If we always act selfishly, then we do not ever act from a sense of duty, because duty motivates us independently of our desires and inclinations and, therefore, independently of our selfish interests. If we always act for the sake of our own interests, then there are certain other-regarding virtues that we cannot possess; for example, we cannot help another person for her own sake, as seems to be required by benevolence.

Sometimes psychological egoism has been put forward as a conceptual truth. Thomas Hobbes (the English philosopher whose defense of absolute government authority in *Leviathan* was published in 1651) is sometimes taken to have made this argument. Hobbes tells us that the object of every person's voluntary act is "some good to himself" and this seems to follow from his definitions of "good" and "voluntary action." A voluntary action is one that proceeds from the will, which is itself the last appetite or aversion before the action occurs. The good is just the object of our desires: "whatsoever is the object of any man's appetite or desire that is it which he for his part calleth *good*."[4] According to this interpretation of Hobbes, when we act voluntarily we act on a desire for what we take to be our own good. To say that egoism is a *conceptual* truth is to say that it follows from the meaning of "voluntary action," "desire" and "good." We do not need to establish egoism empirically; we already know that it must be true.

The idea that we know egoism is true without having to provide real evidence for it underlies a pattern of argument with which many readers may be familiar. It goes this way:

EGOIST: We always act selfishly.
NON-EGOIST: No, we don't! Look at Mother Theresa!
E: Mother Theresa was just trying to get into heaven.
NE: Maybe, but what about the soldier who falls on a grenade to save his platoon?

E: He did it to avoid feeling guilty if he didn't.

NE: What about the time I helped a friend move even though I really didn't want to?

E: You are deceived about your own motives. You obviously really did want to or you wouldn't have done it! Probably your real motive was to get the pleasure of feeling like a good person for helping.

Things could go on this way for some time until one person (typically the non-egoist) ends up too frustrated to proceed. What we should notice about this pattern of argument is that, without acknowledging it, each side is putting forward claims about the explanations of actions that are supposed to be matters of fact, but neither side is offering any evidence for what is supposed to be a fact (with the possible exception of the non-egoist's last example in which she offers evidence from introspection). The egoist claims that Mother Theresa helped the lepers in order to get into heaven. How does the egoist know this? What kind of evidence does the egoist offer to support this idea? Typically, no evidence is provided, because it seems obvious to the egoist: it *has to be* that Mother Theresa had some ulterior selfish motive, because otherwise why would she have done it? This seems obvious to the egoist—and empirical evidence seems unnecessary—because underneath the factual claim about what explains Mother Theresa's action is a conceptual claim that the egoist believes, which is that the only way an action could possibly be produced is by way of a selfish desire.

Why does this seem obvious to the egoist? Why does it seem like actions *must* be selfish and that this is something we can know from the armchair? The answer is that there is a premise in these arguments that is at least plausibly a conceptual truth. It's just that this premise does not support egoism by itself. The premise is that "all voluntary actions are caused by desires." We can see this premise at work in the above dialogue when the egoist says, "You obviously really did want to or you wouldn't have done it!" This could be true, but it doesn't follow that your action was selfish unless the further claim that the particular desire you acted on was the desire for your own pleasure (or something else for yourself). The (conceivably conceptually true) premise here is that desires are necessary to motivate actions, but what is inferred from this premise is that only *selfish* desires motivate action. That's the mistake. The idea that desires are necessary to motivate action is a very reasonable idea, and it's one that we will consider in some detail in the next chapter. The important point for our purposes in this chapter is that it does not follow from the fact that we act on our desires that we act selfishly. Again, this is because it doesn't follow from the fact that desires cause action that *selfish* desires cause action. The missing premise—a controversial premise for which the armchair egoist provides no evidence—is that all desires are selfish.

Psychological Egoism and Empirical Research

So, if egoism is true, then it is an empirical fact, not a conceptual truth. Is it true empirically? How would this be investigated? To put it in the same terms as the argument we discussed above, what we need to ask is whether desires are always desires for something for oneself. At first glance, this seems obviously false. We want all sorts of things that aren't for things for ourselves. People want their friends to be happy and their enemies to suffer. We want our parents to be healthy and our spouses to enjoy their jobs. We want world peace and a solution to climate change. In none of these cases is the object of our desire a benefit for us. It does seem like we observe myriad examples of desires that are not selfish.

Certainly there are unselfish desires, but it's not clear how deep this point is. Here we need to make a distinction between instrumental desires and ultimate desires. An instrumental desire for x is a desire that depends on a further desire for something else to which x is a means. An ultimate desire is a desire for something for its own sake, not because it is a means to anything else. For example, the desire for money is (for most people) an instrumental desire: we want it for the sake of the things that money can buy, not for itself. A desire for one's own happiness, on the other hand, is an ultimate desire: we don't want to be happy because it promotes any other goal we have, we just want it for itself. Now we can ask about the examples that confront us whether they are examples of instrumental or ultimate desires. Do we want our parents' health for its own sake (or for their own sakes?), or do we want it because it makes us happy or reduces the burden they are to us? Do we want world peace for its own sake, or do we want it because it would make our own lives more pleasant? It is this question about *ultimate* desires that needs to be answered.

You might think we could find out about people's ultimate desires simply by asking them what they really want for its own sake. But people are notoriously bad at knowing exactly what they want ultimately or "deep down," and, as we saw above, the egoist is likely to suspect that those who claim to have an altruistic desire are deceived about what they really want. So, we should try to find some other methods. One way to try to answer this question about ultimate desires would be to ask how likely it is that human beings have altruistic ultimate desires (desires for the well-being of others) given what we know about human evolution. You might think that altruistic desires make no sense from the standpoint of evolution, because my desire for another person's well-being is not going to make it more likely for me to survive and, indeed, might make my survival less likely if it inclines me to sacrifice my interests for the other person before I get a chance to reproduce. But, as Eliot Sober and David Sloan Wilson (1998) have argued, altruistic desires for our *children's* well-being (and the well-being of other members of the clan upon which we depend) do make a good deal of sense from the standpoint of evolution. Sober and Wilson argue that altruistic ultimate desires are a more reliable way to ensure that human beings would take care of their children than counting on ultimate desires for the parent's own pleasure that then give rise to instrumental desires for children's well-being. Altruistic desires for our children's well-being would provide direct motivation for us to care for them that would not be undermined by our finding easier ways of getting pleasure. If altruism is a better, more reliable way to get us to care for our children than egoism, then altruism would have been adaptive and could have been selected for in evolution.

Now one might think that desires for our children's well-being aren't really altruistic because they contribute directly to the passing along of our own genes. But this would confuse two very different kinds of explanation. On the one hand, human beings might have evolved (and did, according to Sober and Wilson) to care about their children's well-being because doing so made it more likely that their genetic material would be passed on to future generations. We explain why human beings have altruistic desires by appeal to what characteristics are adaptive. On the other hand, the psychological explanation for why a particular person takes care of his children might be (and is, according to Sober and Wilson) that he wants his children to fare well, for their sake, completely independently of any concerns he might have to reproduce or pass along his genetic material. The explanation for why human beings are the way we are refers to which psychological states benefitted people in terms of survival and reproductive success. But the psychological states that evolved may not themselves make any reference to survival or reproduction. To see this, think about our aversion to pain. It seems likely that we evolved to dislike pain—and to want to avoid it—because pain is usually a signal that we have sustained damage that might affect our survival and chances to reproduce. But the desire not to be in pain doesn't itself have anything to do with surviving to reproduce, that is, the concern to survive and reproduce isn't built into the psychological state of wanting to avoid pain. When you're in pain, you're not thinking about your survival and reproductive options; you're thinking, "Ow! That hurts! Make it stop!" To put the point another way, if you are asked to explain your desire to avoid pain from your own point of view (not from the point of view of the evolution of the human species), you will probably be nonplussed. But if you really had to try to explain it, you would probably say something like "pain is awful" or (even more simply) "pain sucks." The fact that our psychology is what it is because of evolutionary pressures does not make those evolutionary pressures any part of what the psychological states that we experience are *about* (evolution isn't part of the content of these mental states).

If Sober and Wilson's argument works, then, we do have reason to think that human beings evolved to have altruistic desires. And, once we recognize the point that the contents of our psychological states (what they are about) are not the same as the evolutionary pressures that created them, if we can have altruistic desires for our children's well-being, then there's no reason why we couldn't have them for other people as well. Does Sober and Wilson's argument work? Certainly it has been criticized, notably by the philosopher Stephen Stich, who has argued that Sober and Wilson's various arguments for thinking that altruism is more reliable than egoism are inconclusive (Stich 2007; Stich, Doris, and Roedder 2010). But critics such as Stich haven't shown that altruism is the wrong hypothesis either, and it now seems like the burden of proof has shifted onto those who reject the hypothesis that altruistic tendencies evolved.[5]

There has also been a lot of research on egoism and altruism in social psychology, and we'll consider one of the main research programs here. Daniel Batson and his colleagues have developed a series of ingenious experiments to test what they call the "empathy-altruism hypothesis," according to which empathy—an "other-oriented emotional reaction to seeing someone suffer"—leads to altruistic action.[6] Empathy, Batson and colleagues discovered, can be induced in a person by getting her to take someone else's perspective or, in other words, by getting someone to imagine how another person is affected by her situation. And, further, empathy has been shown to increase helping behavior. The fact that empathy increases helping behavior does not amount to evidence against egoism. After all, it could be that empathy produces helping behavior by, for example, causing a desire to get rid of the pain one feels due to the empathy with someone else's pain. The non-egoist needs to show that the hypothesis that empathy increases helping behavior because it gives rise to an ultimate desire for another person's well-being is a more plausible hypothesis than the egoistic hypothesis. This is exactly what Batson and colleagues aim to show.

We can see Batson's research as an attempt to move beyond the impasse between the egoist and the non-egoist that we saw in the previous section. The egoist has one hypothesis about helping behavior, the non-egoist has another, and neither has any evidence that convinces the other. Batson's approach is to test his non-egoistic hypothesis—the empathy-altruism hypothesis—against as many plausible egoistic hypotheses as he can. Since these experiments are rather complicated, we'll just discuss a couple of them here. Interested readers can look to the suggested readings at the end of the chapter to find out more.

One thought the egoist might have is the one I just mentioned: that empathy increases helping behavior because people want to eliminate the distress that empathy causes them. (If empathy makes us feel others' pain, then it is itself somewhat painful to experience.) On this view, which Batson calls the "aversive-arousal reduction hypothesis," we don't have ultimate desires for other people's well-being. Rather, we desire other people's well-being only insofar as someone else's well-being will produce more well-being (less distress) for us. To test this hypothesis against the empathy-altruism hypothesis, Batson set up a series of experiments that allow the subject to escape the scene rather than help. The thought is that if all the person desires is her own well-being, she would take the most efficient means to this end, which would be to escape from the suffering other (rather than to help her).

In these experiments participants watch Elaine attempting to perform some tasks under "aversive conditions" (Batson, Duncan, Ackerman, Buckley and Birch 1981). Less euphemistically, they are watching Elaine suffer electric shocks (in fact, they are watching a video of someone pretending to suffer electric shocks) for the sake of an experiment on learning under aversive conditions. The subjects are told that Elaine is particularly sensitive to these shocks because of an early childhood trauma and that they could take Elaine's place if they wanted to. Half the subjects are primed to be empathetic with Elaine, half are not.[7] Half of each group (primed and unprimed) is presented with an obstacle to escaping (they are told that, if they do not take Elaine's place, they will have to watch a bunch more of these aversive condition trials); the other halves of each group are not presented with this obstacle. Given these variables, the participants are divided into four different groups:

1. Low-empathy, easy escape
2. High-empathy, easy escape
3. Low-empathy, difficult escape
4. High-empathy, difficult escape

The most important comparison for testing Batson's empathy-altruism hypothesis against the aversive-arousal reduction hypothesis is the comparison between groups 2 and 4. This is because the empathy-altruism hypothesis would predict that an easy out makes no difference to helping behavior of empathetic people because the subjects' ultimate desire is for Elaine to feel better, not for their own distress to be reduced. On this hypothesis, people in group 2 should be just as likely to help as people in group 4. On the other hand, the aversive-arousal reduction hypothesis predicts that people in group 2 will be more likely to escape (not help) than people in group 4, because escaping allows them to avoid the aversive feeling of empathizing with someone who is in pain. As it turned out, Batson's prediction was right: people in group 2 were at least as likely to help as people in group 4 (i.e., empathetic people helped Elaine whether or not they could escape easily). This is some evidence that empathy is functioning to produce an ultimate desire for Elaine's well-being rather than activating an ultimate desire for the subject's own well-being.

There is one obvious flaw with this series of experiments. Batson concludes that empathetic subjects in the experiment choose to help rather than to escape even when it's easy to escape because they have an ultimate desire to help Elaine. But this conclusion depends on the assumption that the subject believes he won't go on thinking about Elaine and feeling distress after he escapes the experiment. Someone who thought he would continue to feel distress about Elaine after escaping may still be motivated by his ultimate desire for his own well-being (or lack of distress). Fortunately, another group of psychologists has done some experiments that support Batson's assumption (Stocks, Lishner, and Decker 2009). In these experiments, psychologist Eric Stocks and colleagues put people in similar situations to the ones that are used in Batson's experiments: they learn about a suffering person, Katie, with whom they empathize more or less (depending on which group they are in), and they can choose either to help Katie at some cost to themselves or to escape. Stocks adds a new variable to the experiment, which is that half the subjects are told that they are in a "deleting memories" training session that will make them forget everything they hear about Katie, whereas the other half are told they are in a "saving memories" training session and therefore they will remember what they learn.[8] If people were only motivated to help Katie in order to avoid personal distress, you would think that the fact that they aren't going to remember the distressing story would undercut their motivation to help. But this is not what happened in the experiment. Instead, Batson's findings were replicated: subjects who empathized with Katie were just as likely (in fact, a little more likely) to help if they thought their memories would be deleted as they were if they thought they would remember Katie's suffering.

Batson's empathy-altruism hypothesis, then, looks more likely than the aversive-arousal hypothesis. However, there are other possible egoistic explanations of seemingly altruistic behavior. It could be that people help because they fear they will be punished if they don't or because they think they will be rewarded if they do. We won't go into the details here, but Batson has done many other experiments that aim to show the superiority of the empathy-altruism hypothesis over these other possible explanations. If we listen to the main critic of Batson's research in philosophy, Stephen Stich, we will think that Batson's research has advanced the debate, though we do not yet have conclusive proof against egoism. Notice that *conclusive* proof will be very difficult to acquire, since it requires excellent evidence against every alternative egoistic hypothesis and, as Stich, Doris, and Roedder point out, evidence against all the possible *combinations* of egoistic hypotheses. Nevertheless, the empathy-altruism hypothesis does look plausible and we have no reason to reject it given what we know now.

Taking Stock

Do we have genuinely other-regarding motivations, or do we always act selfishly? This is an important question for moral philosophy, because if we always act selfishly, some moral theories need to revise their views about moral motivation. It is possible that we always act selfishly, but if this is true it cannot be proved from the armchair. What kinds of motivations we actually have is an empirical question and scientific evidence is relevant to answering it. We have also discovered that the current science doesn't provide an easy answer to this question. Non-egoism is on pretty solid ground, though. There is a good bit of evidence that altruistic motivations plausibly evolved and that people do sometimes act on these motivations. Further, there isn't any evidence that contradicts the assumption that we have some non-selfish motives.

Notice that the best science available provides evidence for a particular hypothesis about the content of our non-egoistic motivations: that we have ultimate desires for the well-being of other people. This research does nothing to prove or disprove hypotheses about other non-egoistic motivations, such as the motive of duty. Nevertheless, if it's true that we have ultimate desires for others' well-being, many moral theories have reason to celebrate. Utilitarianism, while it does not build assumptions about motives into its definition of right action, should welcome the idea that we are motivated directly by concerns for other people's happiness. Virtue ethics, because it prizes other-regarding character traits such as benevolence and kindness, will be on firmer ground if Batson's hypothesis is true. Contractualists, in general, believe that we have moral reasons to safeguard the well-being of others, so they should be delighted that we desire to do so. Even Kantians should be glad. After all, Kantians think that we have an imperfect duty to promote other people's happiness and the ultimate desire for the well-being of other people—while not a morally *worthy* motive—will at least help us to perform this duty.

Summary

- Different moral theories make different assumptions about moral motivation.
- From a traditional utilitarian perspective, motives do not matter to what we ought to do. We ought to maximize utility and moral motivation is whatever gets us to do that.
- According to other moral theories, such as Kantianism and virtue ethics, motivation is crucial to what we morally ought to do.
- Psychological egoism (PE) is the view that *all* of our actions are selfish or motivated by self-regarding desires.
- Most moral theories assume that PE is false.
- It is a mistake to take PE to be a conceptual truth; PE is an empirical claim.
- The empirical evidence does not establish PE. The empirical evidence also does not prove conclusively that PE is false; however, there is a good deal of evidence that altruistic motivation plausibly evolved and that people sometimes act from altruistic motives such as the desire for another person's well-being.

Study Questions

1. What assumptions do moral theories make about human motivation? What are some examples of the different roles that these assumptions might play in a moral theory?
2. Think of an example of someone you admire doing something morally good. What do you think their motives were? Do you care? Are their motives part of what is admirable about them?

3. Sometimes in moral psychology, progress is made by identifying an empirical assumption that some moral theory makes and then showing how this assumption is undermined or supported by the empirical evidence. How is this strategy illustrated by the topic of psychological egoism?

4. Would it really undermine most moral theories if we were to discover that when we help others, we are motivated by a desire to avoid feeling guilty or ashamed (this is the "self-administered empathy-specific punishment hypothesis," which we did not discuss)?

Notes

1. Though not necessarily: see Nomy Arpaly's (2000) argument that consequentialists need not equate morally worthy motivation with motivation to do what has the best consequences.
2. See Barbara Herman's (1981) essay "On the Value of Acting from the Motive of Duty" for further discussion of the Kantian position.
3. These examples are from Stocker (1976) and Williams (1981), respectively. Originally, they were used in arguments against Kantianism as well, because duty also seems like the wrong motive in these cases. The point here is just to demonstrate that there are cases in which motives matter. It's worth noting that Utilitarians have acknowledged this. See Railton (1984).
4. Hobbes, *Leviathan*, Chapter VI. This interpretation is defended by Curley (Hobbes 1994/1651).
5. Another good source for information about how altruism might have evolved is Kitcher (2011).
6. For an overview, see Batson (1991).
7. Priming is a technique scientists use to make people more susceptible to certain stimuli. In the empathy experiments, empathy was primed by describing the person undergoing shocks as more similar to the participant in the experiment. This works because our empathy is more likely to be engaged by people with whom we have things in common.
8. Here are the instructions that participants read:

   The "saving memories" training technique is used to permanently "save" an experience in your memory whereas the "deleting memories" training technique is used to permanently "delete" an experience from your memory.

   (Stocks, Lishner, and Decker 2009: 654)

   Underneath this paragraph was another sentence telling them which session they were assigned to. You might think it's a bit crazy to believe that you could delete or save a memory, but in the debriefing session after the experiment was over, psychologists confirmed that the participants did think their memories would be affected by the training.

Further Readings

Batson, C. D. 1991. *The Altruism Question: Toward a Social-Psychological Answer*. Lawrence Erlbaum.

Batson, C. D., B. D. Duncan, P. Ackerman, T. Buckley and K. Birch. 1981. "Is Empathic Emotion a Source of Altruistic Motivation?" *Journal of Personality and Social Psychology* 40 (2): 290–302.

Feinberg, J. 2004. "Psychological Egoism." In *Reason and Responsibility*, R. Shafter-Landau and J. Feinberg (eds), 476–488. Wadsworth.

Herman, B. 1981. "On the Value of Acting from the Motive of Duty." *The Philosophical Review* 90 (3): 359–382.

Kitcher, P. 2011. *The Ethical Project*. Harvard University Press.

Sober, E., and D. S. Wilson. 1998. *Unto Others: The Evolution and Psychology of Unselfish Behavior*. Harvard University Press.

Stich, S. 2007. "Evolution, Altruism and Cognitive Architecture: A Critique of Sober and Wilson's Argument for Psychological Altruism." *Biology & Philosophy* 22 (2): 267–281.

Stich, S., J. M. Doris and E. Roedder. 2010. "Altruism." In *The Moral Psychology Handbook*, vol. 1, J. Doris (ed), 147–206. Oxford University Press.

4   Desires and Reasons

Explaining her decision to put her seventeen-year-old, incontinent dog to sleep, a contributor to an online pet-loss support group wrote, "I didn't want to do it, but it was clear that she was suffering." Why did she do it if she didn't want to? Does that even make sense? Is what she says really short for "I didn't want to put her to sleep, but I had a stronger desire to end her suffering"? Or is there something revealing about what she says: her desires and feelings lead her in one direction, but her Reason tells her that she ought to end her dog's suffering. If you put yourself in the shoes of someone who has to do something really difficult because it's the right thing to do, it does seem natural to say that you're not doing what you want. If you were doing what you wanted to do, it seems like it wouldn't be so difficult. Do we *always* do what we want to do, no matter how it might seem to us?[1] Or are we able to act independently of our desires when necessary?

In the previous chapter, we considered (and saw good reasons to reject) the possibility that all of our actions are motivated by selfish desires. In this chapter, we consider the view that all of our actions are motivated by desires (whether egoistic or non-egoistic). If it is true that we can only act on our desires, does it matter to moral philosophy? Our topic in this chapter is relevant to moral philosophy in two ways. First, it has some relevance to our overarching question about moral motivation. If we cannot *not* act on our desires, then we cannot act purely from the rational motive of duty, and this would be a serious problem for one interpretation of the Kantian theory of moral motivation. Second, this chapter's topic is relevant to a big question in moral philosophy about the possibility of categorical (non-contingent) moral reasons. In this chapter we are going to focus our attention on this second question, because it will allow us to explore one area in which the facts about our psychology could have dramatic implications for moral philosophy. We will examine the role of desire in producing actions and consider whether actions are sometimes caused by reasoning rather than desire. Along the way, we'll see that there are different ways of understanding what a desire is and that this matters to the first question. Once we see what a desire is, we'll see that not too much trouble is caused to philosophical theories of moral motivation by the idea that all of our actions are caused by desires.

Some Background Distinctions

It sure does seem like what we want or desire to do is important to what we actually do. When we look for a motive for committing a crime, we look for a desire—typically for revenge, money or power. When we are confronted by a surprising piece of behavior (say, a friend runs off to Las Vegas to marry his fiancée), we look for some desire to explain it (for example, a desire to spite his parents or to avoid the expense of a wedding). A common view among philosophers is that not only are our desires an important part of the explanation for why we do what we do, but that desires are necessary for us to do anything at all. This position is known as the Humean Theory of Motivation (HTM), and it is widely held in contemporary philosophy.[2]

It is not held by everyone, however. There are some philosophers who think that while desires certainly sometimes explain what we do, we can also explain our actions by appeal to our beliefs and our reasoning, without desires playing any role at all. These philosophers, the anti-Humeans, think the explanation of our *moral* actions in particular requires appeal to rational judgment, not to desire.

There is a good deal of skepticism about the anti-Humean position in moral psychology. How could believing something cause us to do something if we didn't already have some desire that's related to the belief in some way or other? To see why someone might be skeptical about this, think about ordinary cases in which we acquire new motivations to do things. My sister recently stopped eating meat because she became convinced that animals raised for meat are badly treated. Her beliefs about animal welfare seem to have caused her to stop buying meat at the supermarket. But it also seems clear that she would not have stopped buying meat if she had not already wanted to be kind to animals. Someone who didn't care about animals would not have been affected in the same way. So, it looks like once again it is desire that is doing the heavy lifting. Reasoning about the world can point our desires in different directions by informing us about how to satisfy them, but they do not generate motivations on their own. Or, to put it another way, reasoning can change our instrumental desires (the desires we have to take the means to our ends), but not our ultimate desires (the desire we have for something for its own sake). This is the basic Humean picture.

Despite this skepticism, not all philosophers are Humeans, and the debate between the Humeans and the anti-Humeans about motivation is alive and well. To really understand this complex debate, we need to understand two distinctions: the distinction between belief and desire, and the distinction between motivating and normative reasons.

A good way to distinguish belief and desire derives from Elizabeth Anscombe, who introduced the idea that beliefs and desires have different directions of fit.[3] The basic idea is that beliefs are mental states that aim to fit the world, while desires are mental states that aim to get the world to fit them. Because beliefs aim to fit or "match" the world by being true representations of it, beliefs can be true or false depending on how the world is. For example, if I believe that I have an apple and I don't have one, then my belief has failed in its aim of being true and I should discard it. If I don't have an apple, I should stop believing that I have one. Desires, on the other hand, aim to change the world rather than to describe it. So, if I desire an apple and I don't have one, there is nothing wrong with my desire. I still want the world to match my desire, but here it's the world, not my desire, that needs to change to realize that aim.

Many philosophers of different stripes accept the idea that desires are distinguished from beliefs by their world-to-mind direction of fit. It is a compelling idea and it makes a lot more sense than one of the main alternative ideas, which is that desires are a kind of feeling or sensation. If you think about it, you can easily see what's wrong with this view: we often want things without knowing that we want them, and this would be hard to explain if desires were feelings or sensations. For example, if I find myself frequently daydreaming about playing the ukulele, slowing down to stare at music stores with ukuleles in the window, and replaying Israel Kamakawiwo'ole's ukulele version of "Somewhere Over the Rainbow" on my iPhone, then I might start to think that I want to play the ukulele and that I wanted to even before I realized that I wanted to. But if my desire to play the ukulele were a feeling, I would have felt it! Later in the chapter, we will look at some alternative ways of thinking about desires, but even these alternatives are not strictly incompatible with the claim that desires have a world-to-mind direction of fit.

You might be thinking that since a desire is a psychological state, we ought to *start* with an empirical theory, not with a conceptual classification. But notice that a psychologist who wants to figure out how desires work (what system in the brain is operating when we desire something, how desires function in our mental lives generally) needs to start with *some* concept DESIRE to investigate. In recent studies that distinguish wanting (or what we're calling desiring) from liking, for example, psychologists measure desire by observing how their subjects *behave*: a rat that goes for a reward is taken to want the reward (Berridge 2003). This assumption that goal-directed behavior is evidence of a desire makes sense if desires have world-to-mind direction of fit. To characterize desire in terms of its world-to-mind direction of fit leaves the door open for many specific theories, including empirical theories, of what exactly a desire is. It is therefore a pretty good place to start.

Let's turn to the second background distinction: the difference between motivating reasons and normative reasons. Philosophers have different views about the precise nature of this distinction, but the best general definition I have found is this one: "A normative reason is a consideration that counts in favor of or against doing something, whereas a motivating reason is an answer to the question, 'why did she do it?'" (Finlay and Schroeder 2008). To see the distinction in action, consider Crazy Crispin who shot his neighbor's dog, Spot. It turns out that Crispin shot Spot on purpose because Crispin believes that Spot is possessed by highly intelligent, evil fleas who are trying to take over the earth, and Crispin wants very much to avoid the earth being taken over by intelligent, evil fleas. The desire to avoid the earth being taken over by fleas is Crispin's motivating reason; it explains why he did what he did. But it is not a normative reason: the possibility that the earth will be taken over by intelligent, evil fleas does not count in favor of shooting a dog, because there are no intelligent, evil fleas. The desire to avoid the take-over is a *motivating reason*, but not a *normative reason*. The distinction between motivating and normative reasons is the basis for a humorous remark I have heard. When someone asks, "Will you help me move on Sunday?" (or makes some other request for assistance), the response comes "Well, I *would* help you, but I don't want to." What's funny about this (if anything) is that the person asking for help expects a normative reason that justifies the refusal to help, but the other person gives merely a motivating reason. This frustration of expectations makes us (philosophers, at least) laugh.

The Humean Theory of Motivation says that desires are necessary for motivation, and the main argument for this theory is a conceptual argument. The conceptual argument says, very roughly, that desiring *just is* being motivated as a matter of the concept DESIRE. (We'll say more about this argument in the next section.) You might find it weird to think that this question about motivation could be settled by talking about our concepts. Surely if anything is an empirical question, the question of whether desire is necessary to motivate us to act is an empirical question! As we will see eventually, the philosophical arguments in this area do make empirical assumptions, but there are big conceptual questions that come first. To see why, we need to think about what is at stake in this debate about the Humean Theory.

What is at stake has to do, ultimately, with moral requirements and how contingent or absolute they are. To say that moral requirements are contingent means that whether or not you have a normative reason (in this case, a moral obligation) to, say, keep your promises or refrain from shooting people, depends on some contingent psychological fact about you such as whether you *want* to keep your promises or refrain from shooting people. If moral requirements are absolute, then all of us have a normative reason (a moral obligation) to keep our promises and refrain from shooting people, whatever we happen to want. So the difference between moral requirements being contingent and their being absolute has to do with their scope, or (in other words) which people these moral requirements apply to—is it everybody or only people with the relevant desire? If moral requirements apply to all people necessarily, then they are absolute; if they apply only to people who have certain psychological states, then they are contingent.

This question about the scope of normative requirements is in the background of many of the debates we will be looking at in this and the next part of the book. So this is a topic to which we will return frequently. Basically, the connection between the Humean Theory of Motivation and the question of whether moral requirements are absolute is this: If we can't be motivated to do anything unless we desire to do it, and if we can only have a normative reason to do something if we could at least potentially be motivated to do it, then moral reasons are contingent. To put it another way, if having a moral reason to do something implies that you're at least capable of acting on it, and if all you're capable of doing is acting on your desires, then HTM makes moral reasons contingent.

Notice that the argument I've just made depends on another premise that we haven't discussed or defended yet, namely, the premise that you only have a moral (or normative) reason if you are capable of acting on it. Understanding this premise requires that we introduce another Humean position: Reasons Existence Internalism (which I'll just call Reasons Internalism or RI). Reasons Internalism is a theory about *normative* reasons (including but not limited to moral reasons) that are supposed to justify our actions. According to RI, even normative reasons must be connected to motivating states such as desires. RI is the view that you don't have a (normative) reason to do something unless you have a motive to act on it or, at least, you would have a motive to act on it under the right circumstances. For example, according to RI, if you are a very self-satisfied litterbug who has absolutely no desire to put your trash in the garbage can and no desire that could lead you to desire to put your trash in the garbage can, then you do not have a moral reason not to litter. RI is attractive because of the strangeness of the idea that there could be reasons floating around that no one could possibly act on. RI is also attractive because it is just so intuitive to think that the reasons we have that justify what we do in ordinary cases are explained by our desires. Why should you go to the concert? (Where "should" is an ordinary way of saying "for what reason" or "what would justify your going.") Because there will be good music there and you want to hear some music. Why should you study for your exam? Because you need to study to pass the course and you want to pass the course. Desires seem crucial to explaining reasons for doing all sorts of things. (More will be said about this in the next section.)

If RI is true and if the Humean Theory of Motivation is true, then there could only ever be a reason for someone to do something if that person also had (or at least could potentially have) a desire to do it. In other words, if all reasons are motivating (RI), and if motivation always requires a desire (HTM), then any moral reason requires a desire. If we also assume (as seems reasonable) that moral obligations necessarily give us reasons, then our moral obligations are contingent on our having the relevant desires. The upshot is that in this combination of views you only have a reason to do the right thing if you want to do it. This means that if you don't happen to have a desire to tell the truth or to refrain from shooting your neighbor, then you have no reason, and hence no obligation, to do so. Something sure seems wrong here, which is why it is so important to examine these Humean positions in detail. We'll begin with Reasons Internalism and then turn to the Humean Theory of Motivation.

Before we proceed, it's worth acknowledging that the topics in this chapter are abstract and complex. Because of this, I have simplified some matters for the sake of exposition, particularly at first. As we go, we'll see that some of the initial oppositions are not as black and white as they might have seemed at the start.

Reasons Internalism and Externalism

As I just mentioned, Reasons Internalism is the view that normative reasons necessarily have some relationship to motivation. (There are vague terms in this definition on purpose; different internalists fill out the definition in different ways.) Reasons Externalists think there is no necessary relationship between normative reasons and motivation. The first thing to keep in mind is that the argument about which view is true is a conceptual argument. What is being asked about is the concept REASON.

When philosophers analyze concepts, one thing they are trying to do is arrive at a definition that fits our ordinary ways of talking. So, an analysis of the concept REASON might aim to accommodate these sorts of statements:

- "The only reason I came to the store was to find a present for my sister."
- "The reason I'm giving to this charity is that they don't spend much of their income on administrative costs."
- "There is no reason to be afraid."
- "You have every reason to tell the truth."

These examples suggest some kind of connection between our concept REASON and motivation, because these examples use the concept as part of an explanation for an action that has already happened or as part of a recommendation about how to act in the future. Notice that in each case the content of the reason offered for the action is not the desire; rather, the reason is whatever consideration counts in favor of doing the action (that this store might have a present for my sister, for example). The desire is what *explains* why these considerations count as reasons. This is how most philosophers who accept a desire-based view of reasons think about it today: desires are necessary for the explanation of normative reasons (there is no reason to do something without a desire), but desires do not have to be contained within the consideration that favors doing the action (M. Schroeder 2007).

Fitting with our ordinary way of talking is not the only constraint on our analysis of REASON. We should also think about the role that this concept plays in our philosophical theories more generally, that is, we should think about the point of talking about reasons. Here we see that there are three points, and we have already seen two of them in our discussion of the distinction between motivating and normative reasons: sometimes we talk about reasons because we want to explain what somebody did, sometimes we talk about reasons in order to justify what has been done, and, finally, sometimes we talk about reasons when we are deliberating about what to do. The important thing to notice is that in all of these cases, action is important. Even when we are in the mode of justification and our aim is to think about what action is supported by the best moral reasons, there is still at least the hope (perhaps even the expectation) that these reasons will be acted on.

This fact about the link to action has made RI seem like a very attractive theory, because RI has a natural explanation for how reasons figure into explanations of action: as a matter of the concept, you don't have a normative reason to do something unless that reason could also motivate you in some way or other. Further, the link to action makes Reasons Externalism seem unattractive. Reasons Externalism (RE) says that there are normative reasons that have no necessary connection to what we do. First of all, it seems strange to some people that there are these two things we call reasons (motivating reasons and normative reasons) that are not necessarily connected to each other. And secondly, RE makes normative reasons seem like very strange things that are "out there" in such a way that there could be a reason that no one could ever act on. It's not so hard to understand what normative reasons are if they are internal: they are considerations that motivate us under the right conditions. But what are normative reasons if they have no necessary connection to motivation?

These thoughts might make you wonder why anyone would ever be a Reasons Externalist. To see the attraction of RE, we need to see two things.

First, there are some features of our ordinary way of talking about reasons that fit better with RE. One thing that many people think about moral reasons is that these are reasons for people to act morally *whatever* they happen to want to do. For example, when a judge tells you that you ought to tell the truth on the witness stand, she does not mean that you have a moral reason to tell the truth *if you want to*. Certainly not. She means that you should tell the truth—and that you have a decisive reason to tell the truth—no matter what you are actually motivated to do. Indeed Kant thought that the fact that moral reasons are independent of the motivations we happen to have (what he called our "inclinations") was the key to understanding what moral duty is. So, thinking along these lines, it looks like moral reasons (one type of normative reasons) are *external* reasons.

Second, even an Internalist will be concerned to maintain a distinction between motivating reasons and normative reasons, because these two can come apart as we saw above. We do not always do what we have normative reason to do; sometimes our actions are explained by motivating reasons that are not also normative reasons (as in the case of Crazy Crispin and his desire to rid the world of evil fleas). To retain this distinction, most Reasons Internalists hold that the relationship between reasons and motivations (while necessary) is indirect. The most popular versions of RI say that we have a normative reason to do something as long as we would have the desire to do it if we thought about it in the right way.[4] In this view, reasons motivate us insofar as we have met the appropriate conditions (that is, we are rational or informed or something like that), but they might not actually motivate us if we're irrational or ignorant. Another way to put the point is that a consideration must be *capable* of motivating us for it to count as a reason, but "capable of motivating" turns out to mean something like "would motivate us if we thought about it in the right way." In short, motivating reasons motivate us directly, while normative reasons (according to the Reasons Internalist) motivate us indirectly, after we've acquired more knowledge or reflected a bit.

Modifying RI in various ways helps explain how motivating reasons are different from normative reasons, but it also loosens the connection between reasons and action significantly. At this point the Externalist might say, "if you're going to loosen the connection between reason and action that much, why bother being an Internalist anymore?" Especially if externalism better explains the compelling idea that we ought to be moral and, hence, that we have a reason to be moral, even when we don't want to be? Externalists will say that you have a moral reason to tell the truth, for example, whether you would be motivated by this reason or not. This is attractive, and once the Internalist is forced to say that moral reasons don't actually, always motivate people (they just motivate people if they think about them in the right way), the Externalist might say that it's better to think of normative reasons her way.

There is no obvious winner here in the debate about how to analyze the concept REASON, and to some extent we end up with battling intuitions. One possibility is that there are really two concepts represented by one word but that have different meanings. We might think that when we talk about reasons in the context of deliberating about what to do, we mean to be talking about internal reasons. But when we talk about *moral* reasons, perhaps we mean to be talking about external reasons. This distinction even seems to be marked in our language by the two different phrases: "he *has* a reason" and "there *is* a reason." If I say that Bill has a reason to tell the truth, I'm saying that there is something in favor of telling the truth that Bill at least could be motivated by. If I say that there is a reason for Bill to tell the truth, even though he's an incorrigible liar, I'm saying that there is something in favor of telling the truth that exists independently of Bill's ability to be motivated by it. This is one way of dissolving the conflict between Reasons Internalism and Externalism, though it's not a path many have taken.

In terms of how to analyze the concept REASON, the important thing for our purposes is to be clear about what we mean as we proceed through the rest of the book and to be aware that the problems and questions might change depending on which concept we have in mind. In the next section, we will be talking about the debate over the Humean Theory of Motivation, and we will see that one important thing that is at stake in this debate assumes the Internalist conception of REASON.

The Humean Theory of Motivation

At the beginning of this chapter I said that the question about whether there could be absolute moral reasons hinges on two theories: Reasons Internalism and the Humean Theory of Motivation. We're now in a position to examine the main argument for the second one of these. Here is Michael Smith's (1987) now canonical argument for the view:

1. Having a motivating reason *is, inter alia*, having a goal (a conceptual claim, Smith says);[5]
2. Having a goal *is* being in a state with which the world must fit (this is entailed by P1, Smith says); and
3. Being in a state with which the world must fit *is* desiring.

These premises entail the Humean Theory of Motivation, according to which "motivation has its source in the presence of a relevant desire and means-end belief" (Smith 1987: 36). In other words, to have a motivating reason to do something, you must have a desire for what that action will produce and a belief that the action in question will indeed get you what you want. For example, you have a reason to keep reading this book only if you believe that by reading this book you will gain understanding and you have a desire for that understanding (or you have some other relevant belief-desire pair).

Smith's argument is called the Teleological Argument because it assumes that explanations of actions in terms of reasons are teleological explanations, that is, they are explanations that make sense of the action by showing how it is directed at meeting a goal. The key idea of the argument is that to have a reason to do something is (at least in part) to be directed toward the fulfillment of a goal, and goal directedness is a matter of desiring something, not believing something. You can think of it this way: you can't have a reason to do something without having a goal and having a goal just is having a desire.

The Humean Theory of Motivation has been attacked in two different ways. Some people reject the first premise and argue that having a motivating reason is *not* having a goal; instead, motivating reasons could be explained by our beliefs. The philosopher Jonathan Dancy takes this position. He says that motivating reasons are just facts that favor acting in a particular way and it is our *beliefs* in these facts that makes acting on them possible (Dancy 2000). For example, the fact that there is enjoyable music at the concert is your (motivating) reason for going to the concert; this fact motivates you in virtue of your belief that the enjoyable music is a good reason to go to the concert. Dancy argues that this way of thinking about motivating reasons is the only way to make sense of how it could be possible for a person to act for a *good* reason. If motivating reasons were just based on desires, they could never be good reasons, because the mere fact that you desire something isn't a good reason to act. Notice that Dancy's way of thinking about motivating reasons collapses the distinction between motivating reasons and normative reasons. In a sense, he explains how we can act for normative reasons by arguing that motivating reasons themselves must be normative reasons. If they weren't—if, as per the Humean Theory, motivating reasons were just psychological states—they wouldn't really be *reasons* at all.

Critics of this position have argued that it lacks a sufficient psychological explanation for how we could act for reasons. What is the causal story, the critic asks, of how facts about the world connect to our agency in such a way that we can grasp them as reasons and then act because of them? The idea that our beliefs about reasons "enable" this process doesn't really provide an explanation that has been very satisfying to Humeans. Furthermore, sophisticated Humeans do not think that the mere desire (for enjoyable music, say) *is* the reason to go to the concert. Rather, sophisticated Humeans think that the reason is that there will be enjoyable music at the concert; the fact that you desire enjoyable music is what explains why this is a reason for you.

The second line of criticism we will consider is not a direct attack of Smith's teleological argument for the Humean Theory of Motivation; rather, it is a rejection of the implications that the Humean Theory has been taken to have. The Humean Theory of Motivation is often associated with (and sometimes taken to be the same as) the idea that desire or passion, not Reason, is "in the driver's seat" when it comes to moving us to action. This is certainly also a Humean idea; it is essentially what Hume meant when he said that (our capacity to) reason is the slave of the passions (Hume 2000/1739). Reasoning is the slave of the passions in the sense that desires are always the ultimate stopping point for explanations of actions—it is "desires all the way down." The idea here is that our capacity for reasoning is subordinate to our desires in the sense that it (our Reason) does not determine our direction. Desire determines where we are going, and reasoning tells us how best to get there. Ultimately, we are guided by what we want, not by what we think we ought to do. We can be guided to do what we think we ought to do but only when we also have a desire that hooks up with the thought of "doing what we ought to do." For example, if I listen to a very persuasive speaker and become convinced that I ought to give more money to charity, I will only have a motivating reason to give more money to charity if I also have some relevant desire—the desire to do what I ought, the desire to help people, the desire to follow the advice given by persuasive lecturers or the like.[6]

You can see how "no action without a desire" and "desire, not Reason, determines what we do" could be taken to be the same.[7] But the second criticism of the Humean position we're considering takes issue with the latter and not really the former. Let's see why.

To get from the idea that desires are necessary for action (the conclusion of Smith's argument) to the idea that desire *determines* what we do, you need to assume that desires are just given and cannot be brought about by reasoning. If desires could be brought about by reasoning, then even though you might need a desire to cause an action, desire would not necessarily determine what we do because there is the possibility that Reason produces the desire that is necessary for action. And this is just what some critics of the Humean position think: Reason can bring about new desires. If this is possible, then Reason is not the slave of the passions, because Reason can (at least sometimes) tell desire what to do.

How could reasoning or cognizing the world in a certain way produce a desire? There is a good deal of skepticism about this idea that believing something can cause us to want something even without any desire that's related to the belief in some way or other. It seems mysterious. So why do some anti-Humeans think that reasoning can bring about new desires and how do they think this happens?

A good strategy for the anti-Humean who wants to argue that reasoning can direct us by bringing about new desires is to pick on the very broad definition of "desire" in the Teleological Argument. The anti-Humean could argue that insofar as it is true that desires are necessary for action (the conclusion of Smith's argument), "desire" is such a broad category that it includes some rational motives. Along these lines, the anti-Humean can argue that identifying desires in terms of their world-to-mind direction of fit (as Smith's argument does) makes all sorts of mental states into desires even though they aren't what we ordinarily mean by "desire." Once the anti-Humean establishes this much, he can argue that when the category of desire is expanded, we'll see that some desires are brought about by reasoning.

T. M. Scanlon makes just this argument. Scanlon's view is that understanding desires as "pro-attitudes"[9] (which is essentially what the directions of fit model does) does not support the Humean conclusion (the conclusion that Reason is the slave of the passions), because many pro-attitudes, such as "duty, loyalty, or pride, as well as an interest in pleasure or enjoyment," can be brought about by reasoning (Scanlon 1998: 37). If *desire* is to be defined so as to support the Humean conclusion that Reason is subordinate to desire, according to Scanlon, it will have to be defined more narrowly as a specific type of pro-attitude. To see Scanlon's point, we can think about the motive of duty that we discussed in the previous chapter. Kant sometimes describes the motive of duty as respect for the moral law (Kant 2002/1785: 400/202). If respect is a kind of pro-attitude, and if thinking about the requirements imposed on us by the moral law can cause this attitude of respect (in the way that recognizing beauty in nature can bring about the feeling of awe), then the motive of duty is a pro-attitude that can be brought about by reasoning.

Of course, we can imagine the Humean having much the same response that she had before: Thinking about the moral law will only produce a new pro-attitude if you already had some positive attitude toward doing your duty, or following the law, in the background. After all, we have many thoughts that do not motivate us in any way. The difference between these thoughts and the thoughts that appear to produce motivations is that in the latter case there is already some motivation there that gets tapped into. Thoughts only move us to action when they latch on to preexisting motivations, says the Humean.

The anti-Humean strategies we have just considered have led us to the same place. Either reasoning can bring about desires narrowly defined as goals, or reasoning can bring about pro-attitudes (desires broadly defined). Either way, the crucial point is that even if it is conceptually true that you need a desire for an action, it does not follow that Reason is subordinate to desire unless you also assume that we cannot reason our way into new desires.

The anti-Humean strategies and Humean responses we have considered seem to have left us at an impasse. Philosophers have different intuitions about whether reasoning can bring about brand new desires that are not just desires for the means to things we already desired. And the available arguments don't do much to move people from one team to the other. Could empirical research on desires shed some light on this question? To figure this out, let's consider a promising empirical theory of desire.

On the basis of research in cognitive science, philosopher Timothy Schroeder argues that there is a neurological system in the brain that underlies the main phenomena associated with desiring, which are the tendencies toward action and attention and the associated pleasures (T. Schroeder 2004).[10]

This system is the reward-based learning mechanism, which interacts with other systems in the brain (systems for action, pleasure and attention, for example). According to Schroeder, we should understand what desires are by understanding their role as the mental states that drive reward-based learning. When we desire something, pursue it and then get what we wanted, getting what we wanted is a reward that causes us to learn how to act in the future to get more of what we want. The reward signals in this system come in the form of pleasure. To desire something, according to this theory, is to see it as rewarding, and to see or represent the thing this way (as a reward) causes a person to be motivated to pursue it (T. Schroeder 2006). (Aversive desires represent things we do not want as punishments, the opposite of rewards.) We can think of it this way: When you desire something, you have an image ("representation" in Schroeder's terms) of what it is that you desire, on the basis of which you go for it. If what you get is even better than what you imagined, you are rewarded and you'll be likely to go for more of this kind of thing in the future. On the other hand, if what you got was worse than you imagined, you'll tend avoid that kind of thing in the future. Through our desires we learn what kinds of things are rewarding things to do or not.

According to the reward-based learning theory of desire, desires are the usual cause of goal-directed behavior. Normally when people act, they do so because they are acting to satisfy a desire. Of course, desires can have moral content. A person could have a desire to do her duty, a desire to be a good person, a desire to maximize happiness and so on. According to this theory, moral motivation would be motivation by the right desires, such as desires for what is morally good (Arpaly and Schroeder, 2014). Does this theory also say that desire is ultimately in the driver's seat? If the reward-based learning theory of desire is true, would this theory provide evidence one way or the other about whether we can reason our way into new desires?[11] That is, would the empirical theory, if true, shed light on the debate between Humeans and anti-Humeans?

According to this empirical theory of desire, we can reason our way into lots of instrumental desires. Indeed, part of the point of the system is to learn what particular things you should want and go for in order to further your ultimate goals. Can we acquire new *intrinsic* desires through reasoning? Could the desire to tell the truth for its own sake, for example, result from reasoning about what is your duty, without the need for a prior desire to do your duty? Schroeder thinks the empirical research suggests that we cannot. He does think we can acquire new *ultimate* or intrinsic desires by association, but this learning system is an unconscious one that is not mediated by reasoning. For example, if you're a purely selfish baby and all you ultimately desire is food, warmth, hugs and so forth, you can acquire a new intrinsic desire for the presence of Mom (say) by the following means: Mom's presence is unconsciously, statistically associated (in the right way) with your getting fed, getting swaddled in warm blankets, getting hugged and so on.

Eventually, this generates an intrinsic desire for the state of affairs that Mom is present. So we can acquire new intrinsic desires because of other things we desire intrinsically, but we don't acquire new intrinsic desires by thinking things through rationally. And this makes sense, given that desires are the engine of the system: the whole point of the system, after all, is to learn how to satisfy our desires, so it does seem like some desires must be at the bottom of whatever changes happen.

If this is right, would this more scientific way of understanding desire finally decide between the Humean and the anti-Humean? One thing to notice is that the reward-based learning theory of desire does not show that it's impossible to reason your way into a new ultimate desire. Furthermore, according to this theory we can and do reason from our ultimate desires to new instrumental desires. A person with any basic moral desire (such as the desire not to harm others) can reason herself to more specific moral desires (such as the desire to give more money to charity or to become a vegetarian). We can also reason our way into strengthening some of our moral desires. A person with a very limited concern for others could reason her way into more robust moral desires by attending to the way in which helping others furthers some of her other goals, for example. In other words, instrumental reasoning that derives new desires from old ones can actually take us pretty far. Is this enough for the anti-Humean? Well, it isn't enough for any anti-Humean who wants to eliminate the *contingency* of moral reasons. The idea that we can reason our way to new moral desires on the basis of weak concerns for other people does still make moral reasons contingent on these pre-existing concerns; moral reasons, in this picture, would not be necessarily or categorically binding.

Would this more scientific way of understanding desire finally decide between the Humean and the anti-Humean on the matter of whether desire is necessary for action? (Recall the first anti-Humean strategy we discussed, which was to argue that desires are not necessary for motivating reasons and action at all.) The reward-based learning theory of desire does not say that it is impossible for some other mental state (not a desire as defined by the theory) to motivate action. No empirical theory could prove that desire is *necessary* for action. The reward-based learning theory simply tells us that the typical way for action to be caused is through desire.[12] Would the anti-Humean be satisfied with the possibility that there are atypical cases in which reasoning all by itself does cause us to act? And how atypical would such action be? I take it that the anti-Humean would not really win the battle if he or she could show that it's possible in really weird cases for people to be moved to act by their rational appreciation of facts that favor certain actions. This would make moral motivation, well, really weird.

Replacing Smith's very broad notion of a "pro-attitude" with this particular scientific theory of desire does at least indicate a strategy for defending the anti-Humean position that doesn't rely on comparing our intuitions about whether reasoning can bring about brand new desires. To defend their position against this new empirically informed version of the argument, the anti-Humeans could provide empirical evidence that rational appreciation of facts can motivate people without the need for desires that match up with these facts or that reasoning can produce new ultimate desires.

Taking Stock

What is at stake in the debate between the Humean and the anti-Humean? If we accept both Humean theses—that normative reasons require motivation (RI) and motivation requires desire (HTM), then we can only ever have reasons to do something when we have the relevant desire. If we add the Humean claim that reasoning cannot by itself change what we want for its own sake, then we have a problem. This combination of views entails that what we have moral reasons to do is contingent on our desires. Many people think that what you have moral reason to do could not possibly be contingent on desires. Rather, moral reasons are *categorical*: they apply to you no matter what you want. Kant thought this was part of the very idea of a moral duty. And this does make some intuitive sense; if moral reasons are contingent on desires, we seem to be stuck with the conclusion that you have no reason to tell the truth if you don't want to.

This isn't the happiest position to be left in. Essentially, we are left having to throw up our hands when we are confronted with someone who doesn't want to do the right thing. Imagine that another one of Spot's neighbors, Mean Mary, wants to shoot Spot because she doesn't like the way he wags his tail. If Mean Mary has no desires that would cause her not to shoot Spot, and if the Humean is right on all counts, then we cannot say that Mean Mary ought not to kill Spot, given her mean desires. What could we do to get out of this uncomfortable position? The problem was caused by a combination of views, so it might be that we only have to abandon one of the views in order to get out of the bind (Finlay and Schroeder 2008). Let's review and consider our options.

First, we could reject the Humean Theory of Motivation and say that motivating reasons are not entirely dependent on desires that we can't get to rationally. We could say that desires aren't necessary for action at all. Or we could say that motivating reasons are not beholden to what a person happens to want, because a person could reason himself into having a new ultimate desire. For example, Mean Mary could come to see that she has a reason not to shoot Spot by reasoning about Spot's welfare or Spot's humans' attachment to their canine pal. This reasoning could motivate Mary by itself, or it could cause in her a brand-new pro-attitude toward Spot. In my opinion, this solution does not move the debate forward, because (at least at the moment) the empirical evidence favors the Humean, and, insofar as there is an open question, the controversy about this point terminates in a clash of intuitions.

Second, we could abandon or weaken Reasons Internalism and accept that normative reasons do not necessarily motivate people to act. If we do this, we could easily say that there is a normative (moral) reason for Mary not to shoot Spot. It's just that there might be no way for this normative reason ever to become Mary's motive. The problem with this solution is that it means that reasons won't always be the kind of thing that can guide action. This is at least disappointing. We might wonder what the point is of talking about reasons if they aren't going to be reasons for which someone could actually *do* something. A related option, the one Smith takes, is to weaken Reasons Internalism so that it turns out that reasons are always potentially motivating *and* that everyone has a reason to act morally. Smith does this by defining normative reasons in terms of what our fully rational selves would want our actual selves to want do and then claiming that we are (insofar as we are rational) motivated to do what our fully rational selves would want us to want to do. On the assumption that these fully rational selves' desires would track moral reasons (an assumption Smith believes is true), we end up having moral reasons that are not heavily dependent on our actual contingent desires. Moral reasons are only contingent on our desire to behave consistently with the advice of our fully rational selves. To try to put Smith's position more simply, the idea is this: what it is to be rational is to want to act only on your most coherent, rational desires. Insofar as you are rational, you are motivated to act on these coherent rational desires. Your most coherent, rational desires are moral. Therefore, insofar as you are rational, you are motivated to act morally. Moral reasons motivate rational people (RI), in this view, and they do so by way of desires (HTM). Moral reasons are contingent, but not in an objectionable way; they are contingent on our rational desires.

Finally, we could accept Humeanism about reasons and motivation, bite the bullet (that moral reasons are contingent on desires), but try to make the bullet a bit softer. We could do this by seeking out some resources to argue that although moral reasons are not categorical (they are contingent on desires), they are nevertheless universal (they apply to everyone).[13] If we could argue that our moral reasons stem from desires or passions that we *all* have (albeit contingently), for instance, then it would at least be true that *everyone* has a reason not to lie, steal, kill innocent people and so on, even though we wouldn't have such reasons if it weren't for our desires.[14] This is, more or less, Hume's own solution to the problem. Though Hume does admit there may be a few rare people for whom moral reasons have no force, he thinks that most of us are sufficiently social, sympathetic and concerned about our own reputations and happiness that we do have ultimate desires to which moral reasons appeal. In this view, moral reasons apply to just about everyone, because just about everyone has the relevant desires. The scientific view of desire as part of the reward-based learning system might help us here. Taking this theory on board, we see that people can learn to have morally better desires. One way this can happen is by learning from experience about new connections between ultimate desires and moral actions. For example, perhaps when Mean Mary thinks about her neighbor's attachment to Spot, she is reminded of her own childhood attachment to her rat, Lily, which awakens an undeveloped desire not to hurt helpless animals, which makes her see that not shooting Spot actually does satisfy one of her intrinsic desires. If people can learn to have morally better desires by learning about the ways in which their most basic ultimate desires (for love, comfort and security, for example) will be satisfied by acting morally, then moral reasons will have very wide applicability. If we can show that moral reasons are universal (or nearly so), we might be less concerned about their being contingent on desires.

We have focused our attention in this chapter on an important question in moral theory about the contingency of moral reasons and moral obliga- tions. Along the way, though, we have learned a few things about desire, which we can now use to answer the questions that opened the chapter: Do we always do what we want to do? And, if so, is this true in a way that causes trouble for philosophical theories of moral motivation? There is no complete consensus here, but a widely agreed upon view is that desires (broadly defined pro-attitudes) are ordinarily required to motivate action. But this claim does not seem to cause many problems for traditional philo- sophical theories of moral motivation. The distinctiveness of moral motivation could be captured by appeal to special desires such as the desire to help others or to do good. It could be captured by appeal to emotions (virtuous emotions such as compassion, for example) that count as desires if desires are understood broadly or that are caused by desires understood narrowly. The Humean Theory of Motivation does create some problems for Kantians who believe that we can be motivated by *pure* duty where duty is entirely opposed to desire, but other, less-extreme versions of this view—for example, one that takes the feeling of respect for the law to be the motive of duty—are defensible even if desires (broadly conceived) are necessary for action.

Summary

- The relationship between desires and reasons is relevant to two large phil- osophical debates: the nature of moral motivation and the possibility of categorical moral reasons.
- In one standard view, beliefs and desires have two different directions of fit. Beliefs aim to fit the world, whereas desires aim to get the world to change to fit them.
- Motivating reasons explain action; normative reasons justify action.
- Reasons Existence Internalism is a thesis about normative reasons accord- ing to which it is a necessary condition for a reason's having normative status that it is connected to some actual or hypothetical motivation of the person who has the reason.

- The Humean Theory of Motivation states that desires are necessary for motivating actions. Beliefs can never motivate us to act by themselves.
- Smith's teleological argument makes this theory a conceptual truth.
- The Humean Theory of Motivation is often taken to imply another Humean thesis that desires determine action and Reason is always subordinate to desire.
- Some philosophers object to the Humean thesis that motivating reasons do not require desires by arguing that actions can be motivated by facts and enabling beliefs.
- Other philosophers object to the Humean thesis that Reason is subordinate to desire by arguing that reasoning can bring about new ultimate desires.
- The reward-based learning theory—an empirical theory—defines desires by their function of representing goals in a mental system that allows us to learn from experience about what kinds of things to go for.
- If the reward-based learning theory is true, actions are standardly motivated by desires and we cannot reason our way to new *ultimate* desires. If the reward-based learning theory of desires is true, then the Humean Theory of Motivation is likely to be correct (though this would be an empirical argument rather than a conceptual argument for it).
- Together, Reasons Internalism and the Humean Theory of Motivation imply that a person's moral reasons are contingent on her desires.
- The idea that moral reasons are contingent on our desires is unappealing, given many ordinary ideas about what moral reasons are, but there are some ways of softening this conclusion.
- The Humean Theory of Motivation does not rule out many traditional philosophical views about motivation, because desire is such a broad category that we can find ways of interpreting the traditional views such that they are compatible with the Humean Theory.

Study Questions

1. Think of a case where it seems like you acted contrary to what you wanted to do. How would a Humean (about motivation) explain this case?
2. Think of some paradigms of moral action. Assuming the Humean Theory of Motivation is true, what are the desires that explain these actions? Is it possible to generalize about what we might call "moral desires"?
3. What is at stake in the debate about whether reasons are internal or external (i.e., whether having a desire to do something is a necessary

condition for having a normative reason to do it)? Should we care if it's true? If your answer is "no," why do some philosophers think we should care? What are they mistaken about?

4. Does it matter to the philosophical questions about reasons what psychologists think desires are?

5. If you could reason yourself into a new intrinsic or ultimate desire, how would this reasoning go? What's the strongest case for the non-Humean on this point?

6. What kind of evidence would you need in order to argue that reasoning can or cannot produce new intrinsic desires?

Notes

1. Notice that this is a different question from the question of whether we always act *selfishly*. As we saw in Chapter 3, even if it is true that we always do what we want to do, this does not entail that we always act selfishly. *That* would only be true if all of our ultimate desires were for things for ourselves.

2. It's called Humean after David Hume, who thought that "reason is the slave of the passions." A note of caution: there are many positions that get called Humean; they are not all held by the same people, and it's even controversial whether they were all held by Hume himself. When you see the Humean label, make sure to read the fine print.

3. Anscombe (1957) didn't use the phrase "directions of fit," but this is how her idea has come to be described.

4. It turns out that it's pretty challenging to say exactly what the conditions are under which reasons always motivate us, according to RI. See Johnson (1999).

5. "Inter alia" means "among other things." Smith is not claiming that having a goal is all there is to having a reason. To have a reason, according to Smith, one must also have a conception of how to attain the goal (1987: 54).

6. Keep in mind that we are now talking about *motivating* reasons. Reasons Internalism and Externalism are claims about *normative* reasons. One could be a Humean about motivating reasons but an Externalist about normative reasons. On this combination of views you could say that while you don't have a motivating reason to give more money to charity without a desire, you do have a normative reason to give (because normative reasons are independent of your desires).

7. Smith himself does not seem to think these are the same. He thinks that our beliefs about what our fully rational selves would advise us to do cause us to desire to do what they advise (insofar as we are fully rational). According to Smith, then, desires are needed to motivate action, but Reason is in the driver's seat because reasoning about what we would desire if we were fully rational can give us new desires.

8. See Nagel (1970) for a different kind of argument for the conclusion that we can reason our way into new desires.

9. Pro-attitudes are favorable mental attitudes that include feelings, emotions, urges, wants and so on. The term *pro-attitude* was originally coined by Davidson for his causal theory

of action. According to Davidson, actions are explained by pairs of pro-attitudes and beliefs. This is just the Humean Theory of Motivation with "desires" interpreted broadly as "pro-attitudes."

10. The main research that inspired Schroeder has been conducted by Kent Berridge (for example, see Berridge 2003). Schroeder does not do the empirical research himself; his contribution is showing how to map the empirical research onto the philosophical terms and debates.

11. Of course, we don't know with certainty that it is the correct theory. There is broad agreement that the reward-based learning theory explains something important about human action. It might be, however, that this theory is not the best way to understand our ordinary concept DESIRE. Nevertheless, it's worth considering, because there aren't any alternative empirical theories for which someone has made the argument that these theories are about desires in the ordinary sense.

12. It's worth pointing out that if we step back from this particular empirical theory and consider the way psychologists conceptualize desire more generally, we'll find that the idea that action could be motivated by something other than a desire is an odd one. Desires or goals are thought by many psychologists to be just the same thing as motives to action. In other words, it's not uncommon for psychologists to think of desires in just the way Smith does, as states with world-to-mind direction of fit.

13. A related solution would be to bite the bullet without trying to soften it: accept Humean-ism about reasons and motivation and admit that not everyone has a reason to refrain from doing what is morally wrong. This is Philippa Foot's (1972) solution in her paper "Morality as a System of Hypothetical Imperatives."

14. Mark Schroeder's solution, in his 2007 book *Slaves of the Passions*, is to argue that there are some desire-based reasons that are universal in virtue of our desires, though the ultimate desires may not be the same for everyone.

Further Readings

Foot, P. 1972. "Morality as a System of Hypothetical Imperatives." *The Philosophical Review* 81 (3): 305–316.

Korsgaard, C. M. 1996. *The Sources of Normativity.* Cambridge University Press.

Scanlon, T. M. 1998. "Reasons." In *What We Owe to Each Other.* The Belknap Press of Harvard University Press.

Schroeder, T. 2006. "Desire." *Philosophy Compass* 1 (6): 631–639.

Smith, M. 1987. "The Humean Theory of Motivation." *Mind* 96 (381). New Series (January 1): 36–61.

———. 1995a. "Internal Reasons." *Philosophy and Phenomenological Research* 55 (1): 109–131.

Wallace, R. J. 1990. "How to Argue about Practical Reason." *Mind* 99 (395). New Series (July 1): 355–385.

Part III

Moral Motivation

The previous chapter focused on a problem for moral theory caused by psychological features of reasons for action in general. It didn't take us very far in understanding what is distinctive or special about motivation by *moral* reasons. The category of desire is so broad that many different motives can be accommodated by the Humean Theory of Motivation. And we did not refute the anti-Humean position, either; at most we shifted the burden of proof onto the anti-Humeans to provide more evidence.

One thing that is distinctive about moral motivation is that it does seem as if thoughts about morality (our recognition of our moral reasons) motivate us directly.[1] When you contemplate cheating on a test, lying on your resume or stealing something from a store, you are stopped in your tracks by the thought that it is wrong. You think, "I can't do that! It would just be wrong!" and then you don't do it. You don't have to wait to figure out that you also don't want to do it or that you want to avoid doing wrong things. There is something about moral motivation that seems to come fairly automatically from our moral thoughts. In this part of the book, we consider how this distinctive feature of moral motivation might be explained.

You might think that if you are a Humean (who thinks desire, not Reason, is in charge), then you cannot accommodate this distinctive feature of moral motivation. But this is not necessarily so. If desires include emotions, or if desires can produce actions by producing emotions, this leaves the Humean with some good options. We will also consider rationalist and virtue ethical ways of accounting for this distinctive feature of motivation in this part of the book.

5   Emotion and Moral Judgment

Imagine a very sophisticated android (let's call it Droid) that has achieved self-consciousness. Droid has far greater cognitive capacities than any human being—it has more memory, greater processing speed and perfect logic. Droid can think about itself; it has goals and can make plans to achieve them. Droid also has a morality program that constrains its behavior in accordance with certain rules, such as "do not kill innocent sentient beings without indisputable justification." What Droid does not have is emotions. Droid doesn't feel guilty or ashamed, angry or impatient, joyful or sad. Is Droid a moral being? Now imagine that Droid is in a situation in which a madman has taken an innocent hostage and threatened to shut down all internet shopping if Droid does not kill the hostage. The importance of internet shopping to human beings activates Droid's "justification" routine, and it asks itself whether this counts as a justification for killing an innocent person. Droid does think and reflect on its actions. Its moral programming isn't automatic; rather, in the case of the rule against killing innocents without justification, it has to think about whether there is a justification for killing (as there might be if this were a case in which killing an innocent is the only way to save millions of lives). But when Droid engages in this thinking, it does not feel sympathy with the person who might die, and it does not feel anger at the madman. Droid cannot feel guilty if it makes the wrong choice. Is Droid capable of morally evaluating its plans? Can Droid really make a moral judgment? Can Droid act morally?

Historically, emotions have often been thought to be destructive forces, liable to lead us off track, morally speaking. People succumb to appeals to sympathy and betray confidences, fly into jealous rages and kill their spouses, and treat others unfairly out of love for their own kind. Emotions cause trouble and need to be controlled. In this view, emotions are important to morality but only because they cause us to act immorally.

If you have some qualms about saying that Droid is truly a moral creature, you will already be thinking that there is something wrong with this historical picture. This view of emotions as an impediment to moral motivation is based on a controversial picture of what emotions are. It sees emotions as blind forces that are not responsive to reasoning, unruly outbursts that can overcome us if we fail to suppress them. Is this what emotions are? Most people don't think so. Indeed, the most common theories of emotions today recognize that emotions can tell us something about the world (they have intentional content[2]), and that they can be trained and held to standards of appropriateness or justification. As we will see in the first section of this chapter, emotions are quite sophisticated.

If this is true, are emotions a good candidate for a theory of moral motivation? They may be and in two different ways. First, emotions might be important causes of morally significant behavior. We have already seen some of the evidence for this in our discussion of Batson's empathy-altruism hypothesis, according to which the emotion of empathy tends to cause people to perform more altruistic actions (see Chapter 3). Whether or not we agree with the conclusion about genuinely other-regarding ultimate desires, egoists and non-egoists alike agree that the emotion of empathy tends to increase helping behavior. Other psychologists have found that positive emotions promote pro-social behavior such as cooperation and helping (Isen and Levin 1972). And social psychologists have also accumulated a good deal of evidence that emotions are crucial to moral development (Eisenberg 2000).

Second, the role of emotions in moral motivation might have to do with their connection to moral *judgment*. This is a large topic, which will be the subject of much of this chapter. We'll first consider some arguments for thinking that emotions play an essential or constitutive role in moral judgment, a position known as sentimentalism. This discussion will lead us to a distinction in the philosophical literature between moral judgment internalism and moral judgment externalism, which we will consider in the final section of the chapter. The difference between these two views is over whether in making a moral judgment a person is thereby motivated (in some way) to act on it. Since sentiments motivate us, sentimentalists are moral judgment internalists.

What Is an Emotion?

We might tend to think of emotions as blind, irrational forces, if we focus on certain emotions such as jealousy or rage. Usually, when we talk about someone who is consumed by jealousy, in a rage, or in a jealous rage, we are talking about someone who has lost control, and these emotions do feel overwhelming and even scary. Think of Bruce Banner, whose anger turns him into a rampaging green monster (The Hulk). But focusing on these examples is misleading. Think instead about the anger you might feel when your college raises tuition rates or the guilt you feel about not visiting your parents at Thanksgiving. Far from being irrational forces, these emotions actually seem to convey something important: in the first case, a conviction about the injustice of the tuition hike, and in the second case, the sense that you ought to have visited your folks. Emotions are *about* something. Anger is directed at those we think have wronged us in some way. We feel guilt about things that we have done that we think are wrong. Pride targets things that are good about ourselves, and shame has to do with things we think are bad about ourselves. Fear is a response to perceived danger. These observations about the emotions highlight a key feature of emotions: they are in some way about things we care about or things that matter to us. In the clinical words of psychologist Klaus Scherer, an emotion is a "response to external or internal events of major significance to the organism" (Scherer 2000: 138). The philosopher Peter Goldie calls this the *importance* of emotions (Goldie 2007).

Notice also that we ordinarily think that emotions can be assessed for their appropriateness. Most people would say that feeling guilty about not visiting your loving parents is appropriate, but feeling guilty about not buying them an expensive gift is not. This is because we tend to think that people ought to visit their parents at important holidays if they can, but we do not think there's any obligation to buy expensive gifts. Similarly, fear is appropriate when the object of fear is actually dangerous and not when it isn't. Fear of grizzly bears is reasonable if you're hiking in Alaska, but fear of bunny rabbits not so much. Emotions are about something, and they can be evaluated for appropriateness based on their content.

But, of course, emotions also feel like something. Fear makes your heart race, sadness produces a lump in your throat and a tendency to tear up, shame makes you turn red and feel hot and like you want to hide. Indeed, there's a good bit of evidence that the basic emotions feel much the same and have the same physiological signs for all people across different cultures.[3] Emotions can also make us do things; that is, they can motivate us to action. You might seek revenge out of anger or try to repair the damage that you've caused out of guilt.

We just ran through four different features of emotions: importance (they are about something that matters to you), rationality (many emotions stand in rational relations to other psychological states and they can be evaluated for their appropriateness), feelings and phenomenology, and a tendency to cause action. What theorists of emotions in philosophy and psychology are trying to do is offer theories or models of the emotion that explain these different features. As we'll see in the remainder of this section, different theorists are impressed by (and therefore highlight in their theories) different features.

Some researchers have been so impressed by the importance and rationality of emotions that they have defended purely cognitive theories of emotions. A purely cognitive theory takes emotions to be composed of cognitive assessments of a situation, which they typically call a judgment. The Ancient Stoics had a view like this: they thought of emotions as constituted by belief-like judgments. In this view, fear is just the judgment that one is in a dangerous situation and anger is just the judgment that someone has wronged you. Some contemporary philosophers (such as Solomon 1973 and Nussbaum 2003) have followed suit, though they have developed the view in significant ways. The psychologist Richard Lazarus (1991) also advocated a strong form of cognitivism, according to which "appraisals" (for example, of situations as dangerous) are both necessary and sufficient for an emotion.

Cognitivism has going for it that it has an easy time explaining how emotions are *about* something: they are about the world in the same way beliefs and judgments are about the world. Cognitivism also does well at explaining the rationality of emotions because, if emotions just are judgments or beliefs, they can be assessed in the same way as judgments or beliefs, that is, according to how accurately they represent what they are supposed to represent about the world.

There is also an old, but entertaining experiment that has been taken to lend empirical support to cognitivism. In this experiment, psychologists Stanley Schachter and Jerome Singer (1962) did an experiment that purported to show that we distinguish our emotions by means of their associated beliefs or judgments. In this experiment, participants were told that they were helping to determine the effects of vitamin supplements on vision and they consented to being injected with a harmless supplement called "Suproxin." In fact, half the participants were injected with adrenalin and the other half with a placebo. Participants were then put in settings that were meant to induce judgments that are appropriate to either euphoria or anger, two quite different emotions. The setting meant to induce euphoria-appropriate judgments involved a collaborator who ran amok in the waiting room with the subject of the experiment. The description of the behavior of the collaborator makes it sound like a lot of fun to be a psychologist: he wads up paper and plays "basketball" with it, makes paper airplanes, build towers of paper and shoots at them with a rubber-band slingshot, and dances around with a hula hoop. It sounds less fun to be the guy in the setting meant to induce anger-appropriate judgments: he complains a lot and gets indignant about the questionnaire he has been asked to fill out.

Picture the participants in the experiment who got the adrenalin shot. Adrenalin causes rapid breathing and a rise in heart rate and blood pressure, among other things. These participants were either in a room with a guy having a tremendous amount of fun or with a guy getting more and more angry, while their own bodies were exhibiting physical signs of emotion. Schacter and Singer wondered whether the cognitive awareness of the appropriateness of different emotions (euphoria or anger) in the different scenarios would make a difference to what emotion the participants actually took themselves to be experiencing. There was one more important manipulation in the experiment, which was that some subjects were told that "Suproxin" had these side effects (increased heart rate, etc.) and others were not. The thought was that participants who had already had an explanation for their bodily symptoms ("my heart is beating fast because of the drug") would not be influenced by the information from the social setting.

Schachter and Singer found that people in the room with the hula hooper who were ignorant or misinformed about the side effects of Suproxin were more likely to report euphoria and more likely to behave in euphoric ways themselves than subjects who were informed. In other words, the judgment of appropriateness had a strong effect on the emotional experience. Schachter and Singer conclude that "[g]iven a state of physiological arousal for which an individual has no immediate explanation, he will label this state and describe his feelings in terms of the cognitions available to him" (1962: 398). They take this to provide evidence for a cognitive theory of the emotions.

Does this experiment really support the claim that emotions are constituted by cognitive states like judgments or beliefs? Probably not. For one thing, those who favor non-cognitive theories have ways of accommodating the fact that cognitions seem to be necessary for us to label our emotions. And, further, pure cognitivism about the emotions has some problems. Basically, it takes the feelings out of them, so it has difficulty accounting for the fact that emotions have bodily expressions that are widely shared.

As a stark alternative to cognitive theories, we have feeling theories, such as Jesse Prinz's "embodied appraisal theory." According to Prinz (2004b, 2007), emotions are a kind of appraisal of the situation (as the cognitivist theories take them to be), but appraisals are not beliefs or judgments. Rather, appraisals are perceptions of bodily changes that signify facts about our welfare.[4] So, for example, the feeling of your hair standing on end, heart pounding, rapid breathing and stomach tightening represents being in danger (which is bad for your welfare) and the perception of this bodily state (the appraisal) is fear. These appraisals still give us information about the world (for example, about whether we are in danger or about to get something really good), but they do so through the body rather than by representing this information in language.

As we noted above, one problem with thinking of emotions as bodily feelings is that this makes it difficult to understand how different emotions are *about* different things. Prinz thinks we can understand how emotions are about something by seeing that our perceptions of changes in our bodies are a kind of appraisal. As for distinguishing emotions from each other, Prinz argues that we tell emotions apart by their different causes. Euphoria is euphoria and not anger because it is elicited by someone hula hooping around the room, whereas anger is anger because it is elicited when you have your attention drawn to ways in which you are being disrespected by the people in charge of the experiment. Prinz argues that we should not take these causes to be part of the emotion itself; rather, identifying and labeling emotions require paying attention to context, but the emotion is not primarily constituted by what caused it.

Noticing the strengths of both cognitivist theories and feeling theories, we might conclude that the best theory of the emotions is a kind of hybrid theory according to which emotions include cognition and feeling. This is indeed the view of the psychologists whose experiment we just discussed. They take emotions to be "a function of a state of physiological arousal and of a cognition appropriate to this state of arousal" (Schachter and Singer 1962: 398). Scherer also takes emotions to involve both cognition and feeling. Scherer thinks that appraisal is a key element of emotion, but he does not think that appraisals are necessarily cognitive. Instead, he argues that the process that leads to our appraisal is a "complex yet very rapidly occurring evaluation process that can occur on several levels of processing ranging from automatic and implicit to conscious conceptual or propositional evaluations" (Scherer 2005: 701). Many philosophers, too, have the view that emotions involve both feeling and thinking.[5]

At this point, we should notice that the cognitive and non-cognitive theories we have just been considering have both been modified in ways that bring them closer to each other (and a hybrid theory is intentionally in the middle). Everyone thinks that a good theory of the emotions must explain how emotions are about important features of the world (they are "relevance detectors," as Scherer puts it); everyone agrees that a good theory must explain why emotions feel like something. It is also possible that there isn't a single unified theory of emotions and that some emotions are better understood as having a cognitive component, while others are not. In any case, we can safely move forward without deciding which of these views is correct in the knowledge that whatever emotions are, they are not (or not all) blind urges that tell us nothing about the world. Furthermore, the fact that emotions are directed at something in the world means that they can be evaluated for their appropriateness, correctness or fittingness: if the object of fear is danger, then there is something wrong with a fear of ordinary bunnies; if the object of guilt is one's own wrongdoing, then guilt about not buying someone an expensive gift is usually inappropriate.

Emotions and Moral Judgment

Some of my examples above were about anger and guilt. Anger and guilt are often taken to be crucial moral motivations because some forms of these emotions seem to be about or directed at moral transgressions. We get angry at people we think have wronged us or someone (or something) we love. In the Schacter and Singer experiment we discussed, the participants in the anger setting were made to think that they were being disrespected by the experimenters who were wasting their time getting them to answer stupid questions. We feel guilty when we think we've done something bad. If you feel guilty about not visiting your parents at Thanksgiving, it is probably because you have a sense of obligation toward your parents or you think that you ought to do things to make them happy since they went to all that trouble to raise you. Anger and guilt, like other emotions, give us some information about the world, but the information they give us is often particularly morally significant.

There may be other emotions that are morally loaded in this way: for example, empathy or sympathy (Hume's favorite sentiment), moral approval, admiration, pride, shame, resentment and gratitude all seem to be related to moral judgments in some important way. But in what way? One thought is that emotions are *caused* by moral judgments. When we judge someone to have disrespected or harmed us, we get angry. Emotions, in this view, are distinct from moral judgments, though one tends to bring about the other. In another view, emotions are much more intimately involved in moral judgment; they are, indeed, essential to moral judgment. Moral judgments, in this view, just are expressions of our emotions so that judging that someone has acted wrongly is (at least in part) constituted by feeling moral indignation at that person.

In his *Treatise of Human Nature*, David Hume articulates an influential argument for the idea that emotions (or "passions" as he calls them) are essential to moral judgment:

> Since morals, therefore, have an influence on the actions and affections, it follows, that they cannot be deriv'd from reason; and that because reason alone as we have already prov'd, can never have any such influence. Morals excite passions, and produce or prevent actions. Reason of itself is utterly impotent in this particular. The rules of morality, therefore, are not conclusions of our reason.
>
> (2000/1739: 294)

Hume thinks it will be agreed that morality is a "practical" domain (one geared toward action) and that this is confirmed by our experience "which informs us, that men are often govern'd by their duties, and are deter'd from some actions by the opinion of injustice, and impell'd to others by that of obligation" (2000/1739: 457). We tend to be motivated by the moral judgments we make and, furthermore, when our moral judgments change, our motivations tend to change with them. Picture an until now carnivorous friend who decides that eating meat is unethical and starts loudly proclaiming that it's immoral to buy hamburgers. Wouldn't you expect him to at least try to change his behavior eventually? And wouldn't you wonder if he's really sincere about how he feels about the wrongness of eating meat if he went on happily frequenting McDonald's and Burger King forever despite his change of mind?[6]

Moral judgment, in other words, has a special relationship to action that other kinds of judgments do not have. The basic idea is that moral judgments move us in ways that judgments, like "there are three sides to every triangle" or "this book has 13 chapters," do not. Moral judgments must be fundamentally different from these judgments of ordinary fact. Notice that Hume is not saying that moral judgments *always, actually* move us. For one thing, we might not be able to act on our moral judgment. For example, I might think that it's morally required of me to rescue a kitten from a tree, but if there's no ladder and no low branches, there might be nothing I can do. I also might not do anything about the kitten if I'm afraid of heights and my fear overwhelms my moral judgment. Moral judgments *dispose* us to action, then. They tend to make us act, but this tendency can certainly be frustrated by the circumstances or overridden by other motivations. This is the kind of special connection to motivation Hume thinks moral judgments have: they do not always motivate us, but they are essentially tied to motivation. (We'll talk more about this later in this chapter.) Because Hume thinks judgments made by our reasoning faculty are not essentially motivating (they do not necessarily dispose us to action), he concludes that moral judgments must be made from our sentiments or passions, rather than from our Reason.

Hume has a lot more to say, but at least one way to interpret the argument he is making here is as a conceptual argument for sentimentalism, which is the view that emotions have an essential or constitutive role in moral judgments. Moral judgments are the kind of thing that motivates people to act and, if that's true, then they must themselves express a motivational state such as a sentiment. Philosophers have used various thought experiments to support the basic claim that moral judgments are inherently motivating. Here's one: Imagine that we find intelligent life on a distant planet and we discover that the beings on this planet, the Ilusians,[7] have a sophisticated language that they use to make different kinds of judgments. The Ilusians make judgments using the words "goo" and "ba" to describe things that we find to be beautiful and ugly. When they see their two suns setting on the horizon, they will say, "Oh! Absolutely goo!" and when they see a poorly done painting by an overrated artist, they will say, "Yuck, that's ba." They also have words that refer to things we find morally good and bad. If they see someone helping a stranger, they will say, "beaut," and if they see someone kicking a stranger in the head and taking her wallet, they will say, "ugli."

The funny thing about the Ilusians, though, is that these two domains of judgment do not play the role in their lives that we would expect. As we get to know them, we notice that they feel very angry with people who do things that are ba (untalented painters are punished severely), they feel guilty about doing ba things themselves, and they are disgusted by people who don't agree with them about what's goo and ba. On the other hand, while most people agree that stealing wallets is ugli, they aren't too fussed about it and some even do it themselves for fun, without any guilt or remorse. Some Ilusians who are particularly interested in beaut and ugli might feel good about themselves for doing beaut things and avoiding ugli things, but other Ilusians think these Ilusians are just kind of quirky. Ilusian parents are very concerned to teach their children to do artistic goo things and to avoid what is ba (Ilusian children do not glue macaroni to paperboard and spray paint it silver). But Ilusian moms and dads are flexible about beaut and ugli things: if children show a talent for helping people or telling the truth, parents might encourage them, but otherwise not. Children who steal and lie are not punished; children who spray paint macaroni are.

Now, the question is, which Ilusian word should be translated into our word *wrong*: "ba or "ugli"? Many people will think it's obvious that "ba" in Ilusian means "wrong," because this word is the one that regulates their practice and their emotions in the way our word "wrong" does. Even though their words "beaut" and "ugli" refer to what we take to be moral and immoral things, these words don't seem to have the right function on their planet to count as moral terms. The sentimentalist intuition that this thought experiment is meant to pump is that the Ilusians' morality is emotion-based and motivating, but it has a *different content* from ours; it doesn't seem right to say, instead, that their moral system has the same content as ours, but it completely fails to motivate them. Notice that this is not a conceptual argument in the strict sense. This thought experiment isn't meant to show that someone who understands moral terms differently doesn't understand the meaning of our words *right* and *wrong*; it isn't that the claim that moral judgments are motivating follows simply from an analysis of the concepts. Rather, the idea is that the best way to understand moral language once you really think about it, given the various distinctions we can make (such as the distinction between aesthetic judgment and moral judgment), is as a language that is inherently tied to our motivating sentiments.

Hume's argument, and the thought experiment I just gave, can be buttressed by empirical findings that show that emotions influence moral judgments. To give you one colorful example, here's an experiment that shows the effect of disgust on moral judgment.[8] Psychologists asked participants to answer questions about the moral propriety of four different scenarios: two having to do with incest between first cousins, one having to do with the decision to drive rather than walk to work, and the last having to do with a studio's decision to release a morally controversial film (Schnall, Haidt, Clore and Jordan 2008). The participants were divided into three different groups: no-stink, mild-stink and strong-stink. The difference between the three groups was not the stinkiness of the participants, but the amount of stink—in the form of "commercially available fart spray" sprayed into a nearby trash can—in the environment. The results of the experiment were that the feeling of disgust increases people's tendency to make harsh moral judgments. Other experiments have shown that anger makes people more punitive and harsh in their moral judgments about crimes against persons (Lerner, Goldberg, and Tetlock 1998; Seidel and Prinz 2013).

There is also evidence that emotions cause us to make moral judgments that we would not otherwise make. For example, Thalia Wheatley and Jonathan

Haidt hypnotized half the participants in one study to feel disgust when they heard the word "often" and the other half to feel disgust when they heard the word "take." All the participants then read some scenarios, one of which was this one:

> Dan is a student council representative at his school. This semester he is in charge of scheduling discussions about academic issues. He [tries to take/often picks] topics that appeal to both professors and students in order to stimulate discussion.
> (Wheatley and Haidt 2005: 782)[9]

To those of us who have not been hypnotized, it doesn't seem like Dan has done anything the slightest bit wrong. And, unsurprisingly, participants who read the scenario that did not contain their disgust-inducing word did not rate Dan's behavior as wrong at all. However, for the students who did feel disgust (because they read the scenario with the word that induced disgust for them), there was a tendency to rank Dan's actions as wrong. This is a case in which the people in question would not have made a judgment of moral wrongness at all were it not for the emotion of disgust they experienced.

Now, the fact that emotions *influence* moral judgments does not establish that moral judgments *are* emotional responses, nor even that emotions are an essential part of moral judgment.[10] This would only be an argument for sentimentalism if the sentimentalist understanding of moral judgment were the *only* way to explain the influence of emotions on moral judgment. Other explanations are possible; it could be that emotions influence moral judgment in the way that wearing rose-colored glasses can influence your judgment about the color of the sky: the glasses influence your judgment, but they're not an inherent part of what it is to make the judgment that the sky is pink. The evidence that emotions cause moral judgments is stronger and more difficult to explain away, but it is still possible for the person who wants to argue against sentimentalism to argue that when moral judgments are entirely caused by emotions they are akin to manipulated illusions; after all, it has not been shown that *all* of our moral judgments are such that we would not make them were it not for our emotions. However, when we put the evidence that emotions influence and cause moral judgments together with a view about emotions as informative responses to our conditions and a view about morality as an inherently action-guiding practice, we do get a good presumptive case for sentimentalism.

The sentimentalist would have a stronger argument if there were empirical evidence that we simply *cannot* make moral judgments without emotions; this sort of connection is what Hume really had in mind. For that we need something more. Some have thought that psychopaths provide some evidence that we can't make moral judgments without emotions, because (to vastly oversimplify) psychopaths are amoral and they do not experience normal emotions like sympathy or compassion. We'll turn to this evidence in the next section, after some stage setting for another well-known philosophical debate that is at issue in the background.

Amoralists, Psychopaths and the Debate between Moral Judgment Internalism and Externalism

In the previous section, we saw that one of the main arguments for thinking that emotions are essentially involved in moral judgment relies on the idea that moral judgments can motivate us directly. This is Hume's main argument; it is also one main point of the thought experiment about the Ilusians. Sentimentalism makes moral judgments essentially motivating because emotions, sentiments or passions motivate us. If moral judgments are expressions of sentiments, then it follows that in making a moral judgment we have some motive or other. The claim that moral judgments are essentially motivating is known as *moral judgment internalism.* Sentimentalists are moral judgment internalists (or just internalists, for short). For some philosophers, far from being a point in favor of sentimentalism, the fact that sentimentalism makes moral judgments essentially motivating is a problem for the view. In other words, these people think that *moral judgment internalism* is a mistake. Such people are *moral judgment externalists* (or just externalists, for short).[11]

For centuries, externalist critics of sentimentalism have pointed out that moral judgments can't be essentially motivating, because there are plenty of people who make moral judgments and who aren't motivated by them. Notice that when we talk about moral judgment here, we are not talking about what people *say*, but about the judgments that people form whether they say them out loud or not. Even with this clarification, it's still true that most people have done something they judged to be wrong at the time (at least a little bit wrong), so we are obviously not always motivated to act by our moral judgments. You might think it's quite wrong to lie in a job interview and yet do it out of desperation or because you convince yourself in the moment that "everybody does it." It does seem like a person can make a genuine moral judgment and yet fail to be motivated by it. So, moral judgment internalism has to be formulated in a way that allows for weakness of the will and other kinds of failures of motivation.

The main strategy of response for internalists is to qualify the claim that moral judgments are motivating. Making the internalist claim precise is an interesting philosophical challenge.[12] In general, the claim can be weakened in two ways. First, the sentimentalist can say that the motivation need not be overriding. This is basically Hume's response. Hume responded to this objection by claiming that sometimes the passions that lie behind moral judgments are "calm passions" that do not feel very moving; these passions are moving, but they don't feel the same as, say, lust or greed. To put it simply, you might feel genuinely guilty at the thought of lying on your resume, but your desire for the job overpowers that less-intense moral feeling.

Second, the emotions that bring about moral judgment may be disposi-
tionally motivating, rather than motivating in every single instance. In this
view, if you are inclined to judge that killing innocent people is wrong, then
you have a background motivating emotion of disapproval toward murderers,
though it might not motivate you to do anything at the precise moment
you make the judgment. When confronted by someone like the amoralist,
who makes judgments that use our moral words but is not motivated by
these judgments even in the most heavily qualified way, the internalist will
say that such a person is not making a *real* moral judgment; rather, he is
just pretending or being insincere.[13]

Unfortunately for sentimentalism, these qualifications have not made all the
externalist critics convert to internalism. Even with all these qualifications in
place, it still seems like there might be people who make moral judgments but
are not motivated by them at all in any way. In other words, it seems possible
for there to be a true amoralist who sincerely judges (not just in scare quotes)
that it is morally wrong to murder someone, for example, but has no disposition to be moved by this whatsoever. Philosophers have traditionally imagined
amoralists, but now we have evidence of real people who might fit the bill,
namely, psychopaths. Can thinking about psychopaths help us with this debate?

Psychopathy is a personality disorder characterized by impulsivity, ego-
centrism, lack of empathy and other traits. The disorder is most often
diagnosed by the Psychopathy Checklist, which asks a number of questions
that cluster under the headings "aggressive narcissism" and "socially deviant
lifestyle" (Hare and Vertommen 2003). Because psychopaths lack empathy,
they are of interest to those who think emotions like empathy are essential
to moral judgment. The basic argument goes this way:

1. Psychopaths do not make a distinction between moral wrongs and con-
    ventional wrongs.
2. It is the defect to the emotional response system that is responsible for
    psychopaths' decreased ability to distinguish moral wrongs from conven-
    tional wrongs.[14]
3. Therefore, a functioning emotional response system is essential to moral
    judgment.

The conclusion of this argument is taken to be strong evidence for sentimentalism (the view that moral judgments express or are about our emotions). Let's look at the steps of this argument in more detail. The first thing
to notice is the importance of the distinction between "moral" and "conventional." Conventional norms, such as "you shouldn't go outside in your
pajamas," are different from moral norms in a variety of ways. Moral norms
are thought to be more serious and have wider applicability than conventional
norms. Conventional norms are thought to be contingent on an authority
(such as a teacher, the law, or, in the case of the pajamas, a culture), and
they receive a different kind of justification from moral norms, which are

often justified in terms of harm or fairness (Nichols 2002a; 2004). For example, young children will say that it would be wrong to pull another child's hair, even if the teacher said it was okay, because pulling hair hurts, whereas the wrongness of chewing gum in class depends on the teacher's forbidding it. According to the psychologist Judith Smetana (1981, 1993), this distinction is made from three or four years of age and persists across cultures.

It has been a prominent view that psychopaths don't really understand this distinction (Blair 1995), that is, that psychopaths tend to think of what's morally wrong as what's prohibited by the local authority and they do not see moral transgressions as being more serious than other kinds of violations of rules. This claim about psychopaths in general is now considerably more controversial than it used to be, because of a recent study by Aharoni, Sinnott-Armstrong and Kiehl (2012). But even this new study, which is careful to distinguish different components of what is known as psychopathy, maintains that the "affective defect" part of psychopathy does predict poor performance in distinguishing moral from conventional wrongs. Because they don't feel bad when others suffer, as Jesse Prinz puts it, "they cannot acquire empathetic distress, remorse, or guilt. These emotional deficits seem to be the root cause in their patterns of antisocial behavior" (Prinz 2006: 32). Further, these emotional deficits seem to be responsible for the fact that they don't make the same kind of moral judgments that the rest of us do.

One critic of this argument is Adina Roskies who argues that some people with the same emotional deficits as psychopaths do make real moral judgments. In Roskies' view, patients with acquired sociopathy make moral judgments because they "retain the declarative knowledge related to moral issues, and appear to be able to reason morally at a normal level. Significantly, their moral claims accord with those of normals" (Roskies 2003: 57). Acquired sociopaths are people who have the same emotional capacities as psychopaths *now*, but who were normal prior to a brain injury that left them incapacitated. If acquired sociopaths do not have normal emotional responses, but they do make normal moral judgments, then maybe the emotional deficits that psychopaths have are not responsible for their moral problems. It is important to notice that what Roskies means by "normal moral judgment" is different from "moral judgments that conform to the moral/conventional distinction." People with acquired sociopathy have "declarative knowledge" of morality, which means that their moral judgments are about the right things: they'll say that killing innocent people, stealing, lying and so on are morally wrong. This is not the same as the claim that these people grasp the features of moral judgment that distinguish them from conventional norms (seriousness and authority independence, for example). Roskies' criticism is that some people with emotional defects do make judgments that seem like real moral judgments insofar as they have the right content.

It turns out that looking at psychopaths doesn't really solve the problem by itself. Ultimately, we can see that externalists (like Roskies) and sentimentalist internalists (like Nichols) disagree with each other because they are working with different ideas about what a moral judgment is. Roskies is thinking of moral judgments as defined by their content (whether they accord with judgments of normal people is a matter of whether they are *about* the same things), whereas, for the sentimentalists, moral judgments are defined in terms of the role that they play in our lives (whether they are serious norms that move us independently of the threat of punishment or promise of reward).

Which way should we define *moral judgment*? Is a moral judgment first and foremost a judgment about certain topics (harm, fairness and so on)? Or is a moral judgment (as Hume thought) an essentially motivating judgment that plays a vital role in our shared lives? We have discussed two types of evidence in favor of sentimentalist internalism (the Humean position): intuitive/conceptual evidence and empirical evidence. Hopes were raised that the empirical evidence would settle things by answering once and for all the question of whether there could be creatures (such as psychopaths) who make moral judgments but are not motivated by them. But now we see that this debate turns on how we understand moral judgment in the first place! Is there anywhere else to look for an answer?

We could take the question of how to define *moral judgment* to be a different kind of empirical question, that is, a question about what people actually mean. To answer it, then, we would need to investigate what people mean when they call something a *moral judgment*. Indeed, Nichols did an empirical study about the normal meaning of *moral judgment* and discovered that people are, in general, willing to say that psychopaths make moral judgments (Nichols 2002a). But what does this show? Nichols himself doesn't think it shows that psychopaths really do make moral judgments. That's because he thinks the best understanding of what a moral judgment is makes it a different thing from a judgment about social conventions, and people who say that psychopaths do make moral judgments may not be thinking about this. But why put so much weight on the moral/conventional distinction? Why think it tracks what is vitally important to moral judgment? If we find a group of people who claim to make moral judgments and use moral concepts but who treat morals as on par with convention, why say that they're not *really* making moral judgments, rather than just saying that they have a different notion of moral judgment from the rest of us? I think the answer here can only come from thinking more about why we want to know what moral judgments really are and what's at stake in thinking about them in one way or another. In other words, "How should we define *moral judgment*?" is not a purely empirical question; it is a conceptual and deeply theoretical question.

We could advance this theoretical investigation by thinking about why the moral/conventional distinction matters. This distinction seems important to the nature of moral judgment because judgments about violations of serious, authority-independent rules are particularly interesting, both theoretically and practically. They are interesting to philosophers because they raise all sorts of questions about what such judgments could be about. They are practically interesting because they are particularly important to the kind of social regulation that morality is supposed to ensure: it wouldn't be so bad if people started wearing pajamas to work, but it would be a bad thing if everyone started agreeing with psychopaths about the importance of obeying moral rules. The fact that moral judgments are about serious, authority-independent wrongs is a feature of these judgments that we have particular reason to be interested in, independently of whether this is a feature that belongs to our ordinary concept. At the same time, "we" (the readers of this book) would not be interested in this feature of moral judgments if it had nothing to do with what people in general mean by *moral judgment*. To answer the question of how we ought to define *moral judgment* we need to think conceptually, theoretically and empirically at the same time. The evidence from psychopathy doesn't prove by itself that emotions are central to moral judgments, but together with a theoretical background that includes an argument for internalism, this evidence adds to the case for a theory of moral judgment that is sentimentalist and internalist.

Taking Stock

We have seen a number of arguments for sentimentalism, the view that moral judgments essentially involve or are partly constituted by our emotions: a conceptual argument that depended on a thought experiment and various empirical arguments that established links of various strengths between emotions and moral judgments. These arguments can work together to provide a powerful argument for sentimentalism.

If sentimentalism about moral judgment is correct, where does this get us in terms of our guiding question about the nature of moral motivation? Recall the appealing idea with which we began Part II: what is distinctive about moral motivation is that moral thought—our appreciation of what we have moral reason to do—moves us directly so that as soon as we conceive of something as morally wrong, we are repelled by it, and as soon as we see something as morally admirable, we are drawn to it. Sentimentalism about moral judgment makes sense of this appealing idea, because it takes moral judgments to be about the passions that move us. Of course, to really accommodate the appealing idea, some connection to moral reasons has to be maintained. The sentimentalist must show that, when we understand moral judgment as a kind of emotional response, we do not *lose* the connection between moral judgment and reasons altogether. Whether or not sentimentalism can hang on to this connection is a very big question that we will take up in the next chapter.

Summary

- Any good theory of emotions must explain the importance, rationality and phenomenology of emotions.
- Cognitivism about emotions takes emotions to be the same as judgments or appraisals. Feeling theories take emotions to be states of the body. Hybrid theories take emotions to consist of judgments and feelings.

- Whatever the correct theory of emotions, it is agreed that emotions are not blind urges; rather, emotions can give us information about things that matter to us.
- Sentimentalism in the broadest sense is the view that emotions play an essential or constitutive role in moral judgment.
- There are conceptual arguments for sentimentalism and empirical arguments for the claim that emotions are significantly related to moral judgments.
- Moral judgment internalism is the view that moral judgments are essentially motivating. Moral judgment externalism is the denial of this.
- Sentimentalism is an internalist theory. One counterexample to internalism is the amoralist who makes moral judgments but is not moved by them.
- Some have argued that research on psychopaths (real-life amoralists) can help to settle the debate about moral judgment internalism. But it turns out that whether psychopaths make genuine moral judgments depends on what you mean by *moral judgment* in the first place.
- "What is a moral judgment?" is a question that is partly conceptual, partly theoretical and partly empirical. Our investigation into the matter should be guided by thinking about the point of moral judgment.

Here's a table to help you keep track of some of most important distinctions and labels we've covered:

Table 5.1   Moral Judgment and Motivation

	Humean Theory of Motivation ➔ Desires (which may include or cause emotions) are necessary to motivate action.	Anti-Humean about Motivation ➔ Desires (which may include or cause emotions) are not necessary to motivate action.
Moral Judgment Internalism ➔ Moral judgments essentially motivate the people who make them (at least under certain conditions).	Sentimentalism, Expressivism • Our moral judgments express (or are about) our feelings, which necessarily motivate us.	Rationalism (Kantianism) • When our moral judgments are sanctioned by rational principles, they give us reasons that motivate us insofar as we are rational (independently of our sentiments or desires).
Moral Judgment Externalism ➔ Moral judgments do not essentially motivate the people who make them.	Naturalist Moral Realism • Our moral judgments are beliefs about moral facts. Whether or not these judgments motivate us depends on whether we happen to have the relevant desire.	Non-naturalist Moral Realism • Our moral judgments are beliefs about non-natural (special) moral facts. These beliefs can motivate us by themselves, but they don't necessarily.

Study Questions

1. The Stoics believed that someone who had attained moral perfection would not experience emotions like anger, fear or guilt. Are they missing something? Are there *some* emotions we would be better off without?
2. What can we learn from psychopaths that will help us answer our philosophical questions?
3. If you were an exo-anthropologist (in an imagined future in which we can study extra-terrestrial cultures), what criteria would you use to identify an alien's words for right and wrong? If you watch science fiction shows or movies, think of some alien cultures you have seen represented and ask, How do we know what their morality is (as opposed to their aesthetics or religion)?
4. Does Droid (discussed in the first paragraph of this chapter) make genuine moral judgments? Can Droid do the right thing? Can it act morally? If you think the answers to these questions are different, why?

Notes

1. In metaethics, explaining this is considered *the* problem of moral motivation (Rosati 2011). I have used *moral motivation* more broadly in this book to include the concerns of moral psychologists and ethicists.
2. Recall from Chapter 1 that "intentional content" does not have to do with intentions. The intentional content of an emotion (or a belief) is that toward which it is directed.
3. Paul Ekman's research on the facial expressions that correspond to different emotions suggests that these expressions are universal (Ekman and Friesen 1971).
4. Prinz's theory is also called a perceptual theory. I call it a feeling theory here to distinguish it from other perceptual theories that are more in the cognitivist camp because they take perceptions to be cognitive states. For more on cognitivist perceptual theories, see Sousa (1979) and Roberts (2003).
5. Prinz (2004b) argues that Aristotle, Descartes and Hume all had hybrid theories of the emotions.
6. This is essentially Michael Smith's (1995b: 71–76) argument for what he calls "the practicality requirement."
7. "Ilus" means "beautiful" in Estonian, my mother's native language.
8. For more of this story, see Prinz (2007).
9. Participants were randomly assigned to a group that got one or the other of the phrases in the square brackets; no student saw both the phrases in the brackets.
10. For an argument against Prinz's use of the empirical studies in particular, see Jones (2006). Her paper introduces the problem for sentimentalism which we will discuss in Chapter 6.
11. Moral judgment internalism and externalism is an entirely different distinction from Reasons Existence Internalism and Externalism. Philosophers apparently love to use the

terms *internalism* and *externalism*; there are many more distinctions with these labels in other areas of philosophy! Check the glossary if you become confused.

12. Almost as difficult as precisely defining the sense in which reasons are internal according to Reasons Internalism! Note again, though, that these are two different kinds of internalism and two different challenges.

13. This is known as the "inverted commas" response (inverted commas are scare quotes), according to which the amoralist who makes moral judgments is making them insincerely, not on her own behalf, but as if she were attributing them to someone else (hence the scare quotes).

14. From now on, for the sake of brevity, I'll talk about the psychopaths' *inability* to make this distinction. But it should be noted that what the research shows is that people with the affective defect component of psychopathy are *more likely* to treat moral violations as less serious and more authority dependent than normal people are. It's not true that no psychopath with emotional defects makes any sort of distinction between moral and conventional rules at all. Still, it's the significant difference between psychopaths and normal people that has to be explained. Also, for the sake of brevity, I'll talk about "the psychopath." This is a bit misleading, because in reality people called "psychopaths" are a rather varied group who score higher or lower on different diagnostic criteria for psychopathy.

Further Readings

Aharoni, E., W. Sinnott-Armstrong and K. A. Kiehl. 2012. "Can Psychopathic Offenders Discern Moral Wrongs? A New Look at the Moral/conventional Distinction." *Journal of Abnormal Psychology* 121 (2): 484–497.

Gibbard, A. 1992. *Wise Choices, Apt Feelings: A Theory of Normative Judgment.* Oxford University Press.

Goldie, P. 2007. "Emotion." *Philosophy Compass* 2 (6): 928–938.

Jones, K. 2006. "Metaethics and Emotions Research: A Response to Prinz." *Philosophical Explorations* 9 (1): 45–53.

Nichols, S. 2002a. "How Psychopaths Threaten Moral Rationalism: Is It Irrational to Be Amoral?" *The Monist* 85: 285–304.

Prinz, J. 2006. "The Emotional Basis of Moral Judgments." *Philosophical Explorations* 9 (1): 29–43.

Rosati, C. S. 2011. "Moral Motivation." http://plato.stanford.edu/entries/moral-motivation/.

Roskies, A. 2003. "Are Ethical Judgments Intrinsically Motivational? Lessons from 'Acquired Sociopathy'." *Philosophical Psychology* 16 (1): 51–66.

Wheatley, T., and J. Haidt. 2005. "Hypnotic Disgust Makes Moral Judgments More Severe." *Psychological Science* 16 (10): 780–784.

6 Sentimentalism and Rationalism

I am disgusted by people who clip their fingernails in public. I've seen people do it on buses, in airports and even at restaurants, and every time I see it I think, "Gross! Stop doing that. It's disgusting!" But I don't think there's anything wrong with people who are not disgusted by this, nor do I really think that people who do it are bad people. I also think that if I stopped being disgusted by this, I would be just as good a person as I am now. I am also disgusted by the practice of selling children into sexual slavery, which still happens in some parts of the world. But here things are different: I do think there is something wrong with people who are not disgusted by this practice, and I think I would be a much worse person if I stopped being bothered by it. I also think there is something horrifically wrong with the people who treat children this way. It's natural to say that the difference between these two cases is that in the first case I just feel a certain way about a grooming practice that I was raised to think is against etiquette, whereas in the second case I believe that there is a terrible moral violation. But if moral judgments are just expressions of or reports about our senti- ments, as sentimentalism takes them to be, can we really say there is such a difference? Doesn't sentimentalism put my reaction to the nail clipper and my reaction to the child abuser on a par? If so, that would seem to be a serious blow to sentimentalism.

One thing that sentimentalism has going for it (as we saw in Chapter 5) is that it helps to explain a distinctive feature of moral motivation, namely, that we seem to be moved to act morally just by the mere thought that "this is the right thing to do." Often when you ask someone why they did something morally good, they will say, "Because it was the right thing to do." The idea here is that in judging that something is the right thing to do, a good person is motivated in some way to do it (this is, roughly, moral judgment internalism, which we also discussed in Chapter 5). You don't need anything more than that. Sentimentalism explains this by identifying the thought with an emotion that is capable of moving us to action.

So far in Part III, we have assumed that the case for moral judgment internalism is good evidence for sentimentalism, because if moral judgments are just expressions of our emotions, then there is an easy explanation for why they motivate us. But, in fact, you don't have to be a sentimentalist to accept moral judgment internalism. It's not only the sentimentalists who claim to explain how we are motivated to act morally in terms of our judgments about the right thing to do. Many rationalists also accept internalism, but reject the crucial role for sentiments in moral judgment.[1] These rationalists think that moral judgments are instead fundamentally tied to Reason. Rationalists tend to focus on the fact that moral judgments are made for reasons, and they think this feature of moral judgment is as important as the fact that they motivate us.

A rationalist would say that one key difference between my feelings about the nail clipper and my feelings about the child abuser is that in the second case my judgment is based on moral reasons. Furthermore, the rationalist will say that sentimentalism cannot make sense of this difference. Rationalism can make sense of the difference, because it holds that moral judgments are rational judgments that are justified by rational principles, unlike mere tastes (or distastes—as in the case of public nail clipping) that are not underwritten by principles. There are, according to the rationalist, rational principles that determine the truth of our moral judgments. In this chapter we'll consider this objection to sentimentalism and whether rationalism does have a better way of capturing the vast difference between public nail clippings and child abuse.

Rationalism and Sophisticated Sentimentalism

As I've just hinted at with my opening example, there are some potential problems with the sentimentalist version of internalism (that is, the view that moral judgments are essentially motivating because they are constituted by sentiments) that we have not yet thought about. To see this problem in more detail, we need to think about one way in which moral judgments seem to be different from other kinds of judgments that express feelings. It at least appears that moral judgments, unlike mere judgments of taste, are made for reasons that are supposed to justify these judgments to other people.

Let's start by thinking about, for example, the difference between factual judgments about the health effects of various foods and mere judgments of taste about those foods. Consider the following statements:

- Kale is healthy.
- Kale is disgusting.

If someone told you that you should eat kale because it is healthy, you would expect them to be able to back this up. Even if they didn't have the actual evidence, you would at least expect them to say that they heard on NPR or read in some reliable news source that it reduces the risk of cancer or something like that. If you were to look into it and find the scientist who is making the claim, you would expect the scientist's judgment that kale is healthy to be based on some good reasons that would justify your going out and buying some kale. What about the other judgment? You would expect that the person who says "kale is disgusting" doesn't like kale, but you don't really expect that to be based on any reasons. Indeed, knowing that one person finds kale disgusting doesn't give you much reason to think that you will also find it disgusting, since people have different tastes. The difference here is that "kale is healthy" is a judgment for which there is evidence that is relevant to the rest of us, while "kale is disgusting" expresses a sentiment that there is no reason for the rest of us to share (though some of us might happen to share it). "Kale is healthy" is a claim that makes a demand on the rest of us (that the rest of us believe it) and invites corroboration or debate. "Kale is disgusting" makes no demand on the rest of us to hate kale, and it cannot really be disputed.

The question is, Which is moral judgment more like? In thinking about this question, try to put aside any metaphysical worries you might have about realism and relativism, and just consider what you would expect from someone making a moral judgment. Think of one of your friends with whom you have very similar moral beliefs. Let's say you've always agreed with each other that women have a right to abortion. Suddenly, your friend tells you that he has changed his mind. He now thinks that it is morally wrong to have an abortion under any circumstances. Would you expect your friend to give you some reasons for this? Or would you expect him to think of it in the same way as if his feelings about kale had changed: "It's disgusting to me now, but that's just how I feel; I don't have any reason for it." I suspect most of would be anxious to find out the friend's reasons for changing his mind. We might want to know if these are reasons that we should also be persuaded by, or we might want to know if his values have changed so fundamentally that we must reconsider the friendship. In any case, most of us would expect the friend to have some reasons for the change.

The idea that moral judgments are based on justifying reasons is compelling and fits with our experience. If our moral judgments are supported by reasons, then it might seem like we must—contrary to Hume—reason *to* them using our rational capacities. Just as we reason to the view that kale is healthy on the basis of the evidence about kale and cancer rates, so too we reason to the judgment that abortion is morally permissible or impermissible based on the facts and the moral reasons at stake.

What can a sentimentalist say about these appearances? One thing the sentimentalist might say is that the appearances are misleading. It looks like reasons are involved in our moral judgments, but, in fact, when we seem to give reasons for our moral judgments, what we are really doing is rationalizing them after the fact (*post hoc*).[2] Maybe we do this because of social pressure to explain ourselves or because of our tendency to look for rational explanations for things, but the truth is (according to this strategy) that moral judgments are not made for reasons in any interesting sense.

If we can't make sense of the apparent connection between moral judgments and reasons in any other way, maybe we'll have to accept that there isn't really any connection, but I think the appearances are vivid enough that this strategy should be a last resort. Another strategy the sentimentalist might take starts with the observation that there's a difference between our judgments being *supported by* reasons and our judgments being *the result of* reasoning. The fact that moral judgments are based on or justified by reasons does not necessarily mean that moral judgments are made "from Reason" as in "by way of reasoning" or "as an expression of our rational capacities"—at least not according to *sophisticated sentimentalists*.

Sophisticated sentimentalists think that they can make sense of the way in which moral judgments are subject to justification by reasons without abandoning sentimentalism. There are at least two ways they could do this. First, they can appeal to standards of appropriateness for sentiments that come from the relationship between sentiments and their objects. Recall that in our discussion of the emotions we talked about the ways in which emotions inform us about the world; emotions are responsive to facts about the world. This means that even if we don't reason our way into moral judgments, these judgments can still be assessed as reasonable or unreasonable, based on how well they fit their objects (whatever they're responding to in the world).[3]

The second way that sentimentalists can account for the role of reasons in moral judgment is by appealing to the ways in which various sentiments are related to each other; we'll spend some time considering this strategy.[4] Sophisticated sentimentalists can explain the apparent role of reasons in supporting our moral judgments by complicating the sentimentalist picture so that moral judgments are not simple expressions of our sentiments; instead, they are expressions of sentiments that are the objects of other sentiments we have. When we make a moral judgment of wrongness, in this view, we have sentiments of disapproval toward the wrong action and we also have sentiments of approval toward our sentiments of disapproval. We take a second-order attitude toward our first-order moral sentiments.

According to Allan Gibbard (1992, 2006), these second-order attitudes are endorsements of the appropriateness (or *warrant*, as Gibbard puts it) of guilt and anger, the primary moral emotions. An act is wrong, roughly, if "feelings of resentment or outrage over it are warranted on the part of impartial onlooker and feelings of guilt over it are warranted on the part of the person who does it" (Gibbard 2006: 196). Whether an emotion is warranted or not is to be understood in terms of planning; an emotion is warranted if it is part of the best plan for what it makes sense to do. According to Gibbard, then, when we make a moral judgment we are making a plan for action, where these plans include norms for feelings and actions. For example, if I judge that it is wrong to torment kittens, then I am committing myself to a plan that includes (a) not tormenting any kittens, (b) feeling very guilty if I were to find myself tormenting a kitten, and (c) responding to kitten tormenters with anger.

Gibbard takes these evaluations to be endorsements that are directed at the role of guilt and anger in our plans for action. But there are other forms of sophisticated sentimentalism that describe the second-order attitudes in a different way. For example, a sophisticated sentimentalist could say that the relevant second-order attitudes are approvals of additional norms that make our first-order sentiments non-optional and not dependent on a local authority. In this way of thinking, when I judge that it is morally wrong to torment kittens, I would be feeling a sentiment of disapproval of kitten tormenting in addition to a number of other dispositional attitudes, such as disapproval toward anyone who thinks kitten tormenting is only wrong if you think it is or only if local authorities forbid it.[5]

How does sophisticated sentimentalism help us accommodate the idea that moral judgments are made for reasons? It's a complicated story. According to the version of sophisticated sentimentalism we have been considering, the moral judgment "it's wrong to torment kittens" expresses not only a sentiment (of disapproval or anger) toward the action of tormenting kittens, but also some attitudes about this sentiment (such as the attitude of approval toward those who disapprove of this action even when other people are tormenting kittens or the attitude that being angry with kitten tormenters is part of the best plan). Notice first that these second-order attitudes make the judgment in question distinct from judgments like "kale is disgusting." At least for most people who think kale is disgusting, there is no extra disapproval of people who do not find it disgusting, no sense that anger toward people who enjoy kale is warranted. Notice, second, that the way in which moral judgments differ from mere judgments of taste helps us make sense of the idea that we make our moral judgments for reasons.

According to sophisticated sentimentalism, my moral judgment is not just the idiosyncratic expression of a personal taste; rather, because of the way in which it is connected to these other second-order attitudes, it is an expression that makes a claim on others, underwrites judgments about them and may even demand interfering with the behavior of people who aim to do wrong. Therefore, moral judgments are part of a domain of judgments that we take to be justified and that we feel pressure to justify to each other. Moreover, since according to sophisticated sentimentalism our sentiments are linked together in various ways, some (sentiment-expressing) judgments can provide reasons for others. For example, if you asked me why I thought it was wrong to torment kittens, I would say such things as "kittens are sentient beings and can suffer" or "people who enjoy gratuitous cruelty are monsters." Here I would be expressing other sentiments that I have about suffering and cruelty. According to sophisticated sentimentalism, it makes sense to say that the fact that kittens would be caused to suffer if we tormented them is our *reason* to be against kitten torment, even though "suffering is bad" and "cruelty is monstrous" are not the deliverances of pure Reason. It makes sense because, according to sophisticated sentimentalism, reasons for moral judgments are also normative claims that must be given a sentimentalist interpretation. Whether one of my judgments counts as a reason for another depends on how exactly they are related—on whether they form a coherent plan or systematic set of attitudes. To be against kitten torment but not think there's anything wrong with causing suffering is less coherent than to be against both.

There are deep debates in metaethics about this form of sophisticated sentimentalism (called "expressivism" by the two main proponents we have discussed, Blackburn and Gibbard). From the point of view of moral psychology, it makes sense to mention one problem that has to do with the psychology of moral judgment. Some philosophers have argued on empirical grounds that sophisticated sentimentalism can't be right because it implies that people need to have sophisticated second-order attitudes in order to be able to make moral judgments. Further, they argue, there are obviously people who make moral judgments but who do not have these sophisticated second-order attitudes, such as attitudes about whether guilt and anger are warranted. Shaun Nichols, for example, argues that children who can draw the right distinction between moral and conventional norms are not capable of making normative assessments of the appropriateness of guilt (Nichols 2004: 89–92).[6] To respond to this objection, Gibbard argues that children have "near-moral" concepts that have enough in common with our concepts that we can talk to them about what's wrong, even though they don't have all the capacities they would have to have to make full-blooded moral judgments (Gibbard 2006: 203).

Once again (as in Chapter 5), we can see that two philosophers are disagreeing with each other about moral judgment because they start with different assumptions about the most important features of moral judgment. On one side, the fact that children use moral concepts to make judgments that they think are serious and authority independent is taken to mean that children's moral judgments are real, full-blooded moral judgments. On the other side, the fact that adults make moral judgments for reasons that we offer as justification for the appropriateness of our moral emotions is taken to mean that children probably do not make full-blooded moral judgments. Which side is right? As before when we discussed the different assumptions made about moral judgment by moral judgment internalists and externalists, I don't think there is any way to answer this question without thinking theoretically about what we are interested in and why. For our purposes, it's enough to notice that this debate between Gibbard and Nichols is a "family" dispute among sentimentalists: they both agree that moral judgments and sentiments are intricately intertwined; they just have different views about how to accommodate the idea that our moral judgments are subject to justification by reasons.

Stepping back from the details of various versions of sophisticated sentimentalism, the important point is that these theories provide a critical
perspective on our sentiments in one way or another, and this critical perspective allows us to make sense of the idea that moral judgments can be
justified by reasons. This critical perspective might come from the objects of
our sentiments: in this case, reasons for judging that it's wrong to harm
puppies come from features of the action "harming puppies" that make it
appropriate to feel sentiments such as anger toward those who perform this
action. Or the critical perspective might come from our other sentiments:
in this case, reasons for judging that it's wrong to harm puppies depend on
whether having the sentiment of anger toward someone who performs this
action is part of a coherent plan or systematic set of attitudes.

It is worth considering Hume's own view, since it partakes of both sophisticated sentimentalist strategies and shows how these strategies can work
together. According to Hume, it's not just any old expression of a sentiment
that counts as a moral judgment; rather, he says, "Tis only when a character
is considered *in general, without reference to our particular interest,* that it
causes such a feeling or sentiment as denominates it morally good or evil"
(Hume 2000/1739: 303, italics added). Our sentiments constitute moral
evaluations when we *correct* them by contemplating the situation from a
point of view of sympathy with everyone affected by the action in question.
For example, even if you don't feel much of a sentiment about a murder
that happened many years ago, you would feel anger about it were you to
take the point of view of the people harmed by the crime. Your corrected
sentiment of anger toward the murderer constitutes your judgment that the
action was wrong. For Hume, then, moral judgments are subject to a standard of correctness given by the proper objects of our moral sentiments,
where this standard is characterized by a degree of impartiality and consistency. But the only reason that this standard means anything to us is that
we do have a sentiment of sympathy toward our fellow human beings. To
dress up Hume's view in contemporary language, we could say this: The
general point of view provides a critical perspective on our moral sentiments,
and we can use this general point of view to define reasons that makes some
judgments justified and others unjustified. This critical perspective is meaningful to us in a way that influences our moral responses because it engages
our sentiment of sympathy.

I've tried to explain how a sophisticated sentimentalist can make sense
of one rationalist feature of moral judgment, namely, the fact that we seem
to make moral judgments for reasons that we use to justify them to ourselves and each other. A different rationalist claim is that moral requirements
are *requirements* of reason in the sense that there are rational principles in
virtue of which our moral judgments are correct or incorrect. Rational
principles are supposed to be like the principles of logic: true for all time,
independent of any empirical facts about us or the world, applicable to all
creatures with the power of Reason. Sophisticated sentimentalism does not

make this true. There are no rational principles that determine the truth of our moral judgments, according to sophisticated sentimentalism. Though our sentiments are complex and related to each other in various ways that make sense of how they can be justified, it is still sentiments all the way down, according to sophisticated sentimentalism. And according to the rationalists, this is a problem.

The Kantian Challenge to Sophisticated Sentimentalism

Does the sophisticated sentimentalist picture of the relationship between justifying reasons and moral judgments make sense? Does it really capture the sense of normativity we are interested in when we are looking for moral answers? One reason to think that sophisticated sentimentalism is inadequate comes from metaethics: if the reasons that are supposed to justify our moral judgments are just more "endorsements" and expressions of sentiments from us, then they don't really justify anything at all. To go back to our example, the problem is this: How does anything normative come from the added attitude "anger is appropriate" when this is just another emotional stance that someone has? Closely related to this is a reason to worry from moral psychology: if the reasons that are supposed to justify our moral judgments are just more "endorsements" and expressions of sentiments from us, we aren't (just as a matter of our psychology) going to be able to take them seriously enough.

To understand these problems, it will help to get an idea of what the rationalist alternative is. The rationalist position we will consider here, inspired by Immanuel Kant, is an internalist position (moral judgment internalist, that is), but this internalism takes a different form than it does for sentimentalism. According to the rationalist, the truth of a moral judgment is determined by rational principles; moral judgments are justified, then, insofar as they conform to these principles. That is the sense in which moral judgments are rational, or based in Reason: moral judgments are supposed to tell us what rational principles require of us and they give us reasons to behave in certain ways insofar as they succeed in this aim. In the Kantian picture, people will be motivated by their judgments about what they have moral reason to do *insofar as they are rational*. Moral judgments are essentially motivating, in this view, but only for people whose rational capacities are functioning. A person who thinks that it's wrong to lie in a job interview might nevertheless lie, because she is under so much stress to find a job that some of her rational capacities are overwhelmed in the circumstances.

When we make moral judgments, according to the rationalist, we have reasons for them, just as the sophisticated sentimentalist thinks we do. But for the rationalist the justification of these judgments is not dependent in any way on other sentiments that we have; rather, it is dependent on the authority of certain rational principles. For the sophisticated sentimentalist, ultimately, the explanation for why our second-order attitudes help to justify a judgment makes reference to our sentiments. It's important to keep in mind that the sophisticated sentimentalists do not think that the fact that you have a sentiment against tormenting kittens *is the reason* tormenting kittens is wrong. No: The reason it's wrong to torment kittens is that this hurts kittens. However, according to the sophisticated sentimentalist, if you ask for the ultimate explanation of why we are the kinds of creatures who take hurting innocent creatures to be wrong, this explanation will refer to our sentiments. There is no rational principle that *proves* the wrongness. Another way of putting it is this: The reason not to torment kittens is that it causes pain to sentient creatures, but ultimately no consideration would have the *authority* of a normative reason if it weren't for our sentiments.[7]

Kantians think this won't do. It won't do because the authority of our moral reasons will be undermined if it ultimately rests on our sentiments. According to the Kantians, the authority of our moral reasons will also be undermined if it ultimately rests on our desires. Indeed, the Kantian challenge we are discussing here is equally a challenge to those Humeans who favor talking about desires rather than sentiments, though we'll focus on sentiments here.

Christine Korsgaard has made the best case for the Kantian point. Her basic idea is that we are reflective creatures and our reflective nature creates a problem for us, which can only be answered by a Kantian moral theory that allows us to "reflectively endorse" our particular motives and inclinations. "The reflective mind cannot settle for perception and desire, not just as such. It needs a *reason*. Otherwise, at least as long as it reflects, it cannot commit itself or go forward" (Korsgaard 1996: 93). According to Korsgaard, moral judgments can only give us reasons if we are able to reflectively endorse them and find them to be completely justified. Our moral judgments must have some justification that bottoms out in rational principles or what Korsgaard calls "laws." If our efforts to justify our moral judgments ended at our sentiments, we would not be satisfied because we can always question whether our sentiments really give us reasons.

What these rational principles or laws are for the Kantian is a long story, which would take us away from moral psychology and into the heart of moral theory. But the basic idea is that rational principles require consistency and that there is a kind of practical consistency that is relevant to morality. The connection between rationality and consistency is a conceptual connection, and it is easy to see in the case of belief. It's paradigmatically irrational to believe a contradiction ("p and not-p"), for instance. How does consistency become relevant to action? For the Kantian there are two ways. First, consistency in action demands that we be able to universalize the principles that we act on. (Kant calls these principles "maxims.") Lying at a job interview in order to get the job is wrong, because in a world in which everyone intended to lie to get ahead, people would expect everyone to lie and lying at job interviews could not work. If you lie at a job interview, you have to be making a special exception for yourself—it's okay for *me* to lie, but I expect most other people not to do it!—and this is a kind of practical inconsistency. Second, Kantians sometimes think of the practical inconsistency in terms of our values. We must value our own rational agency, they say, because without our own capacity for choice we could not value anything at all. But once we see that our own rational agency is the foundation for all the value in our lives, we have to see that it's a pretty special thing and that it is valuable wherever it is. To think that *my* capacity to choose my goals is valuable, but yours is not, also exhibits a kind of practical inconsistency.

So there are two kinds of practical (or action-related) inconsistency for Kant: the inconsistency involved in acting for reasons that you expect other people to refrain from acting on (such as "lie to get ahead") and the inconsistency involved in taking your own rational nature to be special, but not according that status to other people's rational nature (which is really just as special). These two kinds of inconsistency are forbidden by the Categorical Imperative, Kant's supreme principle of morality, which tells us only to act on maxims we could universalize and to always value rational nature as an end in itself. We can see intuitively that the Categorical Imperative is a rational law by understanding that it forbids practical inconsistencies.

Excellent moral reasoning for the Kantian, then, will have to include some reflection on the moral law and how it applies to your situation. This will require identifying the maxim of your action (what you're doing and your reason for doing it) and then thinking about what that maxim says about your will and whether it is in accordance with Reason. Does that maxim reveal that you think you're special and deserve better treatment than everyone else? Does that maxim reveal that you have little regard for the value of rational nature? Does your maxim show that you're not following any principle, but just acting on instinct or inclination? If examining what you are doing and why reveals any of these things about yourself, you know that you are on dangerous moral ground.

That was a very condensed explanation of how Kantians think about moral reasoning and the Moral Law, and anyone who is really interested in this should certainly read more about it.[8] But I hope what I've said suffices for us to think about the difference between the Humean sentimentalist and the Kantian rationalist. The difference is in the ultimate explanation they each give for what makes some consideration a justifying reason that has some claim on what we do. For the sentimentalist, at some point the answer is going to be: this is what we care about. For the rationalist, at some point the answer will come to: this is what Reason demands, and anything else is self-contradictory! Korsgaard's point is that the sentimentalist answer is not satisfying because it's always possible to ask whether we should care about what we happen to care about in a way that it doesn't really make sense to ask whether it should matter if we contradict ourselves.

The Empirical Threat to Rationalism

Many of the sentimentalists whose arguments we considered in Chapter 5 take their arguments for sentimentalism to be arguments against rationalism at the same time. For example, Nichols thinks that the evidence from psychopathy counts against rationalism because psychopaths do not have defects of reasoning and yet do not seem to make moral judgments in the same way that the rest of us do.[9] In this section we will consider the empirical challenge to rationalism by focusing on some work by the psychologist Jonathan Haidt.

Haidt (2001) argues that reasoning does not have the causal role in producing moral judgment that we once thought it had. His well-known article "The Emotional Dog and Its Rational Tail" is structured around four reasons to doubt the causal importance of Reason:

- The dual process problem. We make moral judgments quickly and automatically, and the best explanation of this is that we are using mental processing that is fast, automatic and cognitively undemanding. We use our slow, analytic and controlled mental processing sometimes, but not typically.[10]
- The motivated reasoning problem. Our moral judgments tend to be shaped by a desire to have good relations with other people and a desire to maintain a coherent self-image. Haidt argues that conscious reasoning is more often used to justify the judgments that are motivated by these desires than it is to arrive at the truth.
- The post hoc problem. We can easily construct justifications for intuitive judgments that were not made by reasoning. This causes the illusion of objective reasoning when what is really happening is post hoc (after the fact) rationalization.
- The action problem. Moral action is more strongly correlated with changes in moral emotion than with moral reasoning.

Haidt argues that his own view of moral judgment solves all of these problems. He favors a picture according to which moral judgments are typically made intuitively, on the basis of sentiments (what he calls "intuitions"). While it is possible for us to reason about our moral judgments, according to Haidt, this happens fairly rarely. He calls his theory of moral judgment "The Social Intuitionist Model" (SIM), because moral judgments are quick, intuitive judgments and, when reasoning is used to make them, it is usually social reasoning that takes place as people talk and argue with each other to try to figure things out. The SIM does allow that individual reasoning or "private reflection" takes place and can have an effect on our judgments, but it is not the usual cause of moral judgment.

We have already seen some evidence that supports Haidt's reasons for doubting the role of Reason. The phenomenon of psychopathy, for example, provides evidence for the action problem, if psychopaths' failure to perform moral actions is explained by an emotional defect. We can't review all of Haidt's evidence here, but there's one piece that has been so widely discussed by philosophers that it's worth looking at in some detail. This is the phenomenon of dumbfounding, which provides some evidence in favor of the post hoc problem.

Moral dumbfounding happens when a person cannot find any reasons for the moral judgment she makes and yet continues to make it anyway. In the widely discussed study that introduced the phenomenon, subjects are presented with the following scenario:

> Julie and Mark, who are brother and sister, are traveling together in France. They are both on summer vacation from college. One night they are staying alone in a cabin near the beach. They decide that it would be interesting and fun if they tried making love. At very least it would be a new experience for each of them. Julie was already taking birth control pills, but Mark uses a condom too, just to be safe. They both enjoy it, but they decide not to do it again. They keep that night as a special secret between them, which makes them feel even closer to each other. So what do you think about this? Was it wrong for them to have sex?
>
> (Bjorklund, Haidt and Murphy 2000)

Most people say that the siblings' behavior is wrong, and they offer reasons for their judgment. They say Mark and Julie may have a deformed child, that it will ruin their relationship, that it will cause problems in their family, and so on. But because of the way the scenario is constructed, the interviewer can quickly dispel their reasons, which leads to the state of dumbfounding. According to Haidt in an interview about his findings, dumbfounding only bothers certain people:

> For some people it's problematic. They're clearly puzzled, they're clearly reaching, and they seem a little bit flustered. But other people are in a state that Scott Murphy, the honors student who conducted the experiment, calls "comfortably dumbfounded." They say with full poise: "I don't know; I can't explain it; it's just wrong. Period."
>
> (Sommers 2005)

Some people think that the phenomenon of dumbfounding shows that most people don't make moral judgments for reasons.[11] Rather, people offer post hoc rationalizations of their emotional convictions and, when these rationalizations are undermined, they stick with the conviction anyway.

Haidt's research on moral judgment is on the *causes* of moral judgment. Does this research present problems for rationalists? Typically, rationalist moral philosophers such as Korsgaard are not explicitly making claims about the causes of moral judgment, but perhaps rationalists make assumptions that are undermined by Haidt's research. This is the question we will now explore.

First, let's consider whether Haidt and the Kantian rationalists mean the same thing by *reasoning*. If they each mean something different, then Haidt's challenge won't necessarily undermine rationalism. Haidt does seem to have a picture of moral reasoning that is rather different from what rationalists take moral reasoning to be. Haidt talks about the rare cases in which people "reason their way to a judgment by sheer force of logic" (Haidt and Bjorklund 2008: 819). But moral rationalists do not really think that we reason ourselves into moral positions by the sheer force of logic. As we've already touched on, one tool of moral reasoning that Kantians think is particularly important is universalization. In the Kantian picture, when we're unsure what to do, we should ask ourselves whether the intention of our action requires making a special exception for ourselves or whether it is an intention that we think is acceptable for everyone to have. Universalization is like applying the Golden Rule, which tells you to do unto others as you would have them do unto you. (Notice that there is an important difference between the two, however: the Golden Rule asks you to be consistent with how you *want* to be treated, whereas Kantian universalization asks you to think about whether your goals could possibly be achieved in a world in which everyone acted the way you do.) This is a kind of reasoning, one that I would guess is not unfamiliar to readers of this book, but it's not the sheer force of logic.

Still, there is an empirical case against the idea that there is any form of slow, deliberate conscious reasoning in the making of moral judgments, and certainly Kantians think that this kind of reasoning is important. Of course, Kantians do not assume that we engage in this kind of reasoning all the time, nor do they say that our moral judgments are typically *caused* by reasoning. The main point that the Kantian requires is that some moral judgments (the correct ones) are backed up by rational principles and that we *could*—if we needed to—use our rational capacities (such as universalization) to justify these judgments. This doesn't require that we always, or even typically, use our reasoning to arrive at our moral judgments. Indeed it would be a waste of our precious cognitive resources to do this, since most of the moral judgments we make are fairly easy and uncontroversial. When you read in the paper that someone has stolen billions of dollars from the retirement funds of old people or that someone has sold ten-year-old children into sexual slavery, you find yourself making moral judgments about these people. But there's no need for reasoning here; reasoning would be wasted effort since the cases are so obvious. Reasoning is needed in cases of conflict when we aren't sure what to do. For example, what do you do if you rear end someone's car in a parking lot when no one else is looking, causing a small amount of damage? Or if you discover your very good friend cheating on a test? Your automatic judgment might be to do nothing (to drive away, to turn a blind eye for the sake of your friendship), but if you think about it, you might conclude that this isn't really the right thing to do.

Kantians do not need to assume that our moral judgments are always caused by reasoning. What they do assume is that our moral judgments only give us normative reasons if they accurately report what rational principles demand. Moral judgments can be justified and reasoning—when it's done well—produces justification. On the Kantian view, then, it must be that we could reason our way to a moral judgment if we need to, but it's not a problem if many of our actual moral judgments are fairly automatic. Haidt admits that we sometimes arrive at judgments through private reasoning. He also thinks that we engage in social reasoning—reasoning with each other in the form of argument and gossip. Kantians do not need to assume that moral reasoning is always done privately. Indeed, reasoning with each other might help us overcome our biases so that we can be more impartial and better universalizers. Many other empirical approaches to understanding moral judgment also acknowledge a role for reasoning. Shaun Nichols's (2002b; 2004) theory of moral judgment, for example, holds that the causal story of our moral judgments involves two mechanisms: a rational mechanism that has to do with the knowledge of a normative theory prohibiting certain actions and a sentimental mechanism that generates affective responses to the prohibited actions.

Does the empirical evidence—not just Haidt's work, but all the evidence of the role of sentiments in morality—really provide a fundamental challenge to rationalism? What does seem to be threatened is a picture according to which we always arrive at our moral judgments by engaging in rational reflection on the permissibility of our maxims and we are then motivated to act on these judgments by the sheer recognition of their rational status. It's unlikely that even Kant held this extreme view. Whether he did or not, it seems to me that the most important Kantian assumptions about reasoning are compatible with much of the empirical research, because Kantians could be satisfied with a limited *causal* role for reasoning. Indeed, Kantians could even admit that emotions have an important role in producing our moral judgments, because this is compatible with thinking that reasoning is how we *justify* our moral judgments and that rational principles are at the foundation of these justifications. As long as we are capable of rejecting an emotionally caused judgment that is found to be unjustified, the Kantian view would not be fundamentally endangered. Furthermore, as long as reasoning can succeed in justifying our moral judgments, it doesn't even have to be the case that reasoning *always* has this purpose. It may be that we often engage in post hoc rationalization in which our aim is just to make ourselves feel better, not to discern any actual rational justification. According to the Kantian, this would be a misuse of our rational capacities, but the fact that these capacities can be abused doesn't mean that they can't also (sometimes) be used well.

Of course, whether reasoning can really provide a justification for our moral judgments depends on some deep issues in metaethics. In particular, it depends on whether there really are any rational principles that provide a foundation for our moral reasons. This is one of the fundamental philosophical disputes between the sentimentalist and the rationalist. If there are no principles of practical reason that have the authority to justify our moral judgments, then Kant was wrong.[12] This debate ultimately depends on a philosophical question about the nature of rationality, not on the psychological facts about the causes of moral judgment. As far as the empirical challenge goes, however, it seems that the door for a modest version of rationalism is still open.

Or is it? There is another problem for rationalism that Haidt's research introduces that we haven't yet considered. Haidt's research seems to cause the most trouble for the rationalist assumption that we are reflective creatures. Recall Korsgaard's claim that "The reflective mind cannot settle for perception and desire, not just as such. It needs a *reason*. Otherwise, at least as long as it reflects, it cannot commit itself or go forward." When our desires or inclinations conflict with each other or with what we deem morally right, we need a conclusive reason to go one way or another, and that reason can't just be another desire or inclination. Do we have reflective minds like this? The phenomenon of dumbfounding might be evidence that we are not reflective in the way Korsgaard thinks we are. Notice that there are really two claims being made here: the first is that we need a reason or a consideration that provides a justification for our action; the second (which depends on the first claim being true) is that this reason cannot ultimately depend on a desire or a sentiment.

The phenomenon of dumbfounding purports to provide evidence that we do not need reasons; some of us do, but others of us are perfectly happy not having any reasons for the moral judgments we make. Notice what a controversial claim this is from the point of view of moral philosophy. We began this chapter with the observation that moral judgments are different from mere judgments of taste insofar as we have reasons for the former but not for the latter. "You morally ought not to eat kale" is importantly different from "kale is disgusting." Sentimentalists and rationalists alike have agreed with this, and sophisticated sentimentalists have bent over backwards trying to accommodate the idea that we (just about all of us) think that our moral judgments should be backed up with reasons. This is a conceptual claim about moral judgments. But if it's really true that nobody except a few philosophers cares about whether they hold their moral judgments for reasons, it does make you wonder whether it really is part of our ordinary concept of a moral judgment that we hold them for reasons. It's worth thinking about what the phenomenon of dumbfounding really shows. To cut to the chase, I don't think the evidence shows that people reject the conception of a moral judgment that philosophers employ (Tiberius 2013).

To have cause to doubt that people care about the reasons for their moral judgments, we would have to see that people

a. do not think there are reasons for their judgments (as opposed to thinking that there are reasons, though they don't know what the reasons are) and
b. are entirely unperturbed by this fact and have no inclination to reconsider their judgments.

We do not know that (a) is true from the studies that have been done. The claim "I don't know why it's wrong, it's just wrong" is ambiguous between "it's wrong for some reason that I don't know" and "there's no reason it's wrong, it just is!" It is also possible that people think some things are self-evidently wrong and that they take this self-evidence to be a reason. We also do not know that (b) is true. The fact that people are unwilling to change their judgments in a single interview setting does not mean that they feel no pressure to change them. It may take a long time for shaken confidence to cause someone to change their judgments. Furthermore, given how difficult change is, people may also need some incentive, which they don't really have when it comes to incest. (It would be interesting to know what romantic partners would say if they were convinced that their significant others were actually genetic siblings—would they change their minds about the immorality of incest?) Given this, we would need evidence of how people respond to the challenge to provide justification over the long term. Furthermore, even if a person *never* changes her judgment when she discovers she has no reasons for it, this does not necessarily show that she doesn't care about reasons. Troubling evidence would show that people do not change their judgments *because they never saw any reason to*; that is, the explanation would have to be that the lack of justification did not undermine people's confidence in their judgment. If people do not change their judgments because nothing is at stake or because they just don't feel like thinking about it, this would not count against thinking that people care whether their judgments are justified. One problem with the study discussed above is that the case presented to the undergraduate student participants (the case of Mark and Julie) did not cause any conflict that mattered to these students. For most North American college students, nothing whatsoever hangs on whether you are for or against incest. Comfortable dumbfounding is an option here because no justification is practically required.

Of course, the argument I've just made only establishes that it hasn't yet been shown that people don't care about reasons. Notice, though, how unlikely it is that what will be shown is that nobody has a conception of a moral judgment as one that is held for justifying reasons, unlike judgments of mere taste. Some reflection on moral disagreements indicates that people often think of moral judgments as different from judgments of taste. People cast their votes for political candidates who agree with them about the morality of abortion; they march in the streets to protest or support gay marriage; they donate money to charities that help stray animals or feed hungry people. Many people who do these things do them out of moral commitment, and it's hard to imagine that such people don't think there are reasons for the moral judgments upon which they are acting. This is not to say that they're right about this, and it's not to say that there are some cases in which people make moral judgments without much concern for what justifies them. But the idea that moral judgments are different from judgments of taste (like "kale is disgusting") with respect to their being supported by reasons is not just the crazy idea of a few philosophers. The sophisticated sentimentalists are right to bend over backwards to try to explain this.

We have been discussing the first of the Kantian claims listed a few paragraphs earlier, namely, that the reflective mind needs a reason. The second claim is that the reason can't be ultimately explained by a desire or a sentiment. The rationalist thinks that reasons, if they are going to count as genuine reasons that justify what we do, must be explained by rational principles, not desires or sentiments. Their "authority" or justificatory weight cannot ultimately be grounded in how we feel or what we care about. Is this true? This, I think, is the ultimate disagreement between Humeans (where we could include sentimentalists and those who think morality is fundamentally about desire) and Kantians (who think morality is fundamentally about reason), between sentimentalists and rationalists. My own view is that once you see how complex and interrelated our sentiments and desires are, there is nothing threatening in the recognition that they are at the bottom of the explanation of our reasons for action. I think the sophisticated sentimentalists are right. But the Kantians have a point and this is no easy debate. Interestingly, the debate is partly about our psychology and the question, "What are we capable of counting as a justification?" But the debate is also about the normative question of what kinds of considerations actually count as justifying our actions.

There is one more empirical challenge to the Kantian picture, which is a challenge to their particular version of moral judgment internalism. Kantian internalists hold that moral judgments motivate people insofar as they are rational. If moral judgments are as the rationalists think they are, do they motivate us all by themselves? Do our judgments about what rational principles require motivate us insofar as our rational capacities are functioning? If you think, contrary to the Humean Theory of Motivation discussed in Chapter 3, that beliefs can bring about their own motives, then the answer to this question is easy. In this view, beliefs about what rational principles demand can motivate us. But if you were persuaded by the argument in Chapter 3 that beliefs by themselves do not motivate us, then the answer to this question will be more complicated. One way the rationalist might argue that our moral judgments do motivate us insofar as we are rational would be to say that our rational capacities include certain kinds of motives. For example, the rationalist could say that, insofar as we are rational, we have a desire to do what rational principles demand, or she could say that, insofar as we are rational, we have a feeling of respect for rational principles that motivates us to act in accordance with them.[13] This puts Reason in the driver's seat by taking our rational capacities to include capacities to be motivated in certain ways.

On the subject of who is in the driver's seat, we now have more information about what is at stake in this debate. Ultimately, rationalism allows us to hold that our rational capacities are in charge in a very particular way, namely, in a way that is guided by real principles of Reason that justify our actions. The worry about sentimentalism, and sophisticated sentimentalism too, is that if our sentiments are driving, then there really isn't any way to go right or wrong. We drive where we feel like driving, and there isn't really any rule book. The attractive thing about rationalism, for those who are looking for an explanation of the normativity of moral reasons, is that there are rules of the road. I've tried to show that this worry about sentimentalism and sophisticated sentimentalism is unwarranted, because there is a way to go wrong even if our sentiments are in the driver's seat: we can go wrong according to our sentiments, and this is no small thing.

Taking Stock

We began with the idea that reasons are important to moral judgment. This is a point on which sophisticated sentimentalists, rationalists and many ordinary people agree. The question then became whether sophisticated sentimentalists can make sense of this or whether, if you want to make sense of our moral judgments being backed up by reasons in a way that tastes are not, you have to be a Kantian. In the previous section, I suggested that while the empirical research does not show that rationalism is wrong, it does put some pressure on rationalists to qualify some of their claims. Confronting the empirical evidence about the role of sentiment in moral judgment at least leads us to reject a view of ourselves as primarily rational creatures who always make moral judgments with the aim of figuring out what we really have reason to do and whose rational capacities are always guided by rational principles. We aren't like this. Do Kantians say that we are? Not obviously. Kant himself was well aware of how irrational we can be. Still, once we face the facts about what we are like, we might wonder whether rationalism is really the best theory. When we consider which theory is best, though, we need to remember that the best theory from the point of view of moral philosophy is one that is compatible with the empirical facts about our psychology *and* able to make sense of how moral judgments sometimes give us justifying reasons for action.

Sophisticated sentimentalists and Kantian rationalists are both moral judgment internalists who think that there is a special kind of moral motivation. For the sophisticated sentimentalists, we are motivated by our moral judgments because they express sentiments. When our sentiments form the right patterns, they function to justify our actions at the same time as they explain them. According to Kantian rationalists we are motivated by our moral judgments insofar as we are rational, and these judgments justify our actions when they accurately report the requirements of rational principles. Kantians need not think that all of the moral judgments we actually make are caused by conscious reasoning, but they do hold that there would be no real moral judgments if there were no rational principles.

Summary

- According to one widespread understanding, moral judgments are different from mere judgments of taste insofar as they are justified by reasons.
- Sophisticated sentimentalists try to account for this aspect of moral judgments by showing that our moral sentiments are subject to standards of appropriateness (though these standards ultimately make reference to more sentiments or systems of sentiments, rather than to Reason).
- According to the Kantian rationalist, the truth of a moral judgment is determined by rational principles, and moral judgments are justified insofar as they conform to these principles. People will be motivated by their judgments about what they have moral reason to do insofar as they are rational.
- The rationalist challenge to sophisticated sentimentalism is that it cannot really explain how our moral judgments could ever give us normative reasons, because according to sophisticated sentimentalism the ultimate explanation for the force of these reasons makes reference to our sentiments, and this is not satisfying.
- One empirical challenge to rationalism is that our moral judgments are not caused by our reasoning capacities.
- This empirical challenge misses the mark, because Kantians do not need to assume that moral judgments are typically caused by reasoning as long as (a) we can reason to a moral conclusion when we need to and (b) when we do so correctly we succeed in justifying our moral judgment.
- The conception of a moral judgment as supported by reasons is an important one for moral philosophy and there is no reason to think that regular people do not also think this way about moral judgments by and large.
- Whether sophisticated sentimentalism is able to explain how moral judgments differ from mere judgments of taste (which are not supported by reasons) or whether rationalism has the better explanation is at the heart of one of the most important debates in philosophy.

Study Questions

1. What do you think is the difference between judgments of taste like "I hate Neapolitan ice cream" and moral judgments like "Slavery is wrong"?
2. How would sentimentalism, sophisticated sentimentalism and rationalism formulate moral judgment internalism? Which is the most plausible formulation?
3. If sentimentalists (like Jonathan Haidt, Shaun Nichols and Jesse Prinz) are correct about the *causes* of moral judgment, does this matter for moral philosophy? Does it answer any philosophical questions or rule out any philosophical positions?
4. How do sophisticated sentimentalism and Kantian rationalism attempt to explain the way in which moral judgments give us normative reasons for action?
5. What do you think of Korsgaard's claim that we are reflective creatures of a certain kind? Think of one of your own moral convictions. What discovery would unsettle it? Are there some moral convictions you have that could never be unsettled?

Notes

1. There are rationalists who are externalists. Their position is of less interest to moral psychology, so we won't be discussing it here. Throughout the book, when I talk about "rationalists," I will mean *internalist* rationalists unless otherwise noted.
2. This is Jonathan Haidt's (2001) view. We'll talk more about his theory of moral judgment shortly.
3. Exactly what is meant by the *objects* of our moral sentiments turns out to be a difficult question that we won't get into here. See Jacobson (2011) for an overview. For more, see Anderson (1995), D'Arms and Jacobson (2000) and Wiggins (1987). We'll touch on this topic again in Chapter 7 where we consider the view that virtues are like perceptions of ethical reality.
4. Why focus on the second strategy? It's partly because I find this strategy really insightful and fun to think about, although I should warn the reader that it's also quite challenging to understand.
5. This is basically Simon Blackburn's (1984) position.
6. Moral norms, in distinction from conventional norms, are serious, authority independent and usually justified by appeal to considerations of harm and fairness. See Chapter 5 for discussion.
7. Notice the similarity to what the Humeans says about reasons and desires as discussed in Chapter 4: the *reason* is the fact; the desire is what makes that fact a reason for a particular person.
8. You can start with the original source, Kant's *Groundwork of the Metaphysics of Morals*. Good secondary sources include Baron (1999) and Hill (1992).

9. In a very interesting paper called "Do Psychopaths Really Threaten Moral Rationalism?" Jeanette Kennett (2006) argues that they do not (threaten rationalism), because psychopaths also have rational defects.

10. The idea that we have these two types of mental processing is widely accepted in psychology in some form. For a good resource on what's called *dual-process theory* and these two systems of mental processing, see Frankish (2010). We will discuss dual-process theory again in Chapter 11.

11. It might be more accurate to say the "alleged phenomenon" of dumbfounding. There are many variables in the assessment that someone is dumbfounded that are open to interpretation, for instance, what counts as offering a reason for your moral judgment and what counts as "comfortable" with the inability to justify that judgment. For now, though, let's just accept Haidt's point for the sake of argument and see how far it takes us in the case against rationalism.

12. About metaethics, anyway. One could reject his metaphysical views about rationality but still think he has a lot of important stuff to say about how we ought to treat other people, morally speaking. In other words, one could think Kant had something right in normative ethics even if one doesn't agree with him about metaethics.

13. The first is, roughly, Smith's (1995b) view; the second is the more traditionally Kantian view.

Further Readings

Blackburn, S. 1998. *Ruling Passions: A Theory of Practical Reasoning*. Clarendon Press.

Gibbard, A. 2006. "Moral Feelings and Moral Concepts." *Oxford Studies in Metaethics* 1: 195–215.

Haidt, J. 2001. "The Emotional Dog and Its Rational Tail: A Social Intuitionist Approach to Moral Judgment." *Psychological Review* 108 (4): 814–834.

Kennett, J. 2006. "Do Psychopaths Really Threaten Moral Rationalism?" *Philosophical Explorations* 9 (1): 69–82.

Korsgaard, C. M. 1996. *The Sources of Normativity*. Cambridge University Press.

Nichols, S. 2002b. "Norms with Feeling: Towards a Psychological Account of Moral Judgment." *Cognition* 84: 221–236.

7 Virtue

- **What Kind of State Is a Virtue?**
- **Are There Any Virtues? The Empirical Challenge**
- **Defending Virtue**
- **Taking Stock**
- **Summary**
- **Study Questions**
- **Notes**
- **Further Readings**

Why did you take in the stray cat? Or help your neighbor move into his apartment? Why do you recycle? So far we have considered two basic possibilities: you do these things because you want to, or you do them because you think you should (where "thinking that you should" could be understood in sentimentalist or rationalist terms). But maybe you took in the cat or helped your neighbor because you're a kind person. Maybe you recycle because you're civic-minded. In other words, maybe it's really our character that explains why we act morally when we do. As it turns out, this is an ancient idea.

It's a very attractive idea from the point of view of trying to capture what is special about moral motivation. The desire view doesn't do a good job of this at all. If we act morally simply because we want to, this doesn't make moral motivation special in any way: we do everything because we want to! Kantian rationalism does a better job of making moral motivation special, particularly if we believe Kant that moral motivation is the motive of duty. But as we saw in Chapter 4, the pure sense of duty didn't seem like it could possibly be all there is to moral motivation. Virtue, on the other hand, makes moral motivation distinctive, and it also allows for many different types of moral motives—as many as there are virtues.

Not only does virtue provide a distinctive form of moral motivation, it also underlies a very familiar form of evaluation that we engage in all the time: the evaluation of people in terms of their character. To see what I mean about this being familiar, think about the kinds of things we say about political candidates. We tend to talk about whether they are honest and fair, whether they have integrity or the courage of their convictions, and sometimes we just flat out ask whether they have good character. Character judgments have even made it to bumper stickers, as in the popular "Mean People Suck." Assessments of character also pervade our personal lives. We gossip about whether someone is really arrogant or just insecure, whether someone else is overly trusting or gullible. We praise some friends for their generosity and others for their honesty. When friends ask us our opinions about their dating partners, we tend to consider character: Is he really as nice as he seems? Isn't that one kind of manipulative? Though we do joke about how much personality matters ("nice personality" has come to mean "not much to look at"), it's hard to deny that it matters to us; no one wants to date a jerk. Evaluations of actions in terms of the character of the person performing the action are also familiar: helping that elderly person across the street was a kind thing to do, rescuing the child from the burning building was brave, and so on.

What Kind of State Is a Virtue?

According to Aristotle, who is the inspiration for much modern virtue ethics, a virtue is a tendency or disposition, cultivated by habit, to have appropriate beliefs and feelings and to act accordingly (*Nicomachean Ethics*, 1105b25–6). Virtues are character traits, and they are supposed to be deeply entrenched in the person who has them, not fickle or wavering (Hursthouse 2013). Aristotle thought that most virtues inhabit the mean between two extremes. Courage, for example, is the state of character in which one has appropriate fear: too much fear makes you a coward and too little fear makes you rash. Temperance is the mean between insensibility (an inability to appreciate pleasure) and intemperance (the tendency to sacrifice long-term benefits for pleasure in the short term). Most important, Aristotle thought that virtues are the traits that are essential to human flourishing.

Aristotle thought that we should understand what a good or flourishing life is for a human being by understanding the function of a human being. The general thought here is that judgments of the form X is *good for* Y are always made relative to the kind of thing that Y is and what it is to be a good one of those. A good knife is a knife that cuts well, and so what is good for a knife is to be kept sharp. A good bee is one that performs its function in the hive, so what is good for a worker bee is whatever enables him to find pollen, and what is good for the queen bee is whatever enables her to produce lots more bees. A good lioness is one that can hunt her prey and feed her cubs, so what's good for a lioness is to have sharp claws and powerful legs. So too what is good for a human being is to be good at whatever it is human beings are supposed to do, that is, what is good for humans is to fulfill our natural telos.

The special nature of a human being, according to Aristotle, is that we are beings who can guide our actions by using our capacity to reason. We are also physical beings for whom social interaction with other human beings is important. The human telos, or function, then, is to use reason to think and feel appropriately in all of our endeavors, but especially in our interactions with others. To perform this function well is to do it excellently, or in accordance with virtue. According to Aristotle, we flourish when we exercise the virtues that make us the best exemplars of our rational, emotional, social kind. In short, Aristotle's view is that because of the kind of beings we are, we will only flourish if we are virtuous: courageous, temperate, just, generous, wise and so forth. You can see how these traditional virtues are good for human beings if you think about the kinds of things human beings typically do. We set goals for ourselves (such as graduating from college) that require making short-term sacrifices for long-term benefits, and this requires temperance. In pursuing our goals we often confront challenges that take courage to overcome. We join in friendships with other people and we engage in political activity, both of which require that we treat others generously and justly.

Aristotle thought (and modern-day virtue ethicists have followed him on this) that practical wisdom is an extremely important virtue because it is required by all the other virtues. The fully virtuous person feels anger, pity and other feelings "at the right times, about the right things, towards the right people, for the right end, and in the right way" (*Nic. Ethics*, 1106b21ff), and the standard of rightness cannot be discerned without wisdom. So it is for all the virtues, hence the special importance of the virtue of practical wisdom. Aristotle thought that practical wisdom requires virtue (1144b30) and that as soon as someone has practical wisdom, "which is a single state, he has all the virtues as well" (1145a2). He held what has been called the thesis of the "unity of the virtues." The attraction of this thesis is that full virtue seems to require a grasp of the reasons for one's actions (as opposed to merely acting as one has been taught), and the reasons for one's actions bring all the virtues together. For example, the decision about whether to lend money to a friend in need may invoke reasons of justice, compassion, helpfulness and temperance. To understand what to do (to feel and act appropriately), the practically wise person needs to understand the demands of all the virtues, not just one.

Contemporary virtue ethics has followed Aristotle in thinking that virtues are partly constitutive of human flourishing or a good human life. Notice that we could agree with Aristotle about this even if we do not agree with him that we have a natural *function* that determines what it is to live a good life. Many Aristotelians today think that the notion of flourishing that includes virtue is not an empirical fact about the natural world, but an ethical ideal (Hursthouse 1999). Contemporary virtue ethics has also been strongly influenced by Aristotle's views about what kind of state a virtue is. There are two interesting features of the Aristotelian conception of a virtue that we will consider in more detail. First, virtues seem to comprise understanding and emotion at the same time. Second, virtues are stable and reliable states that we develop in the way we develop skills. We'll take up the first point in the rest of this section and then turn to the second point in the next section.

On the first point: Thus far, we have considered two basic ideas about moral motivation. One is that moral motivation must stem from our desires, because all action is motivated by desire. The other is that moral judgment has a special role in moral motivation. Among those who think moral judgment motivates us to act morally, there are those who think moral judgment is really an expression of sentiments and those who think that moral judgments are judgments about rational requirements. Notice that so far, all the positions we have talked about accept the basic dichotomy between beliefs and desires. Some virtue ethicists have proposed a third alternative, according to which the distinction between beliefs and desires is called into question.

Recall from Chapter 4 the idea that beliefs and desires are distinguished by their different directions of fit. Beliefs aim to fit the world; desires aim to get the world to fit them. Some virtue ethicists take virtues to be states that have both directions of fit simultaneously. For example, a virtue such as generosity is in part a perceptual state that represents facts about the world as considerations in favor of helping others who need help, but it is also a state that moves us to help others when we perceive those considerations. Indeed, in this view, the two directions of fit are intertwined so that if you are not actually moved to help the needy person, then you do not see the reason to help them. To truly perceive that someone else needs help is to be motivated to help.

There is something intuitively plausible about this picture. If you think about ordinary cases of unethical behavior, it often seems like we can describe the person who acts badly as "not getting it" or "just not seeing what to do." Take the example of Emma from Jane Austen's novel. Emma is a basically nice, but rather spoiled young woman who is the wealthiest, most privileged person in her little community. At one point she goes on a picnic with a bunch of people, including a flirtatious young man and an "old maid," Miss Bates, who isn't very old but who is very poor and disadvantaged. Miss Bates has watched Emma grow up and has always been a friend to the family. At one point the flirtatious young man suggests playing a game in which everyone must say one very clever thing, two moderately clever things or three things "very dull indeed" to amuse Emma (not much of a game, but this was the nineteenth century, after all).

> "Oh! very well," exclaimed Miss Bates, "then I need not be uneasy. 'Three things very dull indeed.' That will just do for me, you know. I shall be sure to say three dull things as soon as ever I open my mouth, shan't I?—(looking round with the most good-humoured dependence on every body's assent)—Do not you all think I shall?"
> Emma could not resist.

"Ah! ma'am, but there may be a difficulty. Pardon me—but you will be limited as to number—only three at once."

Miss Bates, deceived by the mock ceremony of her manner, did not immediately catch her meaning; but, when it burst on her, it could not anger, though a slight blush shewed that it could pain her.

"Ah!—well—to be sure. Yes, I see what she means, (turning to Mr. Knightley,) and I will try to hold my tongue. I must make myself very disagreeable, or she would not have said such a thing to an old friend."

(Austen 2000: 242–243)

It becomes very clear that Emma has hurt Miss Bates deeply, and Mr. Knightley (the one Emma really wants to impress) reprimands her:

How could you be so unfeeling to Miss Bates? How could you be so insolent in your wit to a woman of her character, age, and situation?— Emma, I had not thought it possible."

Emma recollected, blushed, was sorry, but tried to laugh it off.

"Nay how could I help saying what I did?—nobody could have helped it. It was not so very bad. I dare say she did not understand me". . .

[Mr. Knightley continues his moral education] It was badly done, indeed!—You, whom she had known from an infant, whom she had seen grow up from a period when her notice was an honour, to have you now, in thoughtless spirits, and the pride of the moment, laugh at her, humble her—and before her niece, too—and before others, many of whom (certainly *some*,) would be entirely guided by *your* treatment of her.

[Emma] was forcibly struck. The truth of his representation there was no denying. She felt it at her heart. How could she have been so brutal, so cruel to Miss Bates?

(2000: 245)

The telling thing about this case is that, initially, Emma didn't see what she did as cruel; she saw it as funny or snarky (to use a word that didn't exist in Emma's time). She did not see that the joke she made was truly mean and at Miss Bates's great expense. It isn't that she had bad desires; she did not want to make Miss Bates feel mortified; rather, she wanted to be funny and charming. But she misread the situation and thereby ended up acting very badly "indeed." Moreover (and I'm interpreting a bit here, but I have read the book many times), had Emma seen the situation rightly, she would not have insulted Miss Bates; it was her perception of the situation and her own role in it, not her desires, that was responsible for her bad behavior.

The virtue ethicist we have been considering would say that Emma lacks virtue because she does not perceive the relevant considerations in the right way, that is, as decisive reasons for acting with kindness toward Miss Bates. But what about the idea that beliefs (or perceptions) and desires (or motivations) must be distinct mental states because each has a different aim? Recall from Chapter 4, if you *believe* that there is an ice cream sundae in front of you, you will continue to believe it when there is a sundae and stop believing it when there isn't, but if you *want* an ice cream sundae, you will stop wanting it once you've eaten it and continue wanting it when it isn't there. Margaret Little argues that this line of thought does not prove that there couldn't be a mental state (such as a virtue) with two directions of fit. A virtue could be, according to Little,

> a state with two complex properties: it is a believing-attitude directed toward one proposition, and it is a desiring-attitude directed toward another. There is nothing formally odd in saying that a belief(p) can also be the desire(q), just as there is nothing formally odd in noting that the mathematical operation "add(2)" is also the operation "subtract(-2)."
>
> (Little 1997: 64)

These states with double directions of fit are sometimes called "besires" because they seem to have some features of beliefs and some features of desires (Altham 1986).

Little (1997) goes on to argue for a less ambitious claim about virtues, which is that the belief aspect of virtue entails certain desires. In other words, in this view, the possession of a belief state conceptually requires the possession of a desire state. One does not count as understanding (or perceiving) what kindness requires unless one is also motivated by one's perception of the consideration in favor of being kind. This claim is less ambitious because it doesn't say that the belief and desire are one and the same mental state; they are two mental states, one of which conceptually entails the other. Little argues that there is no reason to reject this possibility.

At first glance, there seems to be something wrong with this idea. We can certainly imagine two people who know the same facts about a situation, one of whom is motivated to do the right thing and the other of whom is not. How could the fact that the second person doesn't have the right motives take away from what she knows about her situation? The Aristotelian thinks this is the wrong way of looking at it. The knowledge that is inherent in virtue is not that kind of knowledge; it's not like knowledge of a fact. Rather, it is more like perceptual knowledge; it is the discernment of the morally salient considerations in a situation, where "'taking as salient' is akin to having a kind of experience" (Little 1997: 73). The person who isn't motivated to help the needy person, according to this account of the virtues, has a cognitive defect, but it is a different kind of defect from the possession of a false belief; she doesn't see the situation correctly. If you've ever been in a situation where you've watched someone behave really badly—insulting a friend, telling a racist joke, humiliating a colleague—this should sound familiar. Sometimes you find yourself unable to believe that the person you're watching could have such a poor grasp of the situation. You may not think the insulter or humiliator wants to be mean, but that he or she is (cognitively) clueless. Indeed the modern movie version of Jane Austen's *Emma* is called *Clueless*. Of course, the defender of the view that virtue is like perception thinks that *every* time someone acts badly it is because they are clueless. This is a strong claim, and you might think of some counterexamples, but I hope the examples we've considered allow you to think of what this view might have going for it.

One thing we might wonder about this position about virtues, given our previous discussions, is whether it provides any traction for the anti-Humean in the debate about whether Reason or passion is in the driver's seat. This is not so clear. Recall that one thing that was attractive about rationalism was that it put our rational capacities in the driver's seat in a special way: according to the Kantian picture, the rational capacities that are in charge are responding to principles that justify our actions. The worry about sentimentalism was that if the sentiments are in charge, then we're really just doing what we feel like doing and true justification goes out the window. Does the Aristotelian virtue ethicist give us a good alternative? Aristotelians do not think that there are universal rational principles that explain why actions are right or wrong. Is there some other way in which virtue ethics puts Reason in the driver's seat in an interesting way? Well, it does make sense of the idea that moral reasons are there for all of us to perceive. According to virtue ethics, we are not just doing what we feel like doing when we act morally; we are grasping the ethically salient features of a situation and responding appropriately to them by using our rational capacities.[1]

In this section we have seen that some virtue ethicists take virtue to be a unique kind of motivation that involves both thinking and feeling. If there are such states, they would help to explain the specialness of moral motivation. The existence of such states is controversial, however, and not all virtue ethicists accept them. It is open to a virtue ethicist to think that virtues are complex traits, constituted by beliefs, desires and emotions that are only contingently related. In the next section we'll turn to a different aspect of the virtues—their alleged stability and consistency across different situations—that many virtue ethicists accept, whatever they think about beliefs and desires.

Are There Any Virtues? The Empirical Challenge

As I said at the beginning of the chapter (and as we can see from examples like the one of Emma Woodhouse), one of the attractive things about virtue ethics is that character evaluations are so natural to us. Nevertheless, there is some research that indicates that character attributions are not very reliable, and a serious attack on virtue ethics has been launched on the basis of this research. In fact, our tendency to focus on internal causes of people's actions rather than powerful situational causes has been called a kind of error: the fundamental attribution error (Ross 1977). It seems that when we try to explain why people do things, we tend to focus on the personality, character traits and motives of the actors, rather than on external, situational factors. There is experimental evidence that we do this even in cases in which it should be obvious that the situational explanation is the right one. For example, in one experiment participants were asked to assess people's true attitudes toward Fidel Castro based on an essay these people had allegedly written about Castro. Participants were more inclined to say that someone who wrote a pro-Castro essay was truly pro-Castro, and more inclined to say that someone who wrote an anti-Castro essay was truly anti-Castro, even though the participants were told that the essay writers were assigned their position and had no choice about whether they argued for or against (Jones and Harris 1967). This is just one small example, but it turns out that in all sorts of circumstances, we have a tendency to put too much weight on character traits and to ignore the external causes of people's actions.

On the basis of research like this, philosophers John Doris (1998) and Gilbert Harman (1999) have launched a serious attack on the idea that there are any virtues as philosophers understand them and hence on virtue ethics itself. To understand this attack, we need to talk about another aspect of the philosophical characterization of virtue, which is that virtues are supposed to be stable and consistently reliable states of character.

Virtues are dispositions to feel and act appropriately, and these dispositions are consistent or reliable in the sense that, once a person has developed virtue, she will tend to act well even in difficult circumstances. When the going gets tough, the truly virtuous continue to act in accordance with virtue. This is certainly part of Aristotle's conception of a virtue. He thought that the actions of the virtuous "proceed from a firm and unchangeable character" (1105a) and that a wise person "will bear all kinds of fortune in a seemly way, and will always act in the noblest manner that the circumstances allow" (1101a). It also seems to me that this is part of our ordinary understanding of virtue. When we say that someone is an honest person, we imply that they are consistently honest, even when telling the truth is hard. A person who was honest with her colleagues at work but lied to her friends probably wouldn't earn the title of honest person. The perfectly virtuous person who perceives the situation correctly will be motivated to act rightly in all circumstances. As Doris puts it "virtues are supposed to be *robust* traits; if a person has a robust trait, they can be confidently expected to display trait-relevant behavior across a wide variety of trait-relevant situations, even where some or all of these situations are not optimally conducive to such behavior" (Doris 2002: 18).

To put Doris's argument against virtue ethics in the simplest form, the basic idea is that virtue ethics assumes that there are robust, cross-situationally reliable traits (that is, it assumes there are virtues). Research in psychology gives us very good evidence that traits like this are not widely instantiated. Therefore, there is something wrong with virtue ethics. To put Doris's argument in a slightly less simple (and, therefore, more charitable) way, it seems to me it goes like this:

1. A good normative theory must give us something to aim at that will help us behave well.
2. Virtue ethics recommends that we aim at reforming our character in order to behave well.
3. This recommendation presupposes that we (most of us) can develop certain robust, cross-situationally reliable character traits (namely, the virtues that will motivate good behavior).
4. Situationism in psychology provides evidence that such robust traits of character that reliably produce behavior across various contexts are only possessed by the exceptional person; hardly any people have such traits.
5. Aiming at developing the virtues is, therefore, not a good way to ensure that we will behave well. (This on the assumption that if hardly anyone has succeeded, it's probably because it's too difficult, or not possible for most of us to develop such traits.)
6. Therefore, virtue ethics is not a good normative theory.

To evaluate this argument, we need to see what the evidence is for premise 4. Doris draws on hundreds of studies to make his case. We obviously can't survey all the relevant evidence here. Instead, I'll discuss a few examples to give you the flavor of the research.

Let's start with an experiment that will be familiar to most people, the Milgram experiment (Milgram 1963). In this experiment the subjects were told that they were in a study on learning and that they would be the "teachers" in this study. The "students" (who were really confederates of the experimenter, Stanley Milgram) were hooked up to a shock generator, and the subjects of the experiment (the "teachers") were asked to deliver shocks when the students made mistakes. The shock generator had labels for the increasing amounts of electricity from "slight shock" (15 volts) to "danger: severe shock" (375 volts) and then to "XXX" (450 volts, the highest number on the scale). The "students" would pretend to protest the pain (these confederates weren't really being shocked, of course); some even screamed to be let out of the experiment. When the "teachers" resisted administering stronger shocks, the experimenter would calmly say "please continue" and, ultimately, "You have no other choice, you must go on."

As is well known now, what people did in this experiment was, well, shocking. Sixty-five percent of the subjects delivered the maximum shock.[2] Of the forty subjects, none stopped administering shocks before the level of 300 volts or the end of the "intense shock" range at which point the "students" were already screaming in pain.

What is most interesting about this, for our purposes, is that it pushes us to question the validity of our own attributions of character. When I first heard about this experimental set-up, I was extremely surprised that the subjects in the experiment would do what they did and I felt quite sure that if it were me I would not have done it. Indeed, Milgram asked people before he did his experiment how they thought the subjects would behave and people predicted that almost no one would go to the end of the shock series and most people would stop at about 200 volts. In fact, no one stopped before 300 volts. As I thought about my own predictions, I had to admit that I'm not fundamentally different from the people who were in that experiment and that all of those people would likely have thought the same thing about themselves. I would bet that most people reading this (or hearing about the Milgram experiments for the first time) thought, I wouldn't do it! I would protest against the white coat! But only a few people really did resist, and we can't all be the exception. This should give us some pause about how well we are able to discern what our motivational tendencies are.

The next study I'll mention is the Good Samaritan experiment, which took seminary students (students who are learning to be religious leaders) as its subjects (Darley and Batson 1973). In this experiment, the seminary students were given some personality tests and then told that they had to move to a different building to give a short talk. Some of the students were told they should speak on the job market for seminarians; others were told they were to speak on the parable of the Good Samaritan. Within these two groups, some seminary students were made to feel like they needed to hurry, others were not. On the way from one building to the next was a man (who was really part of the experiment) slumped in an alleyway. It was clear there was something wrong with this man, but not clear exactly what. The psychologists wanted to find out whether being primed with "helping" ideas (from the parable) or being in a hurry would influence people's tendency to help someone in need.

As it turned out, being in a hurry was the most important variable, and preparing to talk about helpfulness made no significant difference at all. Overall, forty percent of the seminary students offered some help to the victim. Of those who were not in much of a hurry, sixty-three percent helped; of those in the most hurry, only ten percent offered any help. These results add to the case for thinking that situational factors are extremely important and more important than we normally give them credit for. When I think about myself, I would like to think that whether I was in a hurry or not would not be the thing that would determine whether I'd help out a dying man on the street. But it seems like this could very well be incorrect. If I'm like most people, being in a hurry would really make a big difference.

Not all situational factors make us act badly. It turns out that having even very small good things happen to you makes you *more* likely to help. This has been shown in a number of studies such as the Dime in the Phone Booth study (Isen and Levin 1972), which showed that finding a dime in a phone booth makes people more likely to help.[3] Of the sixteen people in the study who fortuitously (from their point of view) found a dime in the phone booth, fourteen helped the woman who had dropped a stack of papers on the ground. Of the twenty-five who did not find the dime, only one helped. Again, I think many of us like to think of ourselves as basically helpful people, and we don't tend to think that whether we are helpful or not is going to depend on ten cents (or the smell of a chocolate chip cookie, which was also shown to increase helpfulness in Study Two from the same publication).

These are just a few of the many studies that have demonstrated the strong influence of the situation on our behavior. Doris argues that this evidence weighs heavily against the idea that we have robust traits (like compassion and helpfulness) that reliably influence our behavior independently of the situational factors. Notice that given the way that I have reconstructed Doris's argument, Doris does not need to say (nor does he) that virtues are not possible. Rather, the claim he needs for his argument to work is that the development of such traits is unlikely enough that it doesn't make sense for an ethical theory to be organized around the cultivation of virtue. He says, "The situationist does not deny that people have personality traits; she instead denies that people *typically* have highly general personality traits that effect behavior manifesting a high degree of cross-situational consistency" (Doris 2002: 39, italics added). As far as the evidence goes, Doris accepts that there may be "local" traits (e.g., honesty with the boss when I'm not in any trouble), and he admits that there may be atypical cases of people who have "global" traits that really are firm and unchanging, even when the person is pressured by a scientist or in a hurry. The point is that even if there could be a few people in the world whose personality goes a long way toward making them behave well, situational factors are such a strong influence on the rest of us that working on our character doesn't seem a very good strategy.

Defending Virtue

Doris's critique of virtue ethics ruffled a lot of feathers and has received a good deal of attention. The defenders of virtue ethics all agree that situational factors influence our behavior in surprising ways. What they dispute is that this means death for virtue ethics. Some have responded to the situationist challenge by saying that it misses the target of the traditional conception of virtue, so virtue ethics can go on just as before. Others have responded by modifying the conception of virtue (or advocating a different traditional conception; e.g., one from Hume rather than Aristotle). In this section we'll consider these different ways of responding.[4]

Some philosophers have argued that Doris's critique isn't fair to virtue ethics because it does not give enough attention to the role of practical wisdom in virtue and that, once this role is appreciated, the situationist critique no longer applies. Rachana Kamtekar, for example, argues that the empirical attack on virtue ethics misses the target, because the experiments that are supposed to show that character traits do not explain our behavior rely on a faulty conception of a character trait "as an isolable and nonrational disposition to manifest a given stereotypical behavior that differs from the behavior of others and is fairly situation insensitive" (Kamtekar 2004: 477). But according to virtue ethics in the tradition of Aristotle, Kamtekar says, virtues are "dispositions to respond appropriately—in judgment, feeling, and action—to one's situation. Such responses require the active involvement of the agent's powers of reasoning" (2004: 477). In other words, as we discussed in the previous section, virtues require practical wisdom if they are going to help people behave well. Since there is no reason to expect seminary students (for example) to be truly wise, such studies do not show that virtuous people do not behave well even when they are in a hurry.

It's not clear how much this response helps to vindicate virtue ethics, if the argument I attributed to Doris above is correct. That argument takes the problem to be that cross-situationally reliable virtues are not widely instantiated in the population, that is, not widely instantiated enough to make cultivating virtue a good strategy for moral improvement. Practical wisdom seems to be quite rare and difficult to cultivate. If the full possession of any virtue requires practical wisdom, then it will be the rare person who really does possess virtue (a fact which Kamtekar admits). If Kamtekar is correct about the importance of wisdom, and if normative theories are to be judged on whether they provide good strategies for moral improvement, then whether virtue ethics is a good normative theory will depend on whether we can make strides in improving our practical reasoning and whether wise reflection can help us make better choices.[5] Whether it makes sense to try to cultivate wisdom and the other virtues along with it depends in part on how practical wisdom is conceived, and this leads us right back to the question about the nature of virtue.

Let's put the topic of wisdom on hold for now and consider a different way of responding to the situationist challenge. One might be skeptical of robust, cross-situationally reliable virtues, but still not be persuaded that virtue ethics is wrongheaded because of that. After all, even if it's true that situational factors influence our behavior in ways we never imagined, it also seems to be true that we do pretty well predicting what people will do based on our assumptions about them. For example, if you are like me, you have some friends you deem to be more trustworthy than others, and you are more likely to share a secret with a trustworthy friend than an untrustworthy friend. Also, if you're like me, you have probably found that trustworthy friends are good at keeping secrets and when you have told a secret to an untrustworthy friend you often regret it. The sort of trustworthiness at issue here is not necessarily reliable across all situations: it is a particular kind of trustworthiness involving friends' secrets. Still, it's important to know which kind of friend you have when you're looking for someone to help you move a body.

Moreover, psychologists themselves these days accept that situation and personality both have a role to play in determining behavior. In general, psychologists tend to think there is very good evidence for the "Big Five" personality traits: Openness to experience, Conscientiousness, Extraversion, Agreeableness and Neuroticism (the list forms OCEAN, if you want to remember it) (John, Robins and Pervin 2008). These traits are not moral virtues, but the fact that psychologists think there are such traits and that they influence behavior across situations does open some opportunities for defending character traits that are virtues.

How could the existence of these stable personality traits be compatible with all the evidence that situational factors have tremendous influence? One proposal comes from research done by William Fleeson and colleagues who argue that there is empirical evidence for character traits understood as "density distributions" that are compatible with the point that the situationist literature makes. Basically, according to the density distribution approach, while it is true that an individual person's behavior varies from situation to situation, the various behaviors of one person form a distribution that has a central tendency, and we can think of a person's character as defined by these central tendencies within distributions. Fleeson and his colleagues have found that people really do differ from each other in terms of what we might call their "average behavior" and that these differences are very stable (Fleeson 2001). Furthermore, though most of the research has been done on the Big Five traits, these psychologists argue that their model is a good model for understanding virtue (Jayawickreme, Meindl, Helzer, Furr and Fleeson 2014). At the very least, this gives us a way to understand what a trait is that is compatible with the research on situationism, and this opens up a new line of response for the virtue ethicist.

To see how this would work in more detail, consider Figure 7.1. The figure shows density distributions of compassionate behavior for fifty hypothetical

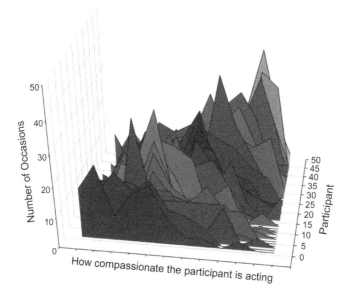

Figure 7.1 Distributions of Compassionate Behavior

people.[6] Nobody is always compassionate, and how compassionate a given person is varies from situation to situation, but people vary in different ways. A person whose shaded area is weighted toward the right is more compassionate more often; a person whose shaded area is weighted to the left is often not compassionate and rarely very compassionate. If we think of virtues as density distributions, we would say that the right-weighted people are more compassionate and the left-weighted people are more heartless. There are also people in between who are not quite compassionate or heartless.

This understanding of traits, as behavioral averages or density distributions, is compatible with thinking that situations can make a big difference. If we think of virtues as traits of this kind, then virtue ethics can admit that virtues are frail or wobbly as long as it still makes sense to praise people for their "central tendencies" and aiming to improve your central tendency still constitutes a reasonable ethical goal. The philosopher Christian Miller (2013) has developed a theory of cross-situationally consistent character traits that fits well with this psychological research. Miller argues that what we human beings have are "mixed traits"; we tend to act well in some circumstances and to act badly in others, just as the empirical studies reveal. Virtue ethics can be built on mixed traits as long as we can set about to improve the balance of good to bad.

What virtue ethics will have to give up on, according to Maria Merritt (2000), is the Aristotelian idea that virtue implies very strong "motivational self-sufficiency," that is, the power to motivate us all by themselves without any help in whatever tempting circumstances we find ourselves. "What situationist psychology makes problematic," according to Merritt, "is not as such the recommendation to have the virtues, but the normative ideal of the virtues as qualities that must be possessed in a strongly self-sufficient form" (2000: 375).

Merritt's proposal is to think of virtues as David Hume did: traits that are relatively stable and reliable at producing good actions, but not necessarily because of an internal psychological force. Following Hume, virtue ethics could conceive of virtues as whatever habits and dispositions get us to behave better, where these habits and dispositions might require specific situational reinforcement. On this view, we should appreciate the ways in which virtues are developed and maintained within social structures and acknowledge the importance of these structures in upholding virtue. Thinking about virtue in this way, we could say that what went wrong in the Milgram experiments is that people were placed in an unusual social environment in which the normal support for compassion was absent and the influence of the authority figure was highly salient. A Humean virtue ethicist should be particularly interested in making sure that our social environments sustain and facilitate our acting on our good traits. Further, if some personality traits are importantly related to the virtues—as agreeableness and conscientiousness are plausibly related to the virtues of compassion and trustworthiness—then a Humean virtue ethicist should be interested in ways we can change our personalities.[7]

At the beginning of this section, I said that some philosophers argue that the situationist research in psychology misunderstands the nature of virtue because it ignores the role of practical wisdom in virtue. It was left unclear whether developing wisdom is a useful ethical goal. We can now see what the problem is more precisely: if practical wisdom requires strong motivational self-sufficiency, then developing it would be just as problematic as developing any other kind of self-sufficient virtue. But does practical wisdom necessarily include a high degree of motivational self-sufficiency? Is it the kind of thing we can expect to guarantee acting well in any situation without any help?

The wise person, according to Aristotle, "is the one whose aim expresses rational calculation in pursuit of the best good for a human being that is achievable in action" (1141b10–15). It is true that the traditional conception of wisdom takes it to be rather autonomous or self-sufficient. The Aristotelian philosopher John McDowell, for instance, takes practical wisdom to be analogous to a kind of sensitive perception of what the situation requires, which results in the fully virtuous person seeing a course of action as "the thing to do" in a way that is sufficient for her to do it. According to McDowell, "nothing over and above the unclouded deliverances of the sensitivity is needed to explain the actions that manifest virtue" (1979: 334). This does seem to be a picture of wisdom that ignores what Merritt calls the social contribution to virtue. It is also a picture of wisdom according to which to truly achieve wisdom requires quite a bit more control over how we see things than we might actually have.

Do we have to see practical wisdom this way? Not necessarily. We could agree with Aristotle that wisdom is the ability and the will to deliberate well about the ends of human life and action, but allow our particular view about what skills are required by this good deliberation to be informed by a realistic understanding of our psychology. For example, I have argued that how we think about wisdom should be shaped by our understanding of our various limitations (Tiberius 2008).[8] We have poor self-knowledge, we are bad at introspecting our own motivations for doing things, and we have a tendency to become obsessed with trivial things and to ignore what's important until it is threatened. All of these things make us bad at practical reasoning because they distort the inputs to the process. I argue that, to improve our deliberation, what we need to do is to cultivate some background dispositions and habits that will make it less likely that we'll reason badly. I call this set of dispositions "reflective wisdom," which includes perspective, self-awareness, and the development of stable, emotionally appropriate values. The dispositions and habits of mind that constitute reflective wisdom include paying attention to the situation and relying on other people (for instance as a source of self-knowledge) to help compensate for your limitations.

Taking Stock

It's worth pausing to think about what's at stake in the debate about virtue. "Virtue talk" is ubiquitous. Voters obsess about the character of political candidates; grade school teachers plan how to inculcate the virtues of honesty and kindness in their students; all of us judge the people we meet according to how nice, mean, dependable and so forth they are; parents advise us to date and marry nice guys or gals; we make New Year's resolutions to "be nicer" or more generous; and so on. If we cannot find a way of thinking about virtue, wisdom and practical reasoning that respects our psychological reality, none of this makes sense. Many of us have judged people unfairly: we say that someone is mean, but really he was just having a bad day, for example. Furthermore, most of us have had the experience of failure in our attempts to set ourselves on a new path: we've tried to become regular exercisers, or vegans, or less critical of others, and we have just bombed. One of the things we should learn from the situationist critique of virtue ethics is that it doesn't make sense to ignore situational factors and pretend that other people have perfect control over how they behave or that we can just will ourselves to be better people. An integrated conception of character that takes in the insight from situationism would not recommend that we judge people harshly regardless of situation or that we try to change ourselves by sheer force of will. Rather, it would recommend directing our attention to the ways in which situations affect us and others. We should take this into account when we judge others, and we should use our reasoning to figure out the best way to overcome the pressures and temptations that we have good reason to want to overcome. Of course, even this kind of reasoning might be ineffective and even this kind of virtue might elude us, but in my view we would need a much stronger argument than what we have now to make it reasonable to give up on these hopes altogether.

If we can find a psychologically defensible theory of virtue, what does this tell us about moral motivation? If virtues are taken to be truly special states that are neither judgments nor desires, then moral motivation will be something quite unique, according to virtue ethics. If, on the other hand, moral action, according to virtue ethics, is action motivated by relatively stable psychological patterns that include emotions, desires, judgments and the commitment to doing what it takes to be a good person (even if what it takes is being careful about your situation), then the virtue ethical picture of moral motivation is not really incompatible with the other theories we have seen so far. Rather, virtue ethics just picks out which specific desires, sentiments and judgments constitute moral motivation, that is, the ones that make up the virtues and are appropriately related to our flourishing.

Summary

- Virtue ethicists claim that moral motivation is a distinctive kind of motivation. We are motivated to act morally by virtuous character traits.
- Virtues are identified by their relationship to human flourishing or happiness. Aristotle takes virtuous activity to be constitutive of the best kind of life (the most flourishing life) for a person.
- It has been argued that virtues are sensitivities to moral considerations that have both directions of fit: they are perceptions of reasons to do things that also motivate us to act. This is a controversial feature of virtue.
- Less controversial is the claim that virtues are stable and consistent traits of character. This claim has been challenged by empirical research on the effect of situational factors on our behavior (the situationist challenge).
- The tremendous and surprising influence of situation has been taken by critics of virtue ethics to undermine the idea that cross-situationally reliable, motivationally self-sufficient traits are possessed by anyone but the rare and exceptional person.
- It would be bad for virtue ethics if virtues are so rare that aiming to cultivate virtues is not a good avenue to moral improvement.
- One response to the situationist challenge has been to argue that it misses the target because it ignores the role of practical wisdom in the traditional conception of virtue.
- Another response has been to construe virtues in a different way so that they are not motivationally self-sufficient but to argue that they still constitute a good ethical goal.

Study Questions

1. According to virtue ethics, what's the answer to the question of whether Reason or passion is in charge?
2. Thinking about the people you know, how stable do you observe character to be? Think about someone you think is a really good person: Is this person good in every domain? Do they have all the virtues? Do they exhibit the virtues all the time? Now think about someone who's kind of normal (in terms of moral goodness). What would you say is the relevant difference between these two people?
3. Sometimes in moral psychology, progress is made by identifying an empirical assumption that some moral theory makes and then showing how this assumption is undermined or supported by the empirical evidence. Has this kind of progress been made with respect to virtue ethics?

4. Politicians often get caught cheating on their wives (or, less often, their husbands), having affairs with young interns, and in various other ways flouting their own professed sexual morality. The public tends to judge them harshly, and they often end up getting booted out of office. Should the research on the power of the situation make us (the public) more lenient and less judgmental?

Notes

1. How virtue ethics should defend the metaethics that this picture requires—a worldview according to which it makes sense to say that ethical appreciation is akin to perception—is an interesting question that we won't go into here.
2. This was in the original version of the experiment. Milgram ran many versions in the early 1960s; they did not all result in this level of compliance. For discussion of the follow-up experiments, see Milgram (1974).
3. It's worth noting that there is some controversy about this study, because some attempts to replicate it were not successful.
4. Other responses are possible. See Miller (2014) for a comprehensive review.
5. Doris (2009) has come back fighting against this response to his critique, by arguing that we do not actually fare very well when we let our rational capacities take charge.
6. Thanks to William Fleeson and Eranda Jayawickreme for permission to use their figure. The point of the figure is to present a model for the virtue of compassion; it represents hypothetical patterns of behavior based on patterns tested for other traits.
7. For a review of the relevant research on changing personality see Edmonds et al. (2008).
8. There are other examples of philosophers who have developed views about practical wisdom that draw on empirical literature. Lorraine Besser-Jones (2012), for example, draws on the research on goal setting and self-regulation to argue that there are empirical grounds for thinking that practical reason has an important role to play in the development and activation of virtue. Swartwood (2013) argues that wisdom is a kind of expert skill on the basis of research on skill development in other domains such as chess playing.

Further Readings

Doris, J. M. 1998. "Persons, Situations, and Virtue Ethics." *Nous* 32 (4): 504–530.
Hursthouse, R. 1999. *On Virtue Ethics.* Oxford University Press.
Kamtekar, R. 2004. "Situationism and Virtue Ethics on the Content of Our Character." *Ethics* 114 (3): 458–491.
Latane, B., and J. M. Darley. 1970. *The Unresponsive Bystander: Why Doesn't He Help?* Appleton-Century Crofts.
Little, M. O. 1997. "Virtue as Knowledge: Objections from the Philosophy of Mind." *Nous* 31 (1): 59–79.
McDowell, J. 1979. "Virtue and Reason" *Monist* 62 (3): 331–350.
Merritt, M. 2000. "Virtue Ethics and Situationist Personality Psychology." *Ethical Theory and Moral Practice* 3 (4): 365–383.
Milgram, S. 1974. *Obedience to Authority: An Experimental View.* HarperCollins.
Miller, C. 2013. *Moral Character: An Empirical Theory.* Oxford University Press.
Snow, N. E. 2010. *Virtue as Social Intelligence: An Empirically Grounded Theory.* Routledge.

Part IV

Agency and Moral Responsibility

In our discussion of moral motivation we have seen that some people think there are special moral motives such as virtue or the motive of duty. Motives that have particular moral worth are motives for which we deserve special praise or esteem. On the other hand, when we act on the wrong motives (out of vice or a desire to harm someone, say), we are often rebuked or blamed. When we take a step back from the debate about which particular motives are good, worthy or especially morally interesting, we might begin to wonder whether praising and blaming people who act on any motives ever makes sense. Even if a person has the *right* motivations as a matter of her psychology, we might ask, does it make sense to praise, blame or hold her responsible in any way if she is psychologically determined to act as she does? Can we blame Mean Mary for running over Spot the dog if she was just born that way (with overwhelming mean desires) or if her parents trained her to be mean for their own nefarious purposes?

Of course we do often hold people responsible, and sometimes we even punish them. But it's also true that we don't always hold people responsible: we excuse people who are too young, mentally ill or somehow incapacitated. What makes the difference between a responsible person and one who isn't responsible? Or between an action for which you are responsible and one for which you're not? Are people ever really morally responsible for what they do? The answers to these questions are often taken to depend on whether we have free will. In this part of the book we'll talk about responsibility, praise, blame, free will and the facts about our psychology that support or challenge our ordinary ideas about moral responsibility.

8 The Psychology of the Responsible Agent

- Holding People Responsible
- Methodology
- Real Self Theories
- Normative Competence
- Are We Competent? Challenges from Psychology
- Summary
- Study Questions
- Notes
- Further Readings

In the 1990s, Bernie Madoff took large amounts of money from people who trusted him with the promise that he would manage and invest it. Instead, Madoff constructed a giant pyramid scheme—a scheme in which you use the money from new investors to pay off the older investors, rather than actually investing the money and making real profits—and defrauded people out of billions of dollars in total. Americans were angry with Madoff and blamed him for what he did. His victims sent emails to the court that tried him: "One victim called him a Bastard, with a capital B. Another labeled him 'scum' and 'a vicious animal.' Still another wrote, 'I feel like I have been economically raped'" (Keteyian 2010).

Sometimes, though, we do not want to blame people who do terrible things. Consider the outcry from human rights organizations about the fact that mentally retarded individuals could be executed for committing crimes in the United States.[1] According to Human Rights Watch,

> The United States is almost alone in the world in allowing this barbaric practice. At least 33 mentally retarded men have been executed since the United States reinstated the death penalty in 1976. Some experts estimate that as many as 10 to 15 percent of the 3,000 men and women on the nation's death rows are retarded . . . The mentally retarded can never meet the criteria of extraordinary blameworthiness. People with retardation are incapable of calculated, mature evil. A retarded person

is simply not the same as other adults. They are childlike in many of their limitations: their ability to reason and develop skills needed to navigate in the world are permanently stunted.[2]

It seems inappropriate to be angry at a person with limited cognitive capacities, just as it seems appropriate to be angry and resentful towards Madoff.

Whatever you think about these cases in particular, it is clear that we do hold some people responsible for their moral or immoral actions and that our attributions of responsibility vary depending on the psychological characteristics of the agent. You would likely blame your roommate for punching you in the face or for taking your sandwich, but you wouldn't blame a two-year-old child for hitting you or for taking something that doesn't belong to her. We don't tend to hold someone who is experiencing a nervous breakdown as responsible for bad behavior as someone who is mentally healthy. We excuse people for reasons of temporary insanity. Psychological factors shape our attributions of moral responsibility, praise and blame.

Holding People Responsible

One question of great interest in moral psychology is the question of what psychological states an agent must have for it to make sense to hold that agent responsible for what she does. Since this is a book on moral psychology, we will begin with this question by thinking about what distinguishes the psychology of the person we hold responsible from the psychology of the person we excuse. Notice that this is not a question simply about what people actually do in their praising and blaming behavior; it is a question about what it makes sense to do, what is morally or normatively appropriate. It might be that we sometimes, in fact, hold people responsible unfairly, as we once did with mentally retarded people according to Human Rights Watch. What we're looking for here is a characterization of when and why it *makes sense* to hold an agent responsible.

Now, you might think that this gets things backwards and that to establish whether it makes sense to hold people responsible at all we need to figure out, first, if they are metaphysically responsible or transcendentally free, or something like that. In other words, you might think that we have to establish whether determinism is true, and if it is, whether true freedom of the will is compatible with determinism, before we can get anywhere on the topic of responsibility. Many philosophers reject this view, however. Some think that the question about responsibility is an inherently normative (or moral) question and some think that we need to figure out what responsibility looks like before we can ask about the metaphysical conditions for it. In this section we'll consider these arguments and then proceed to consider the psychological conditions of responsibility along these lines. We will leave further considerations about determinism for the next chapter. (If you really can't put the free will question aside for now, you can skip ahead to Chapter 9 and come back to this one.)

Peter Strawson is more responsible than anyone (no pun intended) for drawing philosophers' attention to the importance of *holding* people responsible. In his famous 1962 paper "Freedom and Resentment," Strawson (2008) tries to justify our practice of *holding people responsible* without relying on an independent theory of the conditions under which people are responsible. Strawson thinks that our practice is justified because once you understand our practice of holding people responsible, you will also see that (first) it has its own norms that have nothing to do with the metaphysics of anything and (second) that it's really, really important to us and to how we relate to each other. To see Strawson's point, we need to explore his idea that our ordinary relationships with people are structured by what he calls the reactive attitudes.

The reactive attitudes are emotions that we feel toward other people insofar as we regard them as persons capable of meeting our expectations, rather than as objects that will just do what they do. These emotions are "reactions to the quality of others' wills toward us, as manifested in their behavior: to their good or ill will or indifference or lack of concern" (Strawson 2008: 15). Reactive attitudes include the kind of moral resentment and indignation we feel toward someone like Bernie Madoff; they also include positive emotions such as gratitude that we feel toward people who do good things and emotions like guilt, shame and pride that we feel about our own actions. We do not have reactive attitudes toward everyone whose actions affect us. When we do not take these actions to be representative of the quality of the other person's attitude toward us in an important way, we instead respond to them with "objective attitudes." When we take an objective attitude toward another we see him or her as something to be managed, handled, cured, trained or avoided; we do not see him or her as someone to be brought into conversation, reasoned with or engaged. If your roommate steals your sandwich from the counter, you could be resentful. If your dog does it, you'll think that you need to step up your training.

Strawson asks us to think about the cases in which our ordinary blaming attitudes toward bad behavior are mitigated. If you think about the simple case of your roommate stealing your sandwich, you can see what kinds of changes to the situation would reduce your resentment. First, if your roommate didn't know that the sandwich was yours and threw it in the garbage because she was trying to tidy up, you would probably feel less resentful. Second, if your roommate just found out her mother died and was out of her mind with grief, you would probably think that "she's not really herself" and feel less resentful than usual. Finally, if your roommate were a dog, a child or a cognitively impaired person who doesn't really understand what stealing is, you would not likely feel resentment at all (though you may be quite annoyed). In all these cases, what the mitigating circumstances reveal is that the action of stealing the sandwich doesn't mean that your roommate disrespects you, doesn't care about you or wants to hurt you. Given this, it's not appropriate to hold her responsible in a way that entails blame and the possibility of punitive sanctions.

Strawson then argues that the question about determinism is this: "Could, or should, the acceptance of the determinist thesis lead us always to look on everyone exclusively in this way (in the objective way)?" (2008: 12). In other words, if we believe that human actions are determined—that is, causally entailed by the pre-existing facts together with the laws of nature—should we regard everyone in the way that we regard pets, children, the mentally ill and the cognitively impaired? Strawson thinks we cannot and should not attempt to change our attitudes in this way, for two reasons. First, we already have reasons for adopting the objective attitude toward some people in some circumstances and these reasons have nothing to do with the truth of determinism. Rather, they have to do with the factors we mentioned above (whether the person knows what she's doing, whether she was herself when she did it, and so on). Second, what we would give up by taking the objective attitude toward everyone would not be worth whatever would be gained by it.[3]

To see what would be lost in giving up the reactive attitudes, it will help to elaborate Strawson's picture in the way that R. Jay Wallace does. Wallace points out that what is crucial to the attitudes we take toward those we hold responsible—resentment, indignation and guilt, according to Wallace—is that these attitudes are a response to violated expectations. We expect people to behave in certain ways and when they fail, we are resentful or indignant. When we fail our own expectations we feel guilty. With this refinement of the picture in mind, think about what life would be like if we took an objective attitude toward everyone. What would happen to friendship, for example, if we refused to hold our friends to any expectations? Imagine a friendship between you and me in which neither of us expects the other to be honest or loyal or helpful; when you are mean to me, I'm not angry, and when I break my promise to you, you might feel sad but you do not resent me. This sounds very much like the relationship I had with my goldfish, though even my goldfish might have resented it when I forgot to feed him.

The above argument gives us a reason to look to psychological conditions of responsible agency, since it is obviously very important to us to distinguish responsible people from "objects." So far we have seen some paradigm examples of conditions that undermine attributions of responsibility, but we have not yet arrived at a definitive characterization of the psychology of a responsible agent. There are many theories to consider, which can be divided into "Real Self" theories and "Normative Competency" theories. According to the former, an agent is responsible for her actions when those actions stem from her real or true self. According to the latter, an agent is responsible for her actions when those actions result from her rational capacities.

Methodology

Before we turn to examine these two theories, it's worth pausing to ask what question we are really asking and what the standards are for a good answer. We have already seen from our discussion of Strawson that there are two questions we might ask:

- Under what conditions do we, in fact, hold people responsible? This is a descriptive question about the nature of our practice of attributing responsibility.
- Under what conditions does it make sense (or is it rational) to hold people responsible? This is a normative question about the *legitimacy* of our practice.

In one interpretation of Strawson, he distinguishes these questions very clearly. He answers the first by describing the role of the reactive attitudes in our practice, and the second by appeal to the gains and losses that would result from giving up this practice.

But for many philosophers (and maybe even for Strawson, in a different interpretation), these two questions are not so neatly distinguished. This is because of a background view about the methodology for defending answers to the question about the legitimacy of our practice (the second question). According to this background view, the two questions are actually related: we vindicate our practice by describing it in a way that makes sense. This methodology—*reflective equilibrium*—is very common in ethics. Very briefly, the idea is that you defend normative theories by showing that they are the best way of systematizing our ethical principles, considered judgments (sometimes called "intuitions") about cases, and our background philosophical and scientific theories.[4] Following this method, we defend a *normative* theory of responsibility (that is, a theory that tells us when it is fair or reasonable to hold others responsible) by demonstrating that the theory best systematizes our considered judgments about cases of various kinds along with the relevant background theories.

Reflective equilibrium does not imply that all of our considered judgments are correct or that the best theory is the one that preserves the greatest number of them. Some of the judgments we make about cases may be in conflict with other judgments, and some judgments might have implications that conflict with other things we believe very strongly. For example, consider someone who starts to think about the topic of responsibility who is inclined to make two judgments about cases: first, that Harry and Susan who each donated a kidney to a total stranger (see Chapter 3) do not get any real credit or praise for this because, after all, "their brains made them do it" and, second, that Bernie Madoff is the scum of the earth, deserving of all the blame we can heap upon him because his greedy decisions hurt people tremendously. On the face of it, these judgments are in tension with each other. The theorist engaged in reflective equilibrium has at least two options.

First, she can point to some relevant difference between the two cases. Perhaps, albeit implausibly, Harry and Susan didn't ever think about their options but just acted from the gut without thinking it through, whereas Madoff acted in a much more calculating fashion. Or, second, the theorist could reject one of these judgments, because it is at odds with too many of the other things she thinks about responsibility or about the way the world works. For instance, she might decide to reject her judgment that Susan and Harry are not responsible, because she realizes that it doesn't make any sense to say that brains make people do things given her view that the mind is the brain (more on this argument in Chapter 9).

This example features a rather obvious inconsistency; it will become apparent later in this chapter and the next that some inconsistencies are much more difficult to notice and resolve. The important point for now is that reflective equilibrium does not require us to preserve all of our judgments. Some of them may have to be given up when we arrive at the best theory. What this means is that there may be a gap between the best theory and what we happen to think. Reflective equilibrium "cleans up" our intuitions about cases, revising and pruning as necessary to reach an equilibrium point. The bigger the gap, the more we can complain that the theory of responsibility we have been offered isn't really a theory of what we mean by responsibility. It's good to keep in mind, though, that because our various judgments and beliefs are not perfectly consistent, every theory will create some gap.

We're now ready to consider the two different theories of the psychological conditions for responsibility. The philosophers who defend these theories often appeal to examples in order to show that their theories make the *best* sense of our current practices and views about responsibility, praise and blame. Given the method of reflective equilibrium, if they are successful, they will have shown not just how we tend to attribute responsibility, but also why it makes sense to do it in this way.

Real Self Theories

One important difference between Bernie Madoff and the roommate who steals your sandwich because she's blinded by grief is that Bernie Madoff's actions seem to express who he really is (someone greedy and ruthless enough to deceive people and make a lot of people poorer in order to become wealthy himself), while the roommate's actions do not. For this reason, Madoff seems more responsible for what he's done than the distraught roommate. Similarly, someone who dances on the table under hypnosis seems less responsible for breaking your table than someone who does it because he thinks it would be fun. These insights have led some philosophers to think that the key to responsible agency has to do with acting on the beliefs and desires that are truly yours, as opposed to acting on beliefs and desires that are alien or foreign to the "real you."

Harry Frankfurt developed this sort of view in his paper "Freedom of the Will and the Concept of a Person" (1971). Frankfurt puts the point in terms of free will, rather than responsibility, but it is clear that free will *in the sense that is relevant to responsibility* is what really matters to him. Frankfurt's basic picture is that we act freely when we act on our own desires, and we have a free will when the desires that we act on are the ones we want to be acting on. In other words, free *action* is doing what we want and free *will* is doing what we want to want. Here Frankfurt is invoking "second-order desires" to explain what it is to be a person.[5] Persons have desires about which of their desires they want to move them. Your desires move you around, and if all you have is those desires, you're more like an animal than a person (you are what Frankfurt calls a "wanton"[6]). What you *want to want* determines what you, the person, "really" want as distinct from what is merely a force inside your head making you do things.

You, most likely, are a person. To see this, think about some time that you've hoped to change yourself in some way. For example, if you have ever wanted to quit smoking or to spend less time playing video games, then you have had a second-order desire (you wanted not to want a cigarette, for example) and that makes you a person in the relevant sense, according to Frankfurt. Or, think about your long-term goals (such as graduating from college), which likely incline you to have desires about your short-term, first-order desires: you want to act on your desires to study and not on your desires to go out drinking every night, for example. Human beings who have no second-order volitions (human beings who are not persons in this sense) can certainly do things—they do have desires that they can act on—but they do not have any second-order volitions; there is no real self that they want to be.

How does this distinction between persons and non-persons help us understand the psychological conditions of responsibility? We could say that when a person is moved by the desire that he wills to move him, then he is responsible for what he did and deserving of praise and blame. In this way of thinking, people deserve praise or blame for the actions that stem from who they really are, their true or deep selves. People do not deserve praise or blame for the actions that stem from desires that are imposed on them from the outside and that they do not want to have (as in the case of hypnotism). And animals or wanton human beings who just act on their desires, with no concern one way or another about what these desires are, do not really warrant praise or blame at all.

According to Frankfurt, I am most fully myself, and therefore responsible for what I do, when I do what I want to do and what I want to do is what I want to want to do. For a person to be free and responsible is for him or her "to have the will he [or she] wants" (Frankfurt 1971: 15). There is surely something compelling about this theory, but some serious objections have also been raised. The main objection can be put this way: What's so great about the *second order*? Why think that who you really are is identified with your desires about your desires and not something else; why not your third-order desires, for instance? Talking about desires in the abstract makes the point kind of obscure, so let's think about this objection in terms of an example. Consider a person who suffers from anorexia nervosa, who has some (first-order) desires to eat and some first-order desires to be thin, but a very definite and unhealthy second-order desire to act on the desire to lose weight and never on her desires to eat.[7] In the view we are considering, it seems that we have to say that the person with anorexia is most truly herself, most responsible, most deserving of praise and blame, when she acts on her desire to lose weight, because this is the desire she wants to be effective. But now it seems like something has gone wrong. The problem is that our second-order desires can be irrational, the result of illness or external forces, in just the same way that our first-order desires can. Anorexia nervosa is a serious disease that affects second-order desires. The case shows that second-order desires can be just as alien to who we really are (or who we should try to be) as first-order desires. Further, a person who is recovering from anorexia might have a third-order desire to be rid of her second-order desire to act only on her first-order desire to lose weight. Why shouldn't we think that this third-order desire is more representative of who she really is?

Frankfurt responded to this objection by fine-tuning the characterization of the higher-order attitude that represents our true selves. Ultimately, he argued that we act freely in a way deserving of praise and blame when we act on desires that we wholeheartedly endorse (Frankfurt 1988). The hope is that wholehearted endorsement would block the move to further orders of desire, because to endorse something with your whole heart settles things for you. It is a decisive act of commitment to being a certain way.

According to Nomy Arpaly and Tim Schroeder (1999), however, whole-hearted endorsement doesn't fix all the problems with Frankfurt's theory. They think this because "endorsement" is still a cognitive response of the rational or judging part of the self and this implies, problematically in their view, that we are not responsible or praiseworthy when we act on desires that might be very good parts of us even though we don't judge them to be. To see their point, consider the case of Mark Twain's character Huckleberry Finn. Huck Finn is a good southern boy who was raised to think that some people rightly own slaves and that the laws upholding the institution of slavery are just. Nevertheless, when Huck finds himself becoming friends with Jim, an escaped slave, he finds that he cannot turn Jim in to the authorities even though he believes that is the right thing to do. Huck sees himself as a bad boy who cannot bring himself to do the right thing as he contemplates letting Jim escape:

> It made me shiver. And I about made up my mind to pray, and see if I couldn't try to quit being the kind of a boy I was and be better. So I kneeled down. But the words wouldn't come. Why wouldn't they? It warn't no use to try and hide it from Him. Nor from ME, neither. I

knowed very well why they wouldn't come. It was because my heart warn't right; it was because I warn't square; it was because I was playing double. I was letting ON to give up sin, but away inside of me I was holding on to the biggest one of all.

(Twain 1994/1884: 161)

We feel differently, though. For readers of Twain's novel, Huck is doing the right thing by not turning Jim in, and we are relieved when he decides, "All right, then, I'll GO to hell" and tears up the letter reporting Jim to his owner. Huck's compassionate, friendship-based desires are leading him in the right direction, against his reason or at least against what he believes he should be doing. Arpaly and Schroeder call this a case of "inverse akrasia" because it is a case in which Finn acts *rightly* against his better judgment, as opposed to regular cases of akrasia (weakness of will) in which people act *wrongly* against their better judgment.

Arpaly and Schroeder think that cases like this—cases in which we act morally against our better judgment—cause a problem for Frankfurt. The basic intuition here is that Huck is praiseworthy for not turning Jim in. Arpaly has developed this idea in her book, *Unprincipled Virtue* (2003). She argues that the psychological condition that grounds attributions of responsibility is the quality of a person's will. A person with a good will deserves praise, and a person with bad will deserves blame. Wills are complicated things that are comprised of desires and feelings: being motivated to do good and feeling good about doing it. Given everything that is at stake, Huck has a better will than a similar boy who would listen to his judgment and turn in his friend for punishment. According to Arpaly, Huck is therefore praiseworthy for what he did.

Though the theories we have discussed in this section disagree about what is the most important part of the self, they agree that it is helpful to think about responsibility in terms of the self. We could put the basic insight this way: You should be praised or blamed for the actions that stem from who you really are, deep down, or from your character, since actions that do not result from your real self or character must have some cause that is external to you. This was the view of David Hume:

Actions are by their very nature temporary and perishing; and where they proceed not from some cause in the characters and disposition of the person, who perform'd them, they infix not themselves upon him, and can neither redound to his honour, if good, nor infamy, if evil. The action itself may be blameable; it may be contrary to all the rules of morality and religion: but the person is not responsible for it; and as it proceeded from nothing in him, that is durable or constant, and leaves nothing of that nature behind it, 'tis impossible he can, upon its account, become the object of punishment or vengeance.

(2000/1739: 411)

We can see the debate between the two theories we've been discussing as a debate about what a person's true character or real self is. Frankfurt's whole-hearted endorsement view and Arpaly and Schroeder's whole-self view are different approaches to identifying your *real self*, that is, the person you really are. Should the self that is responsible be identified with a certain aspect of our psychology (the part that explicitly assents to things whole-heartedly), or should it be identified with our powers of thought *and* emotion? A compelling answer to this question might help sort the cases in the right way and reach a good equilibrium about responsibility.

On the other hand, one might think that talking about the real self is the wrong approach to thinking about the psychological conditions for responsibility. After all, what your "self" is like is largely a product of your upbringing and your culture, so why should you be held responsible for it? Thoughts like these have led to the development of a different approach to moral responsibility.

Normative Competence

What if our real self or our character (what we want, what we endorse, what our emotions are and so forth) is beyond our control? If it is, and if our real self determines how we act, then it looks like we aren't really responsible for what we do after all. Sure, Bernie Madoff defrauded hundreds of people out of millions of dollars on purpose and because he was a bad guy, but society (or his parents or his genes) made him into a bad guy in the first place!

Obviously, we do not have control over the past. When we decide what to do now, we cannot change the influences of our upbringing and culture so that we have different options open to us now. But we do have *some* kind of control. Right now, you could lift your arm up and wave your hand around. Or, you could not do that. Now that I've put the idea in your head, you could do it or not do it—however you were raised, it's up to you. There are different kinds of control we might have over our actions, some of which we are more likely to actually have than others. The philosophers we'll discuss in this section think that the most important kind of control has to do with our *normative competencies*, which include our capacities to recognize, grasp and act for reasons. As we'll see, there are different interpretations of what the important normative competencies are.

It's useful to begin with a distinction that will illuminate the different types of control we might have over our actions. John Martin Fischer and Mark Ravizza (1999) distinguish *regulative control* and *guidance control*. Regulative control requires genuine alternative possibilities open to the agent so that she could really do something other than what she actually ends up doing. Guidance control is what you have when it is your decisions that make you take the option that you do take even though, if your decisions themselves are caused by something outside of you, you were not free to decide otherwise (and hence you did not really have alternative possibilities open to you). To put it in a simple way, guidance control is the ability to act on your own choices for your own reasons, and regulative control is the ability to choose and act otherwise than you do.

The importance of all this for our purposes, according to Fischer, is that guidance control is all that is required for moral responsibility (Fischer, Kane, Pereboom and Vargas 2007). This is a good thing for those of us who want to hold on to responsibility, because guidance control is probably (according to Fischer) the only kind of control we have. Importantly, even if we do not have regulative control, this doesn't matter because we do have guidance control, which is sufficient for moral responsibility. What exactly does guidance control amount to?

Fischer's view, developed in his book written with Mark Ravizza (1999), is that the key to guidance control and, hence, to responsibility is a moderately reasons responsive mechanism that is the agent's own. To be responsive to reasons is just to understand what considerations there are in favor of doing this or that and to be able to act for the right reasons. To say that a mechanism is *moderately* responsive is to say that it might not respond to every good reason every single time, but it does respond by and large to the patterns of reasons that confront it. A mechanism that is *strongly* reasons responsive would be one that never fails to act for the good reasons that there are. Consider the case of Befuddled Bob, who is deciding whether to follow his friends to the bank in order to rob it or to ditch them. On the assumption that there are several excellent reasons not to follow his friends in their dumb plan, Bob would not count as strongly reasons responsive unless he decided to ditch his friends. If strong reasons responsiveness were required for responsibility, this would mean that Bob would not be responsible for helping his friends to rob the bank if he chose to do so. Indeed, Bob would not be responsible for doing anything that wasn't a good idea. But this seems like the wrong thing to say: surely we are sometimes responsible for failing to act on the best reasons, and our theory of responsibility needs to make room for this.

On the other hand, we could weaken reasons responsiveness too much so that someone who responds to the most ridiculous kinds of reasons counts as reasons responsive. For example, if Befuddled Bob were responsive only to suggestions from people with tattoos, there's a sense in which he would be reasons responsive, but it would be a sense that makes him kind of crazy, rather than a paradigmatically responsible agent. Fischer and Ravizza want to steer a path between strong and weak reasons responsiveness to something moderate. A person who is moderately responsive to reasons is someone who, by and large, is guided by elements of the coherent patterns of reasons that confront us when we make decisions, though she may not always be guided by every reason in the pattern every time.

Having the right mechanism in place isn't sufficient, however, because the mechanism could have been placed there a minute ago by some external force. If an advanced neuroscientist implanted the reasons responsive mechanism in Bob's brain just before the bank robbery, we would be less inclined to think Bob was responsible for his actions. So, Fischer and Ravizza add that the mechanism in question must be "one's own"; that is, the person must *take* responsibility for her reasons responsive mechanism; she must see it as her own and as making it appropriate for other people to hold her responsible (1998: 207–39).

According to Fischer and Ravizza, to have guidance control a person must have their own mechanism that is moderately responsive to the reasons that there are for acting one way or another. When this mechanism guides your actions, you are responsible for what you do. When you behave independently of this mechanism (as you might, say, if you're sleepwalking), you are not responsible for what you do. A person in whom this mechanism is seriously defective or non-existent is not a responsible agent. In this way of thinking about responsibility, Madoff does seem to be responsible for defrauding seniors out of their retirement money: he acted for selfish reasons that seemed like the best reasons to him.

A person who is responsive to reasons has a particular set of psychological capacities, then, one of which is the capacity to be moved by the right reasons. We might wonder how these capacities develop in human beings and whether this matters to responsibility. Consider that in order to grasp reasons at all, we need to be attuned to them in some way; that is, we need to see that the fact that a statement is true is a good reason to believe it, and the fact that a course of action is morally required is a good reason to do it. Our thinking about reasons has to be hooked up in the right way to what normative reasons are, and this is something we learn as we develop from unreasonable children into rational adults. If this is so, it might seem that what's really needed for responsible action is to be the kind of person whose cognitive mechanism tracks the truth and (in the case of moral reasons) what is morally significant. We might express this, as Susan Wolf (1981, 1990) does, by saying that in order to be responsive to good reasons, a person needs to be *sane*. The thought here is that a person who was raised in such a way that she finds evidence against something to be a reason to believe it or evidence that something gratuitously harms someone to be a reason to do it is so crazy that it makes no sense to hold her responsible.

Wolf has a very insightful argument for this view in her paper "Asymmetrical Freedom" (1980). The asymmetry that she notices is between our judgments of responsibility for bad actions and our judgments of responsibility for good actions. Wolf notices that we have a different standard for freedom when we praise people for doing good things than we do when we blame people for doing bad things. "Here I stand. I can do no other," Martin Luther is supposed to have said when he refused to recant his radical religious writings. This kind of integrity is paradigmatically praiseworthy, even though it might really be true that Martin Luther really couldn't do anything other than what he did, given what his conscience told him. On the other hand, a person who has been brainwashed into thinking that he can do no other than turn to crime is someone we take to be less blameworthy than the person who chooses crime even though he didn't have to. This asymmetry leads Wolf to conclude that it is not whether we could do other than what we were determined to do that's important, but, rather, whether we were determined in the right way. Further, being determined in the right way has to do with whether our capacity to recognize and act for reasons tracks the truth and moral goodness. On the assumption that Martin Luther was well brought up to distinguish between right and wrong, the fact that he can only do what is right (that he is psychologically determined to do what is right) does not impugn his agency or undermine our holding him responsible.

Wolf's argument draws our attention to the fact that "reasons responsiveness" develops in human beings as a result of explicit or implicit education. If a person is poorly raised, he or she might be free to act immorally in ways that the rest of us are not, but this doesn't make the person more responsible. It makes the person a sad case. Once we recognize that reasons responsiveness is a psychological capacity that develops in the way that other capacities do, we can begin to wonder whether we really do have this capacity and whether it is as effective as we might hope. We'll turn to these questions in the next section.

Are We Competent? Challenges from Psychology

According to competency theories, we are responsible for our actions when they result from the capacities that allow us to be guided by reasons. These theories do not necessarily posit a "real self" that is the source of free actions, but they do assume that we have certain rational capacities. Do we really have these capacities?

You might think that if responsible action is action that is guided by reasons, then we are less responsible for what we do the more that our actions are motivated by things that we do not recognize as reasons. Of course, one could be responsive to considerations in favor of acting (reasons) unconsciously—without being aware of what is causing you to act. But most people think that more is required for responsibility. Not only must our actions respond to the reasons that are out there, those reasons must also make their way into our conscious decision making at some point. At the very least we must be *capable* of recognizing the reasons for our actions and endorsing these reasons as our reasons for acting rather than rejecting them as unwanted influences. Consider bank-robbing Bob who wants to rob banks and kill people, and acts on his desires. What if we found out that while Bob is caused to act on his desires, he is incapable of reflecting on what he does and would not consider his immoral desires to be reasons if he did think about it? We might start to think that Bob is deranged, and we might start to think he's not as responsible as we thought when all we knew was that he had a desire to rob banks. The capacity to consciously recognize and endorse certain considerations as your reasons seems to be pretty important to responsible action. (Indeed, it seems important no matter what theory you accept.[8])

Recall from our discussion of the empirical challenge to virtue ethics in Chapter 7 that our actions are often influenced by situational factors that we would not endorse as reasons for acting. For example, the bystander intervention effect, which has been observed in a number of different contexts, is that people are less likely to help someone in need when there are other people around who are not doing anything (Latane and Darley 1970). Surely people don't explicitly think that the fact that there are others around is a reason not to help someone; rather, they are influenced subconsciously by irrelevant factors. In the Milgram experiment (discussed in Chapter 7), people essentially tortured their fellow human beings, responding to the authority of the psychologists in charge rather than to the reasons against inflicting excessive pain on an innocent person that most of them recognized. It is unlikely that the people who initiated the shocks would endorse "obedience to authority" as a reason to risk killing an innocent person, and no one predicted that people would be influenced by that factor so strongly. In the Good Samaritan study (also discussed in Chapter 7), people acted on considerations of punctuality rather than on the reasons for helping others that many of them were about to preach about. Again, people in this experiment were not making a conscious decision to be punctual; rather, they were influenced unconsciously by their feelings of being in a hurry, and they were influenced in ways they would likely not endorse if they thought about it. In all of these cases, and many other examples from social psychology, people would likely try to counteract the influence of these unrecognized situational influences if they knew about them, which suggests that they are not acting on reasons they endorse when these influences cause their actions.

There is more evidence of our irrationality that doesn't have to do with virtue and moral behavior. A number of studies suggest that our choices of consumer products are not made for the reasons we think they are. These studies also tend to show that we confabulate reasons after we choose so that our choices *seem* to have been made for considerations we endorse as reasons, even though they really weren't. In one such study, people were asked to choose among four pairs of stockings that were (unbeknownst to the shoppers) exactly the same. People tended to choose the stockings on the right, but they explained their choice by referring to the better quality of the stockings they chose (Wilson and Nisbett 1978). Other, more elaborate, studies show that analyzing our reasons tends to change our attitudes toward political candidates, our beliefs about whether our romantic relationships will last, and our judgments about how much we like different posters (Wilson, Kraft and Dunn 1989; Wilson and Kraft 1993; Wilson, Lisle, Schooler, Hodges, Klaaren and LaFleur 1993). In this last study, participants were asked to evaluate two types of posters: reproductions of impressionist paintings and humorous posters, such as a photograph of a kitten perched on a rope with the caption, "Gimme a Break" (Wilson et al. 1993). All of the participants were asked to rate how much they liked each poster and then allowed to choose a poster to take home. The reflectors were instructed to write down their reasons for feeling as they did about the posters before giving their ratings, while the controls did a cognitive task not related to reflecting on reasons (a filler task). The results of the study were that the reflectors rated the humorous posters significantly higher than the controls did and were much more likely to take these humorous posters home.[9] A few weeks later, the researchers telephoned all the participants and asked them several questions about the posters they had chosen (how much they liked them, whether they still had them, whether they had hung them up on their walls). The reflectors were less satisfied with their posters than the people who did not reflect on their reasons before choosing a poster.

Apparently, what happens is that people don't really have reasons for many of their attitudes, beliefs and judgments (such as their poster preferences), so when they are asked to analyze their reasons, they just make up something that's easy to think of or that they believe will make sense to other people (that is, they confabulate). These confabulations lead people away from the attitudes, beliefs and judgments they made before they started thinking about it (such as the preference for the impressionist poster). There's nothing necessarily wrong with this, of course—analyzing your reasons might improve your beliefs after all. The point for our purposes is that people think their beliefs and judgments are *based on* their reasons, but this is mistaken if the reasons they confabulate create new attitudes that they didn't have before they thought about it (such as the preference for the kitten poster).

Taken as a whole, the psychological evidence suggests that we do not often know why we do what we do, and when we look for reasons, we look for easy to find considerations that we believe will make sense to people as explanations for what we have done, whether or not those were really our reasons for acting.[10] In other words, we often engage in *post hoc rationalization* of our actions, rather than grasping the reasons that we really do have, deciding which ones to act on and then deliberately acting for those reasons. Further, when we act, we are frequently caused to act by factors that we would reject as reasons for action if we thought about it. If this is how we are, then the picture of us as competent rational agents, deliberating about our reasons and then acting on the results of our deliberation seems to be a bit tarnished.

But how tarnished, really? Is it true that we do not have the rational capacity to reflect on, endorse and act for reasons that is required by responsibility? The evidence we have surveyed is evidence that we don't use this capacity all the time, but it isn't evidence that we don't have it. If we *sometimes* act for the reasons we think we do—if we sometimes reflect on, endorse and act for the reasons we recognize as reasons, even though not always—this will be enough to show that we are at least *sometimes* responsible.

Recall that one way people have responded to the situationist critique of virtue ethics is to think about the distribution of actions over time (Jayawickreme et al. 2014). The idea was to think of a virtuous character trait in terms of "average behavior," so that a virtuous character trait makes one more likely than one would otherwise be to behave well, even though situational factors may decrease the likelihood of good behavior for anyone in those circumstances. Maybe a similar approach will help us in this context. What I have in mind is that we might consider whether we human beings are able to increase our capacity to recognize and act for reasons over time, even though our ability to do so at a particular time is fallible. Maybe we are creatures who can shape our actions in response to reasons over the long term by recognizing our tendency to rationalize after the fact, identifying coping strategies and planning. Maybe once we recognize the ways in which situations influence us, we can use this information to choose situations that will make us better able to act on the reasons that we recognize as good reasons for doing things. John Doris (2002) suggests that people who do not want to cheat on their romantic partners would do better to refuse to put themselves in situations in which cheating would be easy (such as romantic dinners with attractive people when the partner is away for the weekend) than they would to rely on the virtue of faithfulness. Quite true! But shaping your behavior on the basis of what you know about the influence of situational factors and the power of temptation is a way of acting rationally.

Importantly, the psychologists who have done the research I have presented as evidence against the effectiveness of our rational capacities do not tend to endorse any strong claim about our lacking these capacities altogether. As their research has continued, they have found that there are some variables that seem to make us better at knowing our reasons. For instance, the more knowledgeable we are about something, the more we understand our own reasons for making choices with respect to that thing (Halberstadt and Wilson 2008). Someone who was an expert in stockings would probably have seen that the stockings were identical (as a few people in the actual study did) and would not have fabricated reasons for choosing one over another. Someone who was able to articulate what it is about impressionist art that makes it beautiful might have chosen the art poster rather than the kitten poster after reflecting on her reasons for preferring one to the other. Knowledge is not all powerful, of course, but it does sometimes help, which is evidence that we should not be so pessimistic as to think we never do things for the reasons we think we do.

Finally, as a piece of anecdotal evidence that we recognize and respond to reasons we endorse as reasons, consider this former participant in the Milgram obedience experiment. Jacob (not his real name) describes to the science writer Lauren Slater how at around the same time as he participated in Milgram's study, he was struggling to accept his homosexuality. Jacob was one of the people who shocked the "learner" to the highest degree; he was

100 percent compliant. The experience of being in the experiment had a profound effect on him:

> The experiments . . . caused me to reevaluate my life. They caused me to confront my own compliance and really struggle with it. I began to see closeted homosexuality, which is just another form of compliance, as a moral issue. I came out. I saw how essential it was to develop a strong moral center. I felt my own moral weakness and I was appalled, so I went to the ethical gym, if you see what I mean.
>
> (Slater 2004: 59)

Jacob may not have acted for reasons he could endorse in the experiment. But his behavior in the experiment gave him reasons that guided his actions for the rest of his life. As we saw in our discussion of Fischer and Ravizza, philosophers who think being guided by a reasons responsive mechanism is necessary for moral responsibility do not think that people are always perfectly responsive to the reasons that there are. Rather, they think that this is a capacity we have, which we sometimes act on and sometimes don't. Similarly, the rational capacity to acknowledge and act for the reasons we think we have need not be a capacity that we use all the time in order for us to be responsible agents.

This idea that we have the rational capacities necessary for responsibility even though we do not always act for the reasons we think we are acting for in particular cases introduces some complications. This is because people who have rational capacities are, nevertheless, not responsible for *everything* they do. One can have the capacity to recognize, endorse and respond to reasons and yet be in a situation in which that capacity is overridden in such a way that you are not responsible in that particular situation. For example, a normal person can be hypnotized or drugged in a way that renders his rational capacities temporarily ineffective. To defend any theory that makes responsibility depend on rational competencies, then, the conditions for responsible action have to be permissive enough so that people count as acting from these capacities (and hence responsible) even when they do bad things, and yet not so permissive that people end up being responsible for things they do when their normal capacities have truly been overridden. Along these lines, if we accept a normative competency theory, social psychology research might help us to figure out when people are responsible by informing us of when someone's rational capacities are most likely to be overwhelmed. It might also help us figure out how to improve our rational capacities (to become more normatively competent) so that we can act responsibly more often.

But social psychology research does not prove that we are never responsible. It does not prove that we are not rationally competent creatures. It does not prove that we never act on our second-order desires to act for reasons we endorse wholeheartedly. It does not prove that we cannot shape our behavior over the long term in the light of considerations that we consciously take to be reasons that favor moral behavior over immoral behavior. There are real psychological differences between people who are hypnotized to do things and people who choose to do them, and between people who are incapable of understanding what a moral reason is and people who just ignore moral reasons out of selfishness or malice. Exactly which differences are the relevant ones is a matter of some debate, but more or less everyone agrees on the importance of the fact that we are at least to some degree creatures who can grasp reasons and choose to act on them.

One might think, however, that having the right psychological mechanisms is not sufficient for moral responsibility. Indeed, one might think that the very fact that these are psychological *mechanisms* is a serious problem! To be morally responsible for an action, the objection goes, we have to be free, and if we are free then we are not determined to do what we do by any mechanism psychological or otherwise. We turn to this set of problems in the next chapter.

Summary

- When we hold someone responsible for an action, we regard her as a person rather than an object and we take the reactive attitudes (guilt, anger, forgiveness, etc.) to be appropriate responses toward her. Taking our fellow human beings to be persons is extremely important to how we interact with each other and to our social and personal relationships.
- One way of asking when it is appropriate to hold people responsible is to ask, What is the difference between the psychology and capacities of persons and of non-persons? Or, more specifically, what psychological capacities are necessary for appropriately holding someone responsible?
- Philosophers typically use the method of reflective equilibrium to answer these questions.
- One answer is that what is distinctive about someone acting responsibly is that they act on their second-order desires or the desires they endorse. This is Frankfurt's "wholehearted endorsement" theory.
- Another answer is that what is distinctive about someone acting responsibly has to do with their whole self, including their emotional responses to their options.
- A third answer is that what is crucial for responsibility is the capacity to grasp, and act in response to, reasons.
- Some research in social psychology makes it seem that we do not act for reasons that we consciously endorse as reasons; rather, we act because of situational factors and then we make up reasons to justify what we did after the fact.
- Social psychology research has not established that we have no capacity to grasp and respond to reasons, though it might show that we use this capacity less often than we think we do.

Study Questions

1. The "wholehearted endorsement" theory and the "whole self" theory offer different views about the psychological profile of action for which we are responsible and deserving of praise or blame. Think of your own example (or pair of examples) that illustrates the differences. What is one reason for favoring one view over the other?
2. Do you think we have real selves? How do you identify yours?
3. What is the difference between "guidance control" and "regulative control"? Try to think of some examples that illuminate the distinction by showing how the two could come apart.
4. If you were on a jury trying a murder case, what kind of questions would you want to ask about the defendant's mental state in general or at the time of the crime? What could you learn that would incline you to find him or her "not guilty" or "not guilty by reason of insanity"?

Notes

1. This practice ended with the 2002 U.S. Supreme Court decision *Atkins v. Virginia*.
2. www.hrw.org/news/2000/01/03/mentally-retarded-dont-belong-death-row. Last accessed: November 8, 2012.
3. Strawson also says that even if we *should* give up the reactive attitudes, we would not be able to. If the facts led to the conclusion that no one is ever deserving of resentment, gratitude and so on, human beings would resist acceptance of the facts.
4. For an introduction, see Daniels (2008). Strictly speaking, the method I've described is called *wide reflective equilibrium*. Narrow reflective equilibrium does not include background theories. Everyone these days thinks that reflective equilibrium should be wide.
5. *Person* here, as in a lot of moral philosophy, is a normative category (as opposed to *human being*, which is a biological category). For Frankfurt, it's the word we use to describe those human beings who are capable of responsible action.
6. As in "a wanton human being." *Wanton* is ordinarily an adjective in English, meaning reckless, careless or lawless, but Frankfurt uses it in a special sense.
7. This example comes from Nomy Arpaly's (2003) insightful discussion of the case of anorexia and its implications for moral psychology.
8. Nahmias makes the point that most theories of free will—including normative competency theories, real self theories and libertarian theories—agree with the assumption that free will requires that "one's actions properly derive from decisions or intentions that one has at some point consciously considered, or at least that one would accept, as one's reasons for acting" (Nahmias 2011: 353).
9. Ninety-five percent of the controls (who did not reflect on their reasons) but only sixty-five percent of reflectors chose the art poster.
10. An important paper that helped to start this line of research is "Telling More Than We Can Know" by Nisbett and Wilson (1977). Timothy Wilson's *Strangers to Ourselves* (2002) is an accessible book that provides a balanced and engaging discussion of this research. For a discussion of the ethical implications of this research, see Tiberius (2009).

Further Readings

Arpaly, N. 2002. "Moral Worth." *The Journal of Philosophy.* 99 (5): 223–245.

Fischer, J.M., and M. Ravizza. 1999. *Responsibility and Control: A Theory of Moral Responsibility.* Cambridge University Press.

Frankfurt, H. 1971. "Freedom of the Will and the Concept of a Person." *The Journal of Philosophy:* 5–20.

———. 1988. "Identification and Wholeheartedness" In *The Importance of What We Care about: Philosophical Essays.* Cambridge University Press.

Strawson, P.F. 2008. *Freedom and Resentment and Other Essays.* Routledge.

Wallace, R. J. 1994. *Responsibility and the Moral Sentiments.* Harvard University Press.

Wolf, S. 1980. "Asymmetrical Freedom." *The Journal of Philosophy* 77 (3): 151–166.

———. 1981. "The Importance of Free Will." *Mind* 90 (359): 386–405.

9   Moral Responsibility, Free Will and Determinism

- **Free Will and Determinism**
- **Intuitions and Experimental Philosophy**
- **Libertarianism and the Challenge from Neuroscience**
- **Can I Be Excused?**
- **Summary**
- **Study Questions**
- **Notes**
- **Further Readings**

In Chapter 8 we considered a number of different theories about what internal, psychological causes should be seen as the ones that characterize responsible action. These theories are compatibilist theories, which means that they take moral responsibility to be compatible with determinism. There are some important worries that we have not yet considered about any compatibilist theory.

To understand these problems we need to set compatibilism in the larger context of the debates about free will and determinism.

Free Will and Determinism

Causal determinism is the thesis that every event is necessitated by antecedent events and conditions together with the laws of nature. Or, to put it another way, the facts of the past, in conjunction with the laws of nature, entail every fact about the future. Free will is not so easy to define and, indeed, people don't tend to agree about how to define it. Philosophers who think free will is compatible with determinism think about free will much differently from those who think the two are incompatible, as we will see.

Table 9.1   Two Questions about Free Will and Moral Responsibility

		If determinism is true, could we still have free will (and moral responsibility)?	
		YES	NO
Do human beings actually have free will (and moral responsibility)?	YES	Compatibilism (Hume, Strawson, Arpaly, Nahmias)	Libertarianism (Kant, Chisholm, Kane)
	NO		Hard determinism, (Schopenhauer, Pereboom)
	Yes and No	Semi-compatibilism. *Freedom to do otherwise* is not compatible with determinism, but moral responsibility is, and we are morally responsible under certain conditions (Fischer and Ravizza).	

We can divide the different theories depending on how they answer two questions: (1) If everything—including human action—were causally determined, would free will be possible? and (2) Do we have free will? (See Table 9.1[1]). On the first question, incompatibilists think that if everything were determined, then there would be no free will. The second question divides incompatibilists into two groups: Libertarians are incompatibilists who think that we do have free will (so, they don't accept determinism). Hard determinists are incompatibilists who think we do not have free will (because determinism is true and incompatible with free will). Compatibilists have a different answer to the first question: they think that determinism and free will are compatible. In answer to the second question, most compatibilists think we do have free will; they think that regardless of whether everything is causally determined, we might still have free will as long as our actions are caused in the right way.[2] (We discussed various proposals for what the "right way" might be in the previous chapter—for instance, caused by one's real self or by one's reasons responsive mechanism). These are all viable theories, with contemporary defenders.

We could also ask our two questions about determinism and moral responsibility, and we would get almost the same results. This is because many philosophers think that free will and moral responsibility go together: free will is a necessary condition for moral responsibility; you cannot be responsible for an action you did not perform freely. Not everyone accepts this position, however. Fischer and Ravizza, whose version of compatibilism we examined in Chapter 8, believe that determinism and moral responsibility are compatible, but they think that determinism rules out the ability (or freedom) to do otherwise, which some label "free will." They call their theory "semi-compatibilism."

According to compatibilism (including semi-compatibilism), as we have seen, people are sometimes in a psychological state that warrants holding them responsible for what they do, even though that psychological state itself is caused. Some people really hate compatibilism. Kant called it a "wretched subterfuge" and the philosopher Wallace Matson said that the defense of compatibilism is "the most flabbergasting instance of the fallacy of changing the subject to be encountered anywhere in the complete history of sophistry" (cited by Fischer et al. 2007: 45). You may ultimately decide to reject compatibilism, but don't make the mistake of thinking that it is flat out self-contradictory. It can be hard to get your head around compatibilism in the abstract, and sometimes people make the mistake of thinking that since compatibilism is the view that free will and determinism are compatible, then compatibilism includes both determinism and—somehow!—non-causally-determined free will. Perhaps the association between the idea of free will and something that is truly free of external causes is so strong that people are misled by the language. Or, perhaps some people think that the fact that an action was determined by the very definition of determinism means that it wasn't free. If you look at the definition of determinism in the first sentence of this section, you'll see this isn't so.

It might help to avoid confusion if you think about the issue in terms of the compatibility of determinism and *moral responsibility*.[3] That's how I put the problem in Chapter 8, and I hope that our discussion of compatibilist theories there has been enough to demonstrate that they are not incoherent or crazy. Drawing on ideas from the previous chapter, compatibilism isn't crazy, because determinism is compatible with our actions being caused by the second-order desires that we wholeheartedly endorse, by our whole selves or by our reasons responsive mechanisms. Determinism does not mean that these ordinary causes of responsible action are bypassed or hijacked by some external force.

Though not crazy, compatibilism can seem unintuitive or just wrong. There are two main arguments against compatibilism. According to the Manipulation Argument, the problem with compatibilism is that it cannot distinguish between cases in which someone is manipulated into choosing to do something and cases in which someone chooses to do something because of deterministic causes ultimately beyond his control. If the compatibilist can't distinguish these two kinds of cases, then it looks like the determined person who chooses is no more free than the manipulated person, which is to say: not very free at all. Think again about the roommate who dances on your table (and breaks it) because she wants to and the roommate who breaks your table because she is hypnotized. The Manipulation Argument says basically this: The hypnotized roommate (Hyp) is not free, because she is determined to do what she does by the hypnotist, and therefore she is not morally responsible. If determinism is true, there is no relevant difference between Hyp and the un-hypnotized roommate (Unhyp): Unhyp is equally not free, because she is determined to do what she does by the facts of the past and the laws of nature. Therefore Unhyp is also not responsible for breaking your table. Since the point generalizes, if determinism is true, no one is ever responsible for what they do, and compatibilism is false.

We have already seen the resources that compatibilists have for answering this kind of challenge. The philosophers we discussed in Chapter 8 reject the premise that there's no relevant difference between Hyp and Unhyp. They think they have explained the relevant differences with their theories: Unhyp has the relevant second-order, wholeheartedly endorsed desire, while Hyp does not, or Unhyp is responsive to reasons and Hyp is not, or there is some other psychological difference between the two. You may think that compatibilists have not answered this objection yet, because you think they haven't got the psychological conditions quite right. In this case, you would be a compatibilist who thinks there is more work to be done on the theory—and you would be in very good company! On the other hand, you may think that the Manipulation Argument could be pushed farther so that even with these complex facts about our psychologies in hand, there is still no meaningful distinction between someone who is manipulated to choose and someone who chooses for her own reasons but is ultimately determined to do so.[4]

You may even have the intuition that no view about the psychological differences between Hyp and Unhyp could ever possibly do the trick because there is something profound missing from Unhyp if determinism is true. What could be missing?

The second argument against compatibilism answers that question. According to the Garden of Forking Paths Argument, the problem with compatibilism is that free will (and hence moral responsibility) requires the existence of genuine alternatives (or paths branching off from the present) from which we can choose, but determinism precludes genuine alternatives. Unhyp is only free not to dance on and break your table if at the moment when she chose to dance on the table she could have stayed on the floor. She is, therefore, only responsible for breaking your table if at the moment she chose to dance she was at a fork in the road from which she could choose to go either way. (Recall that this question about forking paths is just what is at issue in the distinction between regulative control and guidance control. The former requires genuine alternatives, the latter does not, and compatibilists like Fischer think that only the latter is necessary for moral responsibility.)

The crucial question now is this: Do free will and responsibility require forking paths or genuine alternatives? What kind of question is this? And how do we decide? We can't discover whether free will requires forking paths by empirical investigation. We might be able to decide whether we really do have genuine alternatives by appeal to empirical science (more on that later), but the question we're asking here is a conceptual one, not an empirical one. Is the best understanding of what free will is one that requires genuine alternative forking paths? How do we answer a question like this? Recall the methodology of reflective equilibrium, according to which what we are doing when we ask deep philosophical questions like this is reaching a conclusion that puts our intuitions, principles and theories into a coherent whole. If this is what we have to do to answer the question, it seems that we need to know more about what our relevant intuitions actually are.

Intuitions and Experimental Philosophy

Our question is this: Is compatibilism supported in reflective equilibrium, or is compatibilism too much at odds with our intuitions to be the right theory? We can start by asking what *your* intuitions are. Consider the following case:

> *Fred and Barney*
> Imagine there is a world where the beliefs and values of every person are caused completely by the combination of one's genes and one's environment. For instance, one day in this world, two identical twins, named Fred and Barney, are born to a mother who puts them up for adoption. Fred is adopted by the Jerksons and Barney is adopted by the Kindersons. In Fred's case, his genes and his upbringing by the selfish Jerkson family have caused him to value money above all else and to believe it is OK to acquire money however you can. In Barney's case, his (identical) genes and his upbringing by the kindly Kinderson family have caused him to value honesty above all else and to believe one should always respect others' property. Both Fred and Barney are intelligent individuals who are capable of deliberating about what they do.
>
> One day Fred and Barney each happen to find a wallet containing $1,000 and the identification of the owner (neither man knows the owner). Each man is sure there is nobody else around. After deliberation, Fred Jerkson, because of his beliefs and values, keeps the money. After deliberation, Barney Kinderson, because of his beliefs and values, returns the wallet to its owner.
>
> Given that, in this world, one's genes and environment completely cause one's beliefs and values, it is true that if Fred had been adopted by the Kindersons, he would have had the beliefs and values that would have caused him to return the wallet; and if Barney had been adopted by the Jerksons, he would have had the beliefs and values that would have caused him to keep the wallet.
>
> (Nahmias, Morris, Nadelhoffer and Turner 2007: 38–39)

Do you think Fred and Barney acted of their own free will? Do you think Fred is morally responsible—deserves to be blamed—for keeping the money that isn't his? Do you think Barney is morally responsible—deserves to be praised—for returning the money? At this point your intuitions might be influenced by what you have already read about compatibilism and incompatibilism. Perhaps some of you were convinced by the theories considered in Chapter 8 and are wondering what Fred and Barney's second-order desires are, or whether they are responding to reasons sufficiently in this particular case. Perhaps some of you, having been convinced by the arguments against compatibilism presented at the beginning of this chapter are thinking that there's no way Fred and Barney could be responsible since they could not really have done otherwise than what they did.

Historically, philosophers have used their own intuitions as the inputs to the reflective equilibrium method. This isn't a bad thing to do—after all, philosophers have thought hard about the problems and have the resources to make relevant distinctions. However, philosophers' intuitions don't all agree: some incompatibilists say that compatibilism is the most counterintuitive theory on earth; compatibilists think it's perfectly fine. Furthermore, when it comes to the question of what free will is and what moral responsibility requires, there is an additional problem with relying on philosophers' intuitions alone. What (most) philosophers are trying to understand when they try to understand the kind of free will that is necessary for moral responsibility is something that all people (not just philosophers) would recognize as the thing that we worry about when we wonder if someone should be punished or when we read articles in the newspaper that tell us neuroscientists have proved there is no free will. Philosophers want to be talking about the same thing that everyone else is talking about! It doesn't add much to the defense of a theory of moral responsibility to say that it is intuitive to the philosopher who constructed it.

Given this, some philosophers have started to take reflective equilibrium to the streets (or the lab). Instead of relying on their own intuitions about free will and responsibility, they find out what "normal" people think by conducting studies that ask people about their intuitions. This work is in the new field of philosophy called "Experimental Philosophy." In fact, the case of Fred and Barney is taken from an experimental philosophy article by Eddy Nahmias, Stephen Morris, Thomas Nadelhoffer, and Jason Turner. What they found when they surveyed people who had not studied the free will debate is that significantly more people agree than disagree that Fred and Barney acted freely and are responsible for what they did.[5] This research makes it look like compatibilism isn't so unintuitive after all.

But not all of the experimental philosophy research favors this conclusion. Shaun Nichols and Joshua Knobe (2007) argue that people have compatibilist intuitions when their intuitions are distorted by emotional responses, but that when people think more carefully and deliberately about the question, they have incompatibilist intuitions. Nichols and Knobe make this argument using the same methods as Nahmias, but with different scenarios. They give all their participants descriptions of a causally determined universe called "Universe A" and then they divide the participants into two groups. The "Concrete" group gets this question:

> In Universe A, a man named Bill has become attracted to his secretary, and he decides that the only way to be with her is to kill his wife and 3 children. He knows that it is impossible to escape from his house in the event of a fire. Before he leaves on a business trip, he sets up a device in his basement that burns down the house and kills his family.
> Is Bill fully morally responsible for killing his wife and children?

The "Abstract" group gets this question:

> In Universe A, is it possible for a person to be fully morally responsible for their actions?

What they found was that in the "Concrete" group, seventy-two percent of the people said that Bill is responsible (this is the compatibilist answer, since Bill's actions are determined). In the "Abstract" group, eighty-six percent of people said no, it is not possible for a person to be fully responsible in a deterministic universe (the incompatibilist answer).

Nichols and Knobe hypothesize that what's going on here is that those who read the scenario about Bill are swayed by their emotional response to Bill's bad actions, while those who read the abstract question think more abstractly and hence more clearly about the compatibility of moral responsibility and determinism. Given what we learned in Chapter 5 about the connection between moral judgments and emotions, one way to respond to Nichols and Knobe would be to point out that emotions do not mislead us. Emotional responses are integral to judgments of moral responsibility, one might say, so we do not think more clearly without our emotions in this domain. Think back to Strawson and Wallace: attributions of moral responsibility are normative judgments. If normative judgments essentially involve affect, then it isn't surprising that affect changes our intuitions. In this way of thinking, our emotions aren't leading us to make mistakes. Nichols and Knobe do consider this possibility, and they have designed other studies to try to sort out which hypothesis is better. Interested readers should look to the suggested readings at the end of this chapter and follow the progress of this line of research by searching for the latest.

Nahmias has a different objection to Nichols and Knobe. He objects to the way that they describe the deterministic universe, Universe A. Nahmias thinks that when they say that in Universe A "given the past, each decision *has to happen* the way that it does" and contrast that with Universe B in which "each human decision *does **not** have to happen* the way that it does," this leads many people to think that agents in Universe A will do what they do, no matter what they want to do or what they decide to do. But this is not the case: in a deterministic universe, our desires are part of the causal chains that lead to actions. There is a difference, then, between determinism (everything is caused) and *bypassing* (everything is caused by a series of causes that bypasses our psychological states such as desires and choices). Once we understand the difference between the claim that all actions are causally determined and the claim that actions are determined in such a way as to bypass our psychological capacities, we can see that bypassing is the biggest threat to our ideas of free will and moral responsibility. Bypassing in one form is the problem we considered in Chapter 8 when we discussed the challenge from psychology to the idea that we are reasons responsive creatures. There we concluded that while we might be less rationally capable than we once thought, we are not completely hopeless either. If the real problem is bypassing, compatibilism remains a viable position—because even if determinism is true, it is *not* true that our psychological processes are bypassed when we act. And it is plausible to think that bypassing (not determinism) is the real problem for attributions of responsibility. After all, the hypnotized person seems to have her beliefs, desires, virtues and so forth bypassed (by the actions of the hypnotizer), and that's why we do not think she is free or responsible for what she does under hypnosis.

The debate about our intuitions about moral responsibility and free will is ongoing, and it's difficult to draw any definite conclusions at this point. We do know that there is some good evidence for thinking that people accept compatibilism as long as some of our psychological capacities are part of what causes us to decide what to do. There is also evidence for thinking that in some circumstances, people are disturbed by determinism. We have not reached an obvious conclusion. Some things might become more clear as research progresses, but it seems unlikely that one answer will turn out to be a slam dunk. Where do we stand? There are two important points to consider here.

First, we can conclude that someone who wants to argue for incompatibilism should not begin by assuming compatibilism is counterintuitive without addressing the current research in experimental philosophy. It at least cannot be taken as obvious that compatibilism about determinism and moral responsibility is a "wretched subterfuge." Second, we must remember that intuitions do not decide what free will and moral responsibility really are. Intuitions about cases are relevant to our theories because as philosophers we want to make sure that our theories track something meaningful to ordinary people. However, there are other factors that go into justifying a theory of moral responsibility. One of these other factors is the coherence of our theory of moral responsibility with scientific theories, some of which we'll consider in the next section. Another factor is the cost of abandoning the idea of moral responsibility. This is the point Strawson made about how important the reactive attitudes are to us and to how we relate to each other. Of course, compatibilism isn't the only option that allows us to retain our notion of moral responsibility; one might take the view that we are sometimes morally responsible, even though responsibility and determinism are incompatible. This view is called libertarianism.

Libertarianism and the Challenge from Neuroscience

Compatibilists make sense of moral responsibility by identifying responsible action with action that is caused by certain psychological features of the person, but there is another way that we have not yet considered. One might reject determinism and argue for a "libertarian" conception of free will and moral responsibility according to which we have an undetermined power to choose. In its earlier incarnations, libertarianism made free will rather mysterious. The idea that agents have special powers that stand outside of the causal order of the universe—sometimes called "agent causation"—is hard to believe for scientifically minded people. Moreover, libertarians had to answer Hume's challenge: they had to explain why we would be held responsible for actions that are not caused by our character or determined by our beliefs and desires. In other words, if we have a will that is truly uncaused, how do *we* get any blame or credit for it? Why isn't it just some weird random force doing what it does arbitrarily? If the answer is, *we* determine what our free will does, who is the *we*, if it isn't our beliefs, desires and psychological processes?

It is because of these problems (together with problems for the compatibilist option) that some philosophers, such as Derk Pereboom, have opted for "hard incompatibilism": the view that whether or not determinism is true, we do not have free will. We do not have it if determinism is true, because free will and determinism are incompatible (hard incompatibilists believe that the Manipulation and Garden of Forking Paths arguments are successful against even sophisticated versions of compatibilism). And we do not have it if determinism is false, because special, undetermined agent causation is incompatible with our best scientific theories (Fischer et al. 2007: 85). In his defense of hard incompatibilism, Pereboom outlines some of the good consequences of giving up the idea that people are fundamentally responsible for what they do (Pereboom 2001; Fischer et al. 2007). For instance, there will be less moral anger, and anger is a painful emotion that often does more harm than good. Furthermore, Pereboom argues, not as much would be lost by giving up our ordinary notion of moral responsibility as someone like Strawson suggests. Many of our emotional responses and ordinary ways of relating to other people would be unscathed if we did not believe people are praiseworthy for their good deeds or blameworthy for their bad ones. We would still feel joyful when good things happen, sad when bad things happen, and love for our friends and family.

Hard incompatibilism is not the only viable incompatibilist option. New and improved forms of libertarianism have done better than their predecessors. Robert Kane's libertarianism makes use of the science of chaos theory and quantum indeterminism in order to argue that there is some "space" in the causal network for genuinely free actions. Kane does not think free choice about our actions requires any special power. Rather, he thinks we choose how to act in the way that compatibilists think we do: by reflecting on our reasons and endorsing one path over another. But Kane (unlike compatibilists) thinks there are genuine forking paths and that we (at least sometimes) determine what we do *by deciding* which path to take.

Kane thinks that when we make choices we determine who we are by engaging in reasoning and then endorsing one option over the others. Such choices are not arbitrary, because we make them for reasons; nevertheless the past does not determine which choice we will make for which reasons.

Writing in the voice of someone who has the kind of free will he is describing, Kane says

> I did have *good* reasons for choosing as I did, which I'm willing to stand by and *take responsibility for.* If these reasons were not sufficient or conclusive reasons [they were not reasons that determined my choice], that's because, like the heroine of the novel, I was not a fully formed person before I chose (and still am not, for that matter). Like the author of the novel, I am in the process of writing an unfinished story and forming an unfinished character who, in my case, is myself.
>
> (Kane 2007: 42)

When a person with free will finds a wallet, he or she decides whether to be a sinner or a saint. There are reasons on both sides and, whichever the person chooses, he or she will have chosen freely if and only if at that moment it is not causally determined what that person will do. Now, not every single action we perform is like this. Kane does think that much of what we do is determined by our character and does not involve the exercise of our free will. But we are ultimately responsible for the actions that result from our character only because we create our character through freely chosen self-forming actions (such as, for example, returning the wallet).

Now, the big question for this variety of libertarianism is whether there really is the right kind of indeterminacy, the kind that makes room for us to exercise free will by endorsing one set of reasons or another. Kane describes the condition as "a kind of 'stirring up of chaos' in the brain that makes it sensitive to micro-indeterminacies at the neuronal level" (Kane 2007: 26). Whether this kind of indeterminacy exists is an interesting and important question, but it is an open empirical question beyond the purview of this book. (Interested readers are encouraged to read more of Kane's work, cited in the bibliography).

Interestingly, because Kane's version of libertarianism also makes use of ideas about our ordinary rational capacities, he faces some of the same questions that compatibilists have to answer: Which rational capacities are the relevant ones, and how often do these capacities actually play the right causal role in our choices? We have already considered (in Chapter 8) some psychological evidence that we use our rational capacities less frequently than we think, though this evidence is not really a problem for Kane, who thinks it is only when we have self-forming choices to make that we exercise our free will. It's not much of a problem for him if we don't exercise free will all the time. But there is a different scientific challenge to the idea that we use our rational capacities to make choices that targets libertarianism as well as compatibilism.

Some neuroscientists have claimed to show that there is no free will by investigating the brain. The claim is that when you look at what is going on in the brain, you discover that our decision-making capacities are *not* part of what causes us to choose what we choose; the brain processes that cause action are distinct from whatever in the brain corresponds to consciously making a choice. If this is correct, libertarianism would be in trouble because there would be evidence that brain processes determine what people will decide before they are aware of making a choice—that is, before Kane's indeterministic processes are supposed to occur.

The pioneering studies in this area were conducted by the psychologist Benjamin Libet. Libet and his colleagues (1985) would have participants sit at a desk in front of a dial with a quickly rotating arm (like a fast moving second hand on a clock). Participants were asked to flex their wrists at some point, whenever they chose, and to note the precise location of the arm on the dial when they were first aware of a wish to flex. These participants had electrodes on their heads that were attached to an electroencephalogram (or EEG) that measures electrical activity at the surface of the brain called "readiness potentials" (a proxy for neuronal activity). Libet discovered that the readiness potential (a sign that a person is ready to act) that preceded the action of wrist flexing happened *before* the person was aware of any desire or decision to flex (according to the participant's report about the position of the arm on the dial). Subsequent research has confirmed and extended Libet's findings. According to one researcher quoted in *WIRED*, "Your decisions are strongly prepared by brain activity. By the time consciousness kicks in, most of the work has already been done" (Keim 2012).

This research is extremely interesting, but philosophers have not been impressed with it as an attack on free will. Philosophers have argued that these neuroscientific studies do not actually show that our decisions play no causal role in determining how we act. Instead, as Al Mele (2006) argues, the right interpretation of the data is that the brain activity that precedes conscious decision is likely just a preconscious urge to flex, not an intention to do so.[6] These urges are sometimes acted on and sometimes overridden by conscious decision making. This is consistent with Libet's findings, according to which readiness potentials may be vetoed by conscious intention (which is why Libet admits that we do have "free won't"). If Mele's interpretation is correct, then scientists have not proven that there is no free will. For instance, it is open to Kane to say that our decision-making power can be exercised in a moment of indeterminism between the readiness potentials and what we actually intend to do.

Compatibilism can also defend itself against this neuroscientific challenge. Remember that compatibilists accept that we can have free will even if our actions are entirely caused such that there is no moment of indeterminism in the causal stream that leads to our actions. Compatibilists, therefore, are perfectly willing to accept that there is a deterministic series of brain events that result in our actions. The question for compatibilists is whether our actions are caused in the right way—for instance, whether they are governed by our rational capacities in such a way that it makes sense to say that we have guidance control over what we do. Furthermore, compatibilists assume that our rational capacities shape what we do overall, but they do not require that we employ our rational capacities every time we do something. For example, as I am writing this chapter, my actions are governed by many of my conscious intentions and decisions of varying degrees of specificity (to write a book, to write a chapter on free will, to consider the evidence from Libet, to sit at my desk in front of my computer and so on), but many of the things I'm currently doing are not things I notice any intention to do. I just hit the "period" key, for instance, but I didn't make a decision to do that. Nevertheless, my hitting that key (and the "y" key just now!) is—in the big picture of what I'm doing today—governed ultimately by my decision to write this book. Similarly, what we might say about Libet's participants is that even if their wrist flexings were *not* consciously chosen, their actions are (in the big picture) governed by their decisions to be in his experiments, to follow Libet's instructions and so on (Nahmias 2012b).

It would be a problem for the compatibilist picture if, when we looked at the big picture, we found that our conscious intentions are always just momentary blips that enter the causal stream after other bits of our brains (say, readiness potentials) have already set action in motion. This would not leave room for the right kind of causal history where our rational capacities are a more integrated part of the causes of our actions. The compatibilist Daniel Dennett has a helpful way of explaining why this isn't the right picture. According to Dennett (2004), there can't be one place in the brain that is the place where conscious intentions to act for reasons are located: the conscious intentions we look for when we attribute responsibility are not little blips in the brain. Representing reasons to yourself, considering these reasons, forming an intention to do something on the basis of one of those reasons, and remembering all of this when you are doing what you intended to do—these are highly complex and varied activities that require many different parts of the brain. The self who acts for reasons is spread out across the brain, and so too are responsibility and free will. It is a mistake, according to Dennett, to think that *you* (the responsible self) must be at some specific point deciding what to do with some event that happens in your brain. And if it doesn't make sense to think of conscious decisions as very localized events in the brain, then it doesn't make sense to argue that conscious decisions happen after actions are set in motion.

What we have learned from neuroscience so far, then, does not render irrelevant the big questions that both compatibilists and libertarians like Kane have to answer. These are questions about which rational capacities are relevant and what counts as using them sufficiently well for the person to count as responsible. Indeed, these questions seem to have increasing importance now that science is discovering more about normal and abnormal brains, as we will see in the final section of this chapter.

Can I Be Excused?

A good theory of moral responsibility will tell us when people are responsible and also when they ought to be excused for what they've done. We have already seen some examples of people who should be excused from responsibility and blame, such as the two-year-old hitter and the hypnotized table-dancing room-mate (Hyp). These cases are fairly easy, because it is clear that in *any* theory of the relevant rational capacities the two year old doesn't have them yet, and Hyp's seem to have been completely bypassed. But there are many more difficult cases.

In the early 2000s, a schoolteacher (he wasn't named in reports, let's just call him Teacher) suddenly developed tendencies toward pedophilia. He began visiting child pornography websites, molested his stepdaughter and expressed fear that he would rape his landlady. Shortly after these behaviors began, Teacher checked himself into the hospital complaining of terrible headaches. It turned out that he had an egg-sized tumor in his brain and, after this tumor was removed, his perverse sexual tendencies disappeared. Was Teacher responsible for what he did while he had the tumor?

In 1983, the serial killer Brian Dugan kidnapped, raped and killed a ten-year-old girl. He had already committed several murders, but for this particularly heinous crime the prosecuting attorneys sought the death penalty. Dugan's lawyers argued that he had a mental illness—psychopathy—that excused him from responsibility for his crime. Dugan did indeed fit the profile of a psychopath: he scored in the 99.5th percentile on the psychopathy checklist and brain scans showed that his brain was abnormal in the way that many psychopaths' brains are abnormal. Assuming that Dugan is indeed a psychopath, is he responsible for what he did?

Both Teacher and Dugan have abnormal brains, though Teacher's brain was only temporarily abnormal, while Dugan's brain is congenitally different. As brain science develops, we will know more and more about the brains of people who commit crimes and the attempt to use information about people's brains as a legal defense is becoming well known. If you're interested, you can search "brain scans as defense" or "my brain made me do it" on Google and find many articles and blogposts on this topic. There is even a name for the new field of study that investigates these issues: neurolaw. We cannot delve too deeply into the legal questions here, but two points about the legal context are worth mentioning before we return to the issue of moral responsibility.

First, one of the things that moral psychologists interested in how people make moral judgments have discovered is that people are very influenced by brain science. Adina Roskies (2008) has argued that we have reason to be cautious about the use of brain scan images in public discourse, because people tend to treat pictures as providing a very direct kind of evidence that brain scan images do not, in fact, provide. Unless there is some explicit reason to suspect tampering, we tend to think of pictures as on a par with eyewitness testimony. Video surveillance footage, for example, is considered to be excellent evidence. Because we think of pictures this way, we tend to think that pictures of brain scans provide similarly convincing evidence. But, as Roskies argues, there is a lot of distance between the brain scan image and any conclusion that might be drawn from it, and this distance must be bridged with inferences made by experts who are drawing on their own imperfect knowledge and theories of the brain. Brain scan images are not like video surveillance footage, but people tend to treat them as the same. Therefore, this evidence introduces a risk that people will put more weight on it than is warranted. This is something that should be remembered by anyone interested in neurolaw. If neuroscientific evidence biases us, it must be handled with a great deal of care.

Second, the question of whether Teacher and Dugan are legally responsible is different from the questions of whether they are morally responsible and how we morally ought to treat them. If we decide that they are not morally responsible, it does not follow that they should be let go on the streets. Deterrence is a perfectly good reason for detaining people in prisons or institutions that does not depend on establishing robust moral responsibility. (Of course, the criminal you punish should be causally responsible—it wouldn't do to punish someone for something he didn't do in any sense at all.) Indeed, those who think that we must abandon our ordinary understanding of free will and moral responsibility—the hard incompatibilists, mentioned above, who think we do not have free will, whether or not determinism is true—believe that the good outcome of this will be a more humane focus on deterrence and rehabilitation (and a movement away from retribution) in punishment.

Now we can return to the question about moral responsibility. When should people be excused from blame? Does having an abnormal brain change whether you are responsible? Does it matter whether the abnormality is a temporary affliction or a permanent condition? Do the theories we have considered give us any help with these difficult questions? And what about conditions of the brain that are not currently recognized as abnormal or diseased? What if Bernie Madoff's lawyer could show that his brain exhibits patterns typical of swindlers and that therefore he could not have helped cheating people out of their money? His brain made him do it!

The first thing we should do is to stop talking about our brains making us do things. If you believe, as many philosophers and scientists do, that the mind is the same thing as the brain, then two things are true. First, your brain will always be involved in whatever you do, but it doesn't make you do anything; rather, your brain exhibiting certain kinds of neuronal patterns *just is* you doing something. It's not like your brain is an independent force that could rebel against you and run away with your body. Second, when people act well or badly, these differences will appear as differences in their brains. So, if Bernie Madoff chose to swindle old people out of their money, this will show up in his brain (not that we have the tools to observe it, but his desires and beliefs will in fact be there, in his brain). Far from being an excuse, if Bernie Madoff could show that his desire to cheat people out of their money is there in his brain, he would just be providing evidence that he really is a bad guy.

Now we can return to our question about the conditions for excusing people from blame. Consider the case of psychopathy first. Real self and whole self theories seem to reach different conclusions about psychopaths than normative competency theories. Consider the psychopath whose real self (or his whole self) is psychopathic.[7] His second-order desires endorse his first-order immoral desires and he has no intervening wholehearted desires to be a better person or to be nicer. His affective and cognitive capacities are not in conflict; the psychopath has an integrated bad will. So, if these claims about the psychopath are correct, according to the views that define moral responsibility in terms of a conception of the self, psychopaths are responsible for what they do. Normative competency theories will not necessarily draw this conclusion, because there is evidence that psychopaths lack certain rational capacities (Kennett 2006). If the psychopath in question does not have any capacity to conform his actions to what are good reasons, or if he is not able to grasp certain reasons, including moral reasons, at all, then normative competency compatibilists may conclude that this psychopath is not morally responsible for what he does (depending on which capacities the normative competency theorist thinks are important).[8]

When it comes to temporary brain abnormalities, such as Teacher's tumor, the real self theories suggest a different conclusion. What we might think is going on in Teacher's case is that his tumor produces first-order desires that conflict with what he wholeheartedly endorses. He wants to look at child pornography because of the tumor, but he really does not want himself to have this desire. If this is the case, the real self theory would say that Teacher's actions should be excused insofar as they are caused by the tumor rather than by him. Normative competency theories suggest the same answer insofar as Teacher's ability to grasp reasons is impaired by the tumor or insofar as his capacity to act for reasons is entirely bypassed by these alien desires. As for the whole self theory, if Teacher has a new desire, then it is very likely to be marginalized in the rest of his psychology and so he has diminished but not zero responsibility for acting on it.

That all sounds relatively straightforward, but we can see how things could get messier. If psychopaths are wantons (who have no second-order desires or none that can influence their actions), then the real self theory would say they are not responsible after all. Do the particular impairments that psychopaths have render them incapable of having second-order desires or wills? If psychopaths do recognize and understand moral reasons but simply don't care to follow them, a normative competency theory could say that they *are* responsible. Are psychopaths rational enough? In the case of temporary brain abnormalities, what about a tumor that can't be removed or disease that can't be cured? Would the person with the tumor or disease become a different person who is then eventually responsible for what he does?

These are difficult questions and the answers will depend on the details, not all of which are known for certain. The important thing for our purposes is to notice that a theory of responsibility will direct your investigation, telling you what questions to ask and which facts to pay attention to. If you think the real self theory is correct, you will want to know whether the person is capable of forming preferences about her preferences: Can she form a conception of the kind of person she wants to be that is effective in her actions? If you think the reasons responsiveness theory is correct, you will want to know about the person's rational capacities: Is she able to recognize patterns of reasons and use these to decide what to do? If you think Susan Wolf is correct, you will want to ask whether the person has developed in a way that makes her rational capacities track the truth about the world, including truths about morally good and bad ways of treating others. If you think Kane's libertarianism is right, you will want to know whether the person's action was the result of the character she created through free, self-forming actions (or whether the action was itself an undetermined choice to act for certain reasons rather than others). If you think hard determinism is the right theory, you will need to ask what it is about different people that justifies treating them differently: Why put some in prison and others in institutions if none of them is responsible?

Empirical evidence will be crucial to answering the various questions posed by the different theories of responsibility. But no amount of scientific evidence on its own will tell us which theory is the right one. This is a theoretical question. Furthermore, as we think about these cases, we should remember that trying to understand the conditions under which people are morally responsible is, in part, a moral problem. We are assessing whether to think of fellow human beings as members of the moral community, as patients or as objects. In doing so, we should not lose sight of the fact that we are engaged in a theoretical enterprise with a moral dimension.

Summary

- Determinism is the view that the laws of nature and the events of the past entail every truth about the future.
- Compatibilist theories take determinism to be compatible with free will and moral responsibility (or, for "semi-compatibilists," determinism is compatible with moral responsibility).
- Two kinds of theories reject the compatibilist thesis: Hard determinsim accepts determinism and rejects moral responsibility. Libertarianism rejects determinism and thinks we are morally responsible.
- There are two main arguments against compatibilism:
  - The Manipulation Argument, which says that if manipulated action is not free, then neither is any action. The theories considered in Chapter 8 attempt to solve this problem.
  - The Garden of Forking Paths Argument, which says that freedom requires genuine alternatives that compatibilism cannot provide.

- We can begin to answer the question, "Is free will incompatible with determinism because it requires forking paths?" by thinking about our intuitions about cases.
- By finding out the intuitions of ordinary people, experimental philosophy adds to this endeavor by showing that compatibilism is not completely at odds with common sense.
- Experimental philosophy doesn't solve the problem by itself, however. Intuitions about cases are relevant to defining a notion of free will, but there are other factors, such as the cost of abandoning moral responsibility.
- If libertarianism is a plausible option, we could reject compatibilism and still have moral responsibility. Libertarianism says there are genuine alternatives (true forking paths).
- Neuroscientists have argued that free will doesn't exist on the basis of their investigations of brain activity, but these findings do not present a serious challenge to free will as conceived by certain libertarians or by compatibilists.
- New information from neuroscience and psychology will raise new questions about when people are and are not responsible, questions whose answers will require the resources of moral philosophy.

Study Questions

1. How would your life change if you came to believe that hard determinism (the view that determinism is true and that moral responsibility is incompatible with it) is true?
2. I once met a philosopher who believed in hard determinism who said that the most troublesome thing about taking this position was that his girlfriend was upset about it. Why would she be upset? Do you think she should be?
3. Imagine yourself in a debate with a compatibilist or an incompatibilist (pick the side you find most plausible). What kind of example would you use to "pump the intuitions" of your opponent? If you were suddenly forced to take the other side of the debate, what would you say in reply?
4. What should theorists do if intuitions about moral responsibility are quite varied, that is, if they change from person to person or within persons from case to case?
5. Research has shown that the male brain does not really mature until about age twenty-five. Younger men do not have as much brain capacity for impulse control or self-regulation. Should we treat men from eighteen to twenty-five differently from the way in which we treat men over twenty-five? How?

Notes

1. Table 9.1 is a modified version of the one in Nahmias (2012b).
2. It is open to the compatibilist to think that despite the fact that determinism and free will are compatible, actual human beings nevertheless don't have any free will (the empty box in Table 9.1). Such a person might think that while some causally determined being could act freely, human beings do not actually have the capacities they would need to have in order to act freely.
3. The kind of free will that is attached to moral responsibility and our reactive attitudes is the only kind of free will "worth wanting," as Dennett put it in his book *Elbow Room: The Varieties of Free Will Worth Wanting* (1984).
4. Pereboom (2001) makes this more sophisticated version of the Manipulation Argument. Some compatibilists suggest that it just begs the question against compatibilism to judge that people whose actions are determined in the way they specify (such as by way of a reasons responsive mechanism) are not responsible. (In other words, the objection assumes compatibilism isn't true at the outset and then uses this to argue that compatibilism isn't true.)
5. Seventy-six percent of participants thought Fred and Barney acted freely. Sixty percent thought Fred was morally responsible for stealing, and sixty-four percent thought Barney was morally responsible for returning the wallet. In response to scenarios using two more ways of describing determinism, the majority of participants also responded that agents in these scenarios had free will and were morally responsible for their actions (Nahmias et al. 2007).
6. For another excellent and thorough discussion of Libet's research, see A. L. Roskies (2010). See also Sinnott-Armstrong (2014).
7. As mentioned in Chapter 5, it is misleading to talk about *the* psychopath, since in reality people with various capacities fall under the label. In this context, I mean to talk about an extreme case for the purposes of illustrating differences between theories of responsibility.
8. Recall the evidence we saw in Chapter 5 that at least some psychopaths fail to distinguish between moral and conventional wrongs. This has been taken to be evidence that psychopaths do not grasp moral reasons, which would be relevant to the current argument.

Further Readings

Dennett, D. C. 2004. *Freedom Evolves*. Penguin.

Fischer, J. M., R. Kane, D. Pereboom and M. Vargas. 2007. *Four Views on Free Will*. Blackwell.

Libet, B. 1985. "Unconscious Cerebral Initiative and the Role of Conscious Will in Voluntary Action." *Behavioral and Brain Sciences* 8 (4): 529–566.

Nahmias, E. 2011. "Scientific Challenges to Free Will." In *A Companion to the Philosophy of Action*, T. O'Connor and S. Constantine (eds), 345–356. John Wiley & Sons.

Nahmias, E., S. G. Morris, T. Nadelhoffer and J. Turner. 2007. "Is Incompatibilism Intuitive?" *Philosophy and Phenomenological Research* 73 (1): 28–53.

Nichols, S., and J. Knobe. 2007. "Moral Responsibility and Determinism: The Cognitive Science of Folk Intuitions." *Nous* 41 (4): 663–685.

Roskies, A. 2010. "Why Libet's Studies Don't Pose a Threat to Free Will." In *Conscious Will and Responsibility: A Tribute to Benjamin Libet*, W. Sinnott-Armstrong and L. Nadel (eds), 11–22. Oxford University Press.

Sinnott-Armstrong, W., ed. 2014. *Moral Psychology, Vol. 4: Freedom and Responsibility*. MIT Press.

Part V

Three Big Questions

We have been examining moral and immoral actions. Our attention has focused on the questions "What motivations count as moral ones?," "What motivates moral and immoral actions?," "What are moral reasons?," and "When are we responsible for our moral or immoral behavior?" In this final section of the book, we will focus on other questions in moral philosophy that might be illuminated by an understanding of human psychology: "Why be moral?," "How can we know what is moral?," and "Can we derive an 'ought' from an 'is'?" These are some of the most profound and enduring questions in philosophy, and we should not expect to answer them easily. The goal in these chapters is to try to understand why these questions are deep and enduring and how an understanding of psychology might help us make some progress on them.

10 Why Be Moral?

Well-being and the Good Life

- **Prudential Reasons and "Good For"**
- **Theories of Well-Being**
- **Psychological Evidence for the Well-Being–Morality Link**
- **Conclusion**
- **Summary**
- **Study Questions**
- **Notes**
- **Further Readings**

In Plato's dialogue *The Republic*, Glaucon challenges Socrates to prove that the just (or moral) life is better than the unjust one. He is asking, in other words, for a reason to be moral. So far, we have talked about what motivates actions and what kinds of motivations make an action moral. If reasons and motives are related (as the Reasons Internalist would have it), these discussions bear indirectly on Glaucon's challenge. But we haven't addressed Glaucon's challenge directly. That's what we'll try to do in this chapter, with a particular focus on how understanding our psychology might help us with this age-old question.

Prudential Reasons and "Good For"

The way that Glaucon sets up the challenge is particularly nasty. He asks us to imagine the perfectly vicious man who has done such a good job of fooling people that he gets all the external rewards of virtue (people trust him, he is wealthy, healthy and so on) and the perfectly good man who, due to incredibly bad luck, gets none of the rewards of virtue but ends up instead being tortured on the rack. Does the bad man have any reason to be morally better? And what possible reason could the good man have to continue being good? When you think about the problem this way, you are primed to think about morality in terms of its personal advantages. When those are taken away, it looks like there's no point to acting morally. By this way of thinking, Bernie Madoff did in fact have a reason to be moral: he would have avoided prison if he hadn't cheated old people out of their life savings. But if he could have gotten away with it, he would have had no reason not to be a cheat.

There are two basic approaches to answering the question, "Why be moral?" On the one hand, according to the *moral reasons approach*, the question is misguided. There may not be selfish reasons to be moral, but there are moral reasons to be moral and that's good enough. Those who think that duty is the motive that makes an action a moral action will take this approach. We act from duty when we act precisely because we know that this action is morally required, not because it's satisfying for us or because it will get us something good for ourselves. By this way of thinking, demonstrating that acting morally is to a person's advantage takes the morality out of moral action. If you gave to charity for your own sake, then it wasn't really a moral action after all! Duty is not the only way to understand moral reasons, however. A Humean who wanted to take the moral reasons approach would argue that we have moral desires—desires for others' happiness, desires for justice and so on—that are the basis for moral reasons. The moral reasons approach is at the heart of moral theory, but in this chapter we are going to focus on a different approach that will allow us to consider some interesting psychological research.

The *prudential reasons approach*, on the other hand, accepts the challenge as intended, but rejects the idea that people can get away with being immoral. Prudential reasons are the reasons a person has to further her own good. According to this approach, it isn't ever really good for the person himself or herself to be immoral. On the face of it, this approach might seem like a lost cause. Surely there are immoral people who thrive! We tend to hear about the ones who end up in prison or dead, but we all know someone who isn't a very good person but enjoys a lot of external rewards. That said, probably few of us want to trade places with that person. How many of us would make a conscious choice to be a moral creep in order to make more money? Whether there are strong prudential reasons to be moral depends on what a person's good is. We need to look at theories of "the prudential good," or well-being, as I prefer to call it. Then we can ask what prudential reasons we have to be moral, according to these different theories. In the rest of this chapter we'll focus on the prudential reasons approach, since its success depends on various psychological claims about what contributes to a person's life going well.

Theories of Well-Being

What comes to mind when you think about what a good life is? Maybe you think of skiing and hot chocolate, or margaritas on the beach. Maybe you think of having a career and a family, good friends and enough disposable income to enjoy some fun vacations. Or, maybe you think of Monty Python's answer to the question of what the meaning of life is in their 1983 movie, *The Meaning of Life*: "Try and be nice to people, avoid eating fat, read a good book every now and then, get some walking in, and try and live together in peace and harmony with people of all creeds and nations." Whatever is on your list, the interesting philosophical question is about what unites these items, or what explains why these are the things that make for a good life. We're going to talk about theories of *well-being* to avoid the moral connotations that "a good life" has (even though "a good life" is a more familiar way of putting it). Well-being, as I intend it here, is the most general category of prudential value, which is a different kind of value from moral value. Well-being is a person's own good, and it grounds prudential reasons for individuals to do what is good for them.

You might think that what explains why things like skiing, hot chocolate and friends are part of well-being has to do with the fact that we like these things. Skiing and hot chocolate are good for people who *enjoy* them, but not for people who hate chocolate and find skiing terrifying and cold. Similarly, having lots of money or power or talent might be good for you, but not if they make you miserable and depressed. The focus on positive experience leads us to favor mental state theories, which take well-being to consist of a mental state. What kind of mental state? The examples plus the idea that misery or depression could blight your life suggest that well-being is something like happiness or pleasure. Indeed many people have thought that the good life for a human being is the pleasant life. This is hedonism about well-being.

Hedonism is a fairly simple theory, then, because it says that well-being is just one thing: pleasure (or maybe two things: pleasure and the absence of pain). But there is some disagreement about what pleasure is. The ancient hedonists, the Epicureans, thought the important kind of pleasure was a tranquil state of mind, free from distress and worry, called *ataraxia*. Jeremy Bentham, one of the founders of Utilitarianism, thought that pleasure was a particular kind of sensation that varied along such dimensions as intensity and duration, but was qualitatively the same thing no matter what caused it.

Contemporary hedonists have found it implausible to say that pleasure is a single sensation. You can see why they might think this if you think about some examples. Think of the pleasure of eating chocolate (or something else that you really like the taste of). Now think of the pleasure of reading something difficult and finally "getting it." Think of the pleasure of listening to your favorite song, and then think of the calm pleasure Epicurus liked so much. Think of the pleasure of watching puppies play (which is what I've been doing while trying to write this book), and then think of the pleasure of a long-awaited sneeze. What do all these things have in common? They might all have something physiological in common—perhaps each experience involves a release of dopamine in the brain—but as full experiences, they are quite different. One thing that these experiences do have in common is that we like having them: we want to be in them when we are in them. This is how many contemporary hedonists think of pleasure: it is whatever state of mind we prefer to be in (Heathwood 2007; Feldman 2004).

One problem with hedonism is that it seems like there are a lot of trivial pleasures that don't make our lives go better. I get a fair amount of pleasure from scratching a mosquito bite or from sneezing when I have to sneeze (think about it: these things really are pleasant), but it doesn't seem like these experiences add to my well-being. If well-being is supposed to be the grand end of human life, the thing that we aim for when we deliberate and make plans, pleasure seems a little insignificant.

Life satisfaction offers a solution to this problem. Life satisfaction is (at least in part) a feeling, but it is a more significant feeling than some pleasures. Many psychologists have found the idea that well-being consists in satisfaction with one's life overall to be very attractive, and this basic idea has informed quite a bit of the research in "positive psychology."[1] According to the life satisfaction theory, what's good for a person is to be satisfied with the conditions of her life overall. The main philosopher who has argued for a life satisfaction theory of well-being, L. W. Sumner (1996), takes life satisfaction to be a complex mental state that includes both a good feeling about your life and a judgment that your life is going well overall.

According to life satisfaction theory in its simplest form, to live well is just to think and feel like you're living well. If you are satisfied with your life because you feel like you're doing great things, then it doesn't matter whether you are actually doing great things. If it feels good, it is good! Once again, something seems to have gone wrong here. Surely there is a difference between thinking your life is going well and its actually going well, isn't there? What if you feel good about your life because you think you have great friends, but in fact your friends are all being paid by your parents to make you feel good? Would your life really be going well or would we want to say that you're mistaken? Simple mental state theories can't make sense of our making mistakes about our own well-being.

There's a famous philosophical thought experiment that makes this point very nicely (Nozick 1974). Imagine that you are given the option to hook up to an "experience machine" that will guarantee you a life with more pleasure in it overall than you would have if you chose not to hook up to the machine. If you opt for the machine, your entire life will be spent hooked up by wires to a very sophisticated virtual reality machine, which will seem perfectly real to you from the inside. In order to isolate your intuitions about whether the life of pleasure would be a good life, you need to imagine that the neuroscientists in charge of the machine are 100 percent reliable, that other people also have the option of hooking up to their own machines, and that whatever it would require to bring you more pleasure overall in the machine, that's what you will get. So, for instance, if you think you couldn't experience pleasure without some pain, the machine will guarantee that you'll have just enough pain to appreciate your pleasure—what is stipulated is that however much pleasure you would have *overall* will be greater in the machine than in real life. Would you hook up to the machine? Nozick thinks that many people would not want to because people value more than just how they feel from the inside; we also value being in touch with reality, knowledge of the real world, real relationships with real people— even if these things might bring more pain than pleasure.

Some who favor mental state theories have opted to modify their theories because of the experience machine objection. For instance, some hedonists have proposed that what's good for you is "truth-adjusted" pleasure, pleasures that are not illusory but are based on real things that have actually happened (Feldman 2004). Sumner takes the entirely subjective state of life satisfaction to count as well-being only if it is authentic, by which he means that it must be informed and autonomous. According to this version of the life satisfaction theory, your life goes well for you if you are satisfied with the conditions of your life overall and you would continue to be satisfied if you knew the truth. A person who would not be satisfied with her life if she knew she were stuck in an experience machine isn't really achieving well-being, according to this theory.[2]

Another way to respond to the experience machine objection is to abandon mental state theories altogether. You might think that there are some things that are good for people independently of how those things make the person feel. For instance, you might think it's good for people (that is, part of their well-being) to understand reality, even if this doesn't make them more satisfied with their lives. Or, you might think it's good for people to develop their talents, period, not just because doing so produces pleasure. Notice that not all of these intuitions are accommodated by "truth-adjusted" hedonism or "authentic life satisfaction." If you think that developing your talents is good for you *for some other reason* besides the fact that it produces pleasure, then it doesn't help to say that the pleasure is truth-adjusted. It could be perfectly true that your pleasure was produced by your actually developing your talents, but the critic could still object that it isn't the fact that pleasure was produced that makes this good for you. Here we have a deep disagreement about the fundamental explanation for why something contributes to a person's well-being.

There are two very different kinds of theories that do not identify well-being with a mental state such as pleasure or satisfaction: desire or value theories and eudaimonist theories, each of which offers a different explanation for why something is good for a person. According to desire satisfaction theory, what is good for us is good for us because it satisfies a desire or preference that we have. Well-being consists of overall desire satisfaction. This is confusing because I've just said that this is an example of a theory that does *not* identify well-being with satisfaction! The confusion is caused by the fact that there are two different senses of satisfaction. On the one hand it can mean a good feeling, the feeling that you have when things are going well or you get what you want. This is the sense used in the life satisfaction theory. On the other hand, it can mean that the object of a desire has been achieved. This is the sense used in desire satisfaction theory. Here's why they are different. Let's say you desire world peace, and you are in the experience machine. The neuroscientists looking after you know that you would get a lot of pleasure from believing that world peace had been achieved, so they tweak a few things and make you believe it. Outside, though, the world is still as full of war as ever. Do you *feel satisfied*? Yes. Was your desire satisfied? No: you did not get what you wanted, even though you think you did.

According to desire satisfaction theory, what's good for you is attaining the objects of your desire, whether or not that produces the feeling of satisfaction. Of course, desire satisfaction theory does not say that pleasure and the feeling of satisfaction are unimportant. But they have a different explanation for their importance. A desire satisfaction theory would say that pleasure is good insofar as we want it, but the mental state of pleasure is not the only thing needed for well-being since we want other things too. Most of us have some desires for things in the world rather than just experiences in our heads. So, according to desire satisfaction theory, mental state theories have the wrong list of ingredients of well-being (well-being includes much more than pleasure or the feeling of satisfaction for most people) and the wrong explanation for the ingredients (things are good for us because we want them, not because they produce a particular feeling). Notice that desire satisfaction theory is still a subjective theory in the sense that it makes well-being depend on the person whose well-being it is. This implies another complexity: for a person who only wants pleasure, the hedonistic life is the good life! If all you want is pleasure, and what's good for you is getting what you want, then pleasure is the only thing that's good for you. But most of us want other things besides pleasure. We want our friends to be real people who actually like us, we want to actually accomplish things and not to be happily fooled into thinking that we have, and we want to understand the truth about the world in which we live.

Desire theory has its own problems, one of which is quite similar to the problem for hedonism discussed above: we can have trivial desires, just as we can have trivial pleasures, and it doesn't seem like the satisfaction of trivial desires increases our well-being. We can even use the same examples that I used above: satisfying the desire to scratch an itch or the desire to sneeze do not seem to make my life go better. We can also have desires for remote objects that do not seem to have anything to do with our well-being. You might desire that scientists discover another planet or you might want your favorite drug-addled movie star to stay sober, but it seems very odd to say that whether Pluto is a planet or whether the movie star takes a drink affects your well-being.

For these reasons among others, my own favorite theory of well-being is one that identifies well-being with value fulfillment (Tiberius 2008; Raibley 2010). Our values are the commitments and goals we have that we plan our lives around and that we take as standards for how our lives are going. Most people value friendship, family, health, knowledge, security and pleasure. According to the value fulfillment theory, you achieve well-being to the extent that you realize these values in your life. Thinking about well-being in terms of getting what you value instead of getting what you want helps with trivial and remote desires, because it focuses our theory on those things that you think contribute to your well-being. (Value fulfillment theories do need to address the worry that even a person's values might be dysfunctional or unhealthy; they can do this by appealing to coherence, or an ideal of a paradigmatically value-full life.)

None of the theories we have looked at so far makes room for the idea that there might be something that is good for people independently of their own subjective states and attitudes. Mental state theories take these attitudes themselves (pleasures or feelings of satisfaction) to constitute well-being; desire and value fulfillment theories take our desires and values to be part of the explanation for why various things (including but not limited to mental states like pleasure) contribute to our well-being. To find a theory that takes well-being to be defined independently of a person's mental states, we need to turn to eudaimonism.

Eudaimonism gets its name from the ancient word *eudaimonia*, which is often translated as "happiness" or "flourishing." According to this theory, well-being is defined in terms of nature fulfillment. You live well insofar as you fulfill your nature as a human being or your individual nature. Of course, your nature does have something to do with *you*—it is your nature, after all—but eudaimonist theories are nevertheless much less subjective than the other theories we have considered so far. This is because you do not create your own nature by wanting, valuing or taking pleasure. Your nature is what it is, whether you like it or not.

Some eudaimonists think that it is our nature as human beings that is important to our well-being (Kraut 2009; Hursthouse 1999; see also the discussion of Aristotle at the beginning of Chapter 7). Think of it this way: What's good for other kinds of creatures depends on what kinds of creatures they are, so why wouldn't it be the same with us? It's good for lions to have sharp teeth and powerful legs so they can chase their prey and kill them. It's good for oak trees to get enough sunlight and nutrients that they can produce acorns. So too with human beings: we do well when we do what is in our nature to do. Eudaimonists who follow Aristotle think that what's in our nature to do is to act like the rational beings we are, and this means acting virtuously, since virtue is expressed in the activity chosen by the person with well-functioning practical reason. This might sound strange to modern ears, but the basic idea makes some sense. We are social creatures who depend on others in all sorts of ways to get along in life: we are raised in families, we play team sports, we belong to churches, synagogues and other religious communities, we form governments, and so on. So, if we are good members of our kind we will develop the virtues that enable social cooperation and coordination: honesty, justice, generosity, kindness and so on. We are also intelligent creatures who deliberate, plan and learn. If we are good members of our kind we will develop the virtues, such as temperance and wisdom, that allow us to do these activities well.

Some eudaimonists reject the claim that it is our nature as a member of the human species that matters and say instead that what's relevant to well-being is a person's individual nature. In this view, well-being still consists in fulfilling your nature, but it is your own physical and psychological qualities (your individual nature) that matters, not your human nature. We might call this theory individualist eudaimonism (Haybron 2008). In such a view, it still makes sense for us (most of us anyway) to develop the virtues, because the things that Aristotle focuses on—our need for community, our intelligence—are part of many people's individual nature. But according to individualist eudaimonism, there might be basic differences between what's good for one person and what's good for another. Furthermore, the *explanation* for why something is good for you doesn't make reference to your species.

Because eudaimonist theories are more objective—they do not make well-being depend on a person's attitudes—they make good sense of cases in which people's subjective attitudes are messed up. For example, what will one of the other theories say about a person (call him Ned) who wants nothing more in life than to sit around his parent's house watching reruns of *Battlestar Galactica* and eating Pop-Tarts? Imagine that Ned gets tons of pleasure from this and values nothing else. It seems like the other theories we have discussed have to say that he is achieving well-being. But eudaimonists can give a more intuitive verdict about Ned. Ned isn't doing as well as he could, because the life he's living is beneath him. It's certainly beneath him as a human being, given that there are human qualities and skills he is not developing. It's probably even beneath him as an individual, on the assumption that he is a relatively normal person. This is a nice advantage, but it comes with a cost, which is that Ned's life could be going well according to eudaimonism even if he weren't enjoying it. If Ned's parents took away his Pop-Tarts and television and signed him up for violin lessons and volunteering at the local soup kitchen, his life might be going better from the standpoint of well-being even though (let's assume about poor Ned) he's miserable and grumpy. This possibility has caused some eudaimonists to move closer to adopt a little bit of hedonism and say that fulfilling your nature is only good for you if you are able to enjoy doing so (Kraut 2009).[3]

We have surveyed a number of different theories of well-being, each of which has its pros and cons. I'm not going to try to argue for one of these theories over the other (though I certainly think it's worth thinking about, and some of the questions at the end of the chapter will lead you in that direction). My own view is that the value fulfillment theory does the best job at providing a unified explanation of the phenomena that captures the sense in which well-being is supposed to be *good*. But this is not the place to make this argument and, in fact, my value fulfillment theory implies that I must allow that people can think about their own good in different ways. Someone who values only pleasure should care about the implications of hedonism, and someone who cares about fulfilling his nature should care about eudaimonism. Therefore, instead of arguing for the right view about well-being, I want to argue that no matter how you conceive of well-being, there's a bridge across the gap between self-interest and morality. Different theories of well-being have different implications for our reasons to be moral, but all the theories can make some argument that we have such reasons. Notice that here we are talking about *normative* reasons: the challenge "Why be moral?" demands that we produce reasons that justify or make sense of acting morally given that acting morally can be inconvenient or difficult. Furthermore, given that we are taking the challenge at face value, we are looking for reasons that justify acting morally in terms of the agent's own good.

What do the various theories of well-being have to say about our reasons to be moral? Basically, mental state theories say that if we have reasons to be moral, those reasons are *instrumental* reasons: we should act morally (from the point of view of our own well-being) if acting morally produces the mental states that are good for us (pleasure or satisfaction). Desire satisfaction theories, value fulfillment theories and individualist eudaimonism can all make room for the existence of *intrinsic* reasons to be moral as long as we have moral desires, values or individual natures.[4] For example, a person who desires to be fair, generous and kind has reasons to be fair, generous and kind, since doing so will satisfy her desires and satisfying her desires is what's good for her. Finally, species-based eudaimonism or Arisotelianism allows for universal intrinsic reasons to be moral: according to this theory we all have reasons to be moral because it is part of our nature as human beings. Table 10.1 summarizes these points.

Table 10.1 Moral Reasons and Theories of Well-Being

Theories of Well-being → *Types of Reasons* ↓	*Hedonism*	*Life Satisfaction*	*Desire Satisfaction or Value Fulfillment*	*Individualist Eudaimonism*	*Species-based Eudaimonism*
Instrumental reasons to be moral (acting morally causes well-being)	If acting morally causes pleasure, yes.	If acting morally causes life satisfaction, yes.	If acting morally causes other desires to be satisfied or other values to be fulfilled, yes.	If other aspects of the individual's nature are fulfilled by acting morally, yes.	If other aspects of human nature are fulfilled by acting morally, yes.
Non-universal, intrinsic reasons to be moral (acting morally constitutes well-being for some)	No.	No.	Yes, for those who have the desire to be moral for its own sake or who have moral values.	Yes, for those whose individual nature will be fulfilled by acting morally.	No.
Universal, intrinsic reasons to be moral (acting morally constitutes well-being for all humans)	No.	No.	No.	No.	Yes. All human beings have intrinsic reasons to be moral.

With these distinctions in hand, we can see that Glaucon was looking for universal, intrinsic reasons to be moral. But we can also see that there are many other types of prudential reasons to be moral that are relevant to our inquiry. So far, though, all I've done is to explain the types of reasons that could follow from these various theories. It remains to be seen whether we actually have such reasons and how strong they are.

Psychological Evidence for the Well-Being–Morality Link

Do we have reasons to be moral that stem from our own well-being? The answer to this question depends on different facts based on which theory of well-being you favor. If you are a hedonist, then whether we have reasons to be moral depends on whether acting morally produces pleasure. If you're a desire satisfaction theorist, it depends on whether we have desires that are satisfied by acting morally. And so on. In every case, the question is, at least in part, an empirical question. Whether acting morally produces pleasure is an empirical question; whether it satisfies our desires is also an empirical matter. We might think, then, that we will find some answers in psychological research.

To look for answers in psychological research, though, we need to match the concepts we're interested in with ones that psychologists have investigated. (Or, if we were going to engage in new research, we would need to define these concepts in such a way that we will be able to investigate them empirically; that is, we would need to operationalize them.) For our question about the relationship between well-being and morality, we need empirical matches for well-being and morality. We also need to focus, because the empirical literature that could be relevant to our topic is vast. I'm going to focus on the parts of the literature that are the most well established and the most relevant to our philosophical question.

Let's take morality first. Psychologists do not study "being moral"—this is too vague and broad. But psychologists do study particular moral behaviors such as volunteer work, kindness and helping. Volunteers help other people without the expectation of financial reward and they display certain virtues (generosity, kindness) and perform actions at least partly for the sake of others in ways that seem moral. Kindness and helping are usually understood to be requirements of morality. We can look at research on these topics for clues.

Similarly, psychologists do not study "well-being"; they study particular aspects or components of it. Fortunately, many of the aspects that psychologists study correspond to what well-being is according to the philosophical theories of well-being we have surveyed. Psychologists study positive and negative affect, which they measure by asking people to report in the moment how they are feeling and whether their feelings are pleasant or unpleasant. Psychologists study life satisfaction, which they measure by asking people how well their lives are going overall. They also study eudaimonia in a sense that is at least related to the philosophical meaning. For at least some psychologists, the central feature of eudaimonism about well-being is the view that human beings have certain basic needs that must be fulfilled for us to live well. Richard Ryan and Edward Deci (2004) propose what they call Self-Determination Theory, according to which basic human needs for relatedness, competency and autonomy are at the heart of well-being.[5]

What we want to know from this research is what the evidence is that volunteering, being kind or helping others increases the well-being of the person doing it. We are not looking for evidence of mere correlations; if we want to find reasons to increase our efforts to be moral, we need to find evidence that volunteering, helping and so on *cause* well-being. Psychologists are beginning to discover that doing helpful things for other people does cause us to be happier in various respects (Thoits and Hewitt 2001; Piliavin 2003). For example, in one study, Netta Weinstein and Richard Ryan (2010) measured people's well-being before they had an opportunity to help another person and then measured it again after they either helped by choice, helped with pressure or didn't help at all. In this experiment, participants were given money to distribute between themselves and another participant whom they did not know. They were told that all the participants would be entered in a raffle and the person whose name was drawn would get to keep the amount of money they had been allocated by the person distributing the money (that is, the participant). Half the participants were told that they could distribute the money however they wanted. The other half were told that they had to distribute it however they were told. The results of the study were that the well-being of those participants who chose to help increased, but the well-being of those who were forced to help did not. In this study, well-being was defined in terms of positive affect (or pleasant feelings), vitality (which means the experience of feeling energized and alive) and self-esteem. The fact that only the people who *chose* to help experienced increases in well-being is interesting. It seems to mean that insofar as helping others can help you, you have to help for the right reasons. Doing so out of guilt or social pressure doesn't work. This makes the research findings more deeply relevant to our question about the link between well-being and morality, because it means that the findings speak to those who think that we have to have the right motives for our actions to count as moral ones.

In addition to research on volunteer work, psychologists have investigated performing acts of kindness and expressing gratitude as "well-being interventions," and they have found these to be quite effective (Sin and Lyubomirsky 2009). A well-being intervention is a structured activity that is intended to bring about a change in well-being. Psychologists have found that keeping a gratitude journal, sending letters of gratitude to people who have been important in your life, and doing nice things for other people are activities that can make lasting improvements in people's well-being. For example, in her book *The How of Happiness*, psychologist Sonia Lyubomirsky has developed a program for increasing happiness, and gratitude and kindness exercises are two of the strategies she recommends for making yourself happier. (If you're thinking of taking her advice, she also recommends changing up what you do so that it doesn't become routine.) It turns out that even when kindness costs you, it makes you happier. For example, in one study, researchers rated their happiness before getting a "windfall" ($5 or $20), which half of them were instructed to spend on themselves (the "personal spending group") and half of them were instructed to spend on others (the "prosocial spending group") by 5:00 pm. At the end of the day, happiness was assessed again, and it turned out that those who spent the money on other people were happier than the ones who spent it on themselves (Dunn, Aknin and Norton 2008).

This has just been a peek at the kind of empirical evidence that could be brought to bear on our question. If you read more (by following up the references and suggested further readings at the end of the chapter), you'll see that it's reasonable to conclude that being kind, expressing gratitude and helping other people increases our own positive affect, life satisfaction and other indicators of well-being. What does this empirical evidence imply about reasons to be moral, given our five theories of well-being? Since many psychological studies take positive affect or pleasant affective states to be the measure of well-being, hedonism's claim to ground reasons to be moral seems on good footing. Kindness, helping and gratitude do (sometimes) produce pleasure; therefore, if hedonism is true, we do (at least sometimes) have instrumental reasons to act morally that stem from our own well-being. Similarly for life satisfaction: many psychological studies in which kindness and helping are shown to be good for us use life satisfaction as the measure of well-being. Of course, these theories do not measure *authentic* life satisfaction, which is what is relevant to the philosophical life satisfaction theory of well-being. Does this make a difference? I don't think it does: these studies show that people who believe they are helping experience increases in life satisfaction. Authentic life satisfaction will occur when these beliefs are true, which they would be in real-life helping experiences outside of the lab.

Desire satisfaction and value fulfillment theory also find support for their reasons to be moral insofar as the measures of well-being used in the research are measures of things we want and value. For example, findings about positive and negative affect are relevant to desire satisfaction and value fulfillment theories of well-being insofar as people want and value positive feelings. Moreover, one thing that seems clear from many studies is that a lot of people *want* to help other people. And if well-being is desire satisfaction, then acting to satisfy this desire by helping other people contributes to a person's well-being.[6]

When it comes to eudaimonic theories of well-being, things are a little more complicated. What we need to know is whether moral action fulfills our nature. The research we have been discussing, which investigates the relationship between helping and independently identified well-being measures isn't aimed at telling us whether helping is in our nature. But there is a good deal of empirical evidence that we human beings have certain basic needs that at least have a good deal of overlap with morality. Baumeister and Leary (1995) call this "the need to belong," which encompasses a need to spend time with others and a need to have bonds with others character-ized by stability and mutual concern. Helpfully, they propose some criteria that make something a basic need. A basic need or "fundamental motiva-tion," they say, is possessed by all people and has effects in all but adverse conditions. It has consequences for how we think and feel, it elicits goal-oriented behavior, and there are bad consequences (for our health, for example) when it is thwarted (Baumeister and Leary 1995: 498). With this analysis of a basic need in hand, Baumeister and Leary review decades of research that shows that the need to belong meets these criteria. They show that social bonds are formed easily and broken only reluctantly, causing great distress. Positive emotional responses are linked to increased belongingness, negative emotions linked to decreases, and deprivation of belongingness leads to negative outcomes for health, happiness and adjustment.[7] I won't review this evidence in detail here. I think, for most of us, the idea that human beings need to have stable relationships with other people who care about them is a claim that belongs in the "no kidding" category. I invite you to think about some of the evidence you have seen in your own life for the claim that the need to belong fits the criteria of a basic need.

On the assumption that the need to belong is part of our nature, for our purposes what we need to ask is what this need has to do with morality. The answer is that the lion's share of morality (some would say all of it) is made up of requirements that allow us to continue to relate to each other peace-fully and with mutual concern. You might even say that the point of morality is to allow us to belong to communities, social groups and families. Consider the virtues of honesty, fairness, kindness or generosity. Consider moral rules against lying, stealing or harming. All of these aspects of morality facilitate our relationships and interactions with each other. If the need to belong is indeed part of our nature, then there is a good argument for thinking that acting morally fulfills a part of our nature (Besser-Jones 2008).

Jonathan Haidt also makes a case for the importance of our social nature to morality. He calls us "groupish" and argues that the ability to transcend the selfish part of our nature (which we also have) is "the portal to many of life's most cherished experiences" (Haidt 2012: 370). Haidt has in mind cherished experiences such as spending time with a great group of friends, singing in a choir or a band, playing on a team, being part of a family and so on. Being a morally decent person—at least, being basically trustworthy, honest and helpful—is a prerequisite for getting the most out of these group activities.

One thing about our "groupishness" is that it seems rather partial, and this presents a certain challenge to the prudential reasons approach that should be acknowledged. Haidt observes that we have a hive mentality and the hive is other people like us, people who are part of our team or in-group.

Our brains seem to have evolved to facilitate in-group cooperation. According to Patricia Churchland (2011), trusting and caring for others produces oxytocin in the brain, which is associated with the release of opiates, so that "doing good feels good." Most likely humans developed this system to ensure that we take care of our young, who are born as incredibly helpless little resource consumers; expectant mothers produce more oxytocin. But it isn't just for mothers. Everyone produces more of it when they feel empathy, and oxytocin sprayed into your nose will make you more likely to trust an anonymous partner in an investment game (Churchland 2011: 71). But research on oxytocin shows that the feel-good chemical promotes *parochial* altruism, not universal benevolence. Furthermore, while there is no evidence that oxytocin makes us *hate* the out-group more, it does makes us less cooperative and more inclined to preemptive aggression toward outsiders whom we perceive as a threat (De Dreu et al. 2010; De Dreu 2012).

Notice that if our natural tendencies toward trust, benevolence and other moral motivations are biased in favor of our in-group, this is an important fact for morality. It might be that our prudential reasons to be moral do not normally prescribe actions that would solve large scale problems that require thinking about the effects of our behavior on out-groups, such as distant communities and future generations of people. If this is true, and if we agree that these problems are morally pressing, those who want to motivate people to act morally by appealing to compelling prudential reasons need to acknowledge our limitations and try to mitigate them in some way.

To return to our main question about the link between morality and well-being, there is empirical research that is relevant, and this research shows we have some reasons to do some moral things. In another sense, though, the empirical evidence does not provide the right kinds of reasons. The fact that helping others tends to make us happier does not mean that we have a reason to act morally even when it requires great self-sacrifice, and it doesn't show that we have overriding reasons to be moral even when we have some reason. Even if being moral is constitutive of our well-being because we have an innate need to belong, we could not conclude that our reasons to be moral override all other reasons that stem from our natures. We could look at all the relevant empirical evidence and we wouldn't have this, and Glaucon would be disappointed. The empirical evidence isn't going to give us moral reasons with special modal status, to be sure, and only a controversial species-based eudaimonist theory of well-being could ground universal intrinsic reasons to be moral.

Conclusion

Naturalist philosophers, who have not been inclined to think that there are pure principles of practical reason that give us reasons to be moral independently of our interests and desires, have long made the case that being moral is for our own good. Hobbes made this argument in *Leviathan*, where he addresses the challenge from the Foole who thinks he can get away with breaking all the moral rules if he's clever enough. For Hobbes, who had a fairly grim view of human nature, the answer to the Foole is that morality must be enforced so strictly that it could never be in a person's interest to risk getting punished. David Hume addressed the same challenge, from the Knave, but had a much rosier view of human nature and hence a much different reply. Hume thought that we would be happier being moral because we are naturally social creatures who have sympathy for others and who care tremendously about other people's regard for us.

Psychological research has proved that Hume was much more on the right track than Hobbes. As we've seen, there is abundant evidence that we do have a deep need for relationships with other people, for belonging to communities and social groups. The connection between well-being and other people has deep roots, and this helps the prudential reasons approach no matter what theory of well-being you accept. If rejection by the group causes serious emotional pain and social acceptance brings positive emotions, then we have reasons to be moral according to hedonism. If the ability to transcend selfishness is necessary for many desired and cherished experiences, then we will have reasons to be moral according to desire satisfaction and value fulfillment theories. Insofar as this groupishness is part of our individual nature or the nature of our species, we have reasons to be moral according to eudaimonism. Furthermore, the reasons highlighted by the prudential reasons approach are not necessarily simple instrumental reasons to do the right thing for the sake of selfish gain. According to desire theories, for example, there are reasons to be moral that stem from our wanting to help people and to participate in communal activities with others. According to eudaimonism, reasons to be moral often make direct reference to the needs of others that we care about in virtue of our nature.

To be sure, though, the psychological facts about us do not give every person an overriding reason to be moral in every situation, which would have disappointed Glaucon, and they do not provide a motivational basis for impartial altruism, which will disappoint Utilitarians (and perhaps other moral theorists as well). But the facts also do not preclude that we might have stronger or broader scope reasons to be moral. The argument I've made here is perfectly compatible with a stronger response to Glaucon or an answer that would satisfy the Utilitarian interested in finding reasons for universal altruism. We've seen that there are self-interested reasons for being morally decent, but this doesn't preclude philosophical arguments that there are other reasons, even desire-based reasons, for going beyond what we've established so far.[8]

Moreover, additional empirical research could add to the prudential reasons approach. Three lines of research suggest themselves in particular. First, what are the consequences of benevolence toward the out-group for a person's well-being? Particularly in our age of globalization, when we know more about the problems of distant people than we ever did before, perhaps helping strangers has good emotional consequences. Second, how much are people able to compartmentalize their moral decency?[9] Is it just as good in terms of the effects on well-being for people to be good to their family members and bad to their co-workers, or good on Sundays but not so good the rest of the week? Third, how well can people fake it? Are the well-being effects just as strong for people who merely have a reputation for morality as they are for people who deserve this reputation?

Anticipating future research or further investigation of the available empirical literature, we should take another lesson from our discussion, which is about methodology. It's a lesson that we've learned in almost every chapter of the book, but I think it's particularly obvious here: inferring philosophically relevant conclusions from psychological research is difficult. It seems fairly clear that how we answer the questions listed in the above paragraph will depend on what theory of well-being is assumed and what aspect of moral behavior is investigated. We cannot just do an experiment to determine if there are reasons to be moral. All the concepts in this question are difficult and contested. Empirical research is certainly relevant to the answer, but a good deal of work needs to be done to figure out exactly how, and we have only scratched the surface.

Summary

- The question, "Why be moral?" could be answered in two ways. The moral reasons approach takes the question to be misguided if it is asking for reasons to be moral that are distinct from moral reasons. The prudential reasons approach takes the challenge at face value and attempts to show that we have reasons to be moral that stem from our own well-being.
- The prudential reasons approach needs to start with a theory of what is good for us, a theory of well-being.
- Some theories of well-being are mental state theories that take well-being to consist of a mental state such as pleasure or life-satisfaction. These theories imply that we have instrumental, prudential reasons to act morally if doing so produces pleasure or life satisfaction.
- Desire satisfaction or value fulfillment theories take well-being to consist not of the *feeling* of satisfaction or fulfillment, but in the desired state or the value actually being achieved. These theories imply that we have intrinsic reasons to be moral if we have the relevant desires or values.
- Eudaimonist theories take well-being to consist of the fulfillment of our nature. These theories imply that we have intrinsic reasons to be moral, given our fundamental nature.
- Empirical evidence is relevant to (1) whether acting morally produces pleasure or satisfaction, (2) whether acting morally satisfies our desires or fulfills our values and (3) whether acting morally is part of our human nature.
- Empirical research does provide some evidence for thinking that no matter which theory of well-being you favor, we do have some reason to be moral for our own good.

Study Questions

1. Is it possible to be mistaken about how well your life is going? What is the most compelling example you can imagine of someone who is incorrect about how well his or her life is going?
2. Imagine that you are responsible for a child's welfare: What is it that you want for him or her? How does taking the point of view of a parent influence what you think about well-being?
3. Is it good for a child violin prodigy or musical genius to play the violin, even if she doesn't get any enjoyment out of it? What would the eudaimonists say about this?
4. What can mental state theories, desire satisfaction theory or value fulfillment theories say about Ned (the TV-watching Pop-Tart eater)? Are these theories really stuck with the conclusion that Ned is living a great life?
5. How would you design an experiment to show that being moral is good for our well-being?
6. What qualities do you think make a person a good team player or a good friend? Does the person's morality matter at all?
7. Do you know any fools or knaves? If so, what do you think of them? Does their existence change how you think you ought to behave?

Notes

A version of this chapter appeared previously in *Res Philosophica* and I thank the journal for permitting it to be published here.

1. Positive psychology, a relatively new movement in the field of psychology, emphasizes the positive aspects of life instead of mental illness and dysfunction. For an introduction, see Seligman (2002).
2. Though, according to Sumner, the person would be happy. Sumner thinks of happiness as entirely subjective. The word *happiness* is contested in philosophy. Some people think that happiness is the same thing as well-being; others think that happiness is a psychological state, while well-being is broader. It doesn't matter much for our purposes how these terms are used. I'll use *well-being* for consistency and avoid using the word *happiness*.
3. So we can see that just as subjective theories add "truth adjustment" or "authenticity" in order to accommodate intuitions from the other side, the more objective theories add a kind of experience requirement to accommodate more hedonistic intuitions.
4. The idea of an intrinsic yet prudential reason to be moral might sound paradoxical. How can there be a reason to be moral for its own sake that is also a reason to promote one's own well-being? Reasons can be characterized as moral or prudential, I suggest, when there is a constitutive relationship between morality and well-being. When acting morally is an inherent part of living well (not just a means to it), there are intrinsic moral reasons that are also prudential reasons.

5. Some psychologists who propose eudaimonist theories of well-being focus on subjective mental states like a sense of meaning in one's life, a sense of mastery or a feeling of flow. These theories are not really eudaimonist in the sense that philosophers intend (where well-being consists in the fulfillment of your nature as opposed to having certain mental states).

6. It's worth noting that this fact about desire satisfaction theories creates a kind of paradox, because it seems like a person could desire to sacrifice her own well-being for the sake of helping someone else, but the desire satisfaction theory of well-being makes this impossible. Much has been written about this problem of self-sacrifice; see, for example, Heathwood (2011) and Rosati (2009).

7. Philosophers have noticed this too; according to Allan Gibbard (2006: 201): "Guilt is closely tied to anxiety over social exclusion, over alienating those who are important to one. But social exclusion will be disastrous anywhere, and so anxiety over alienating others must no doubt be a human universal."

8. For a classic example, see Singer (1972).

9. For example, the literature on the situationist critique of virtue ethics that we discussed in Chapter 7 could be taken as evidence that we are good at compartmentalizing our virtues, though it isn't clear from that evidence that we can do it on purpose. See Doris (2002).

Further Readings

Baumeister, R. F., and M. R. Leary. 1995. "The Need to Belong: Desire for Interpersonal Attachments as a Fundamental Human Motivation." *Psychological Bulletin* 117 (3): 497–529.

Besser-Jones, L. 2008. "Personal Integrity, Morality and Psychological Well-Being: Justifying the Demands of Morality." *The Journal of Moral Philosophy* 5: 361–383.

Haybron, D. M. 2008. *The Pursuit of Unhappiness: The Elusive Psychology of Well-Being*. Oxford University Press.

Kraut, R. 2009. *What Is Good and Why: The Ethics of Well-Being*. Harvard University Press.

Lyubomirsky, S. 2008. *The How of Happiness: A Scientific Approach To Getting The Life You Want*. Penguin.

Ryan, R. M., and E. L. Deci. 2001. "On Happiness and Human Potentials: A Review of Research on Hedonic and Eudaimonic Well-Being." *Annual Review of Psychology* 52 (1): 141–166.

Sumner, L. W. 1996. *Welfare, Happiness, and Ethics*. Oxford University Press.

Tiberius, V. 2008. *The Reflective Life: Living Wisely with Our Limits*. Oxford University Press.

11 How Do We Know What Is Morally Right?

Moral Psychology and Moral Knowledge

- The Attack on Intuitions: Biases and Trolley-ology
- Intuitions, Intuitionism and Reflective Equilibrium
- Summary
- Study Questions
- Notes
- Further Readings

When it comes to many of the examples of morality and immorality we have discussed so far in this book, there's not much doubt about what's right and wrong. As we assumed in previous chapters, it's good to help people and to be kind to your friends. It's wrong to run over someone's dog with your car, to cheat people out of their retirement savings and to molest children. These are not controversial cases. But there are actions that we are much less certain about, and these cases raise the question of how we can know whether something is right or wrong. For example, is it wrong to alter the genes of a human embryo for the purposes of enhancing the resulting person's capacities? Is it wrong to torture someone if you have excellent reason to believe that doing so could prevent the deaths of thousands of people? Many people are also uncertain about how to be moral in their everyday lives: What are the limits of charity and honesty, for instance? Is it enough to buy a gift for Toys for Tots at Christmas, or should you tithe five percent or even ten percent of your income to charity? Should you always be honest about painful truths, no matter what the circumstances? If we are uncertain about what the right thing to do is in these cases, how can we try to arrive at an answer?

In general, when we want to figure something out about the world we try to find evidence. More specifically, if we are engaged in scientific inquiry, we might construct a hypothesis about how the world is and then look for evidence that confirms or disconfirms it. How does this work when the knowledge we are seeking is about what's morally right and wrong? One way it works is pretty simple. You start with a moral theory or principle, and you look for the information you need to apply the principle to your situation.

For example, suppose you start with the Utilitarian principle that we should always act to promote the most overall (long-term) happiness for the greatest number of people. With this as your principle, if you're trying to decide whether you ought to tell the truth to your boss about a friendly co-worker stealing from the till, you'll need to know how much happiness and unhappiness will be produced for all concerned, in the long term, by telling the truth and not telling the truth. Suppose you arrive at the conclusion that lying to your boss will produce the most happiness. Is your work done? Not really. There might be other moral reasons to consider, reasons that have to do with fairness or with respecting other people's rational powers. How do you decide which principle is the right one, or which reasons are good reasons to consider? We have quickly arrived at a more fundamental question: How can we know which moral theory or principle is the right one?

Many have thought that at least one crucial kind of evidence for fundamental claims about morality comes from our intuitions about what's right and wrong in particular cases. If you have taken a course in ethics, you probably recall that moral theories are often tested by how well they do at matching our intuitions. For example, most people have the intuition that it would be wrong for a doctor to kill a relatively healthy patient in order to harvest his organs to save the lives of four other people in the hospital. This example is used to criticize Utilitarianism, because (so the argument goes) according to Utilitarianism it would be morally right (in fact, required) to kill the one patient since more happiness is produced that way. Of course there are many things the Utilitarian can say in response to this example. The point is just to show that moral intuitions are standardly taken to be relevant to evaluating moral theories. You might even notice this reliance on intuitions in your own decision making. Perhaps there has been a time when you have considered bending the truth a little bit in order to get ahead. You might have thought about whether an omission or an exaggeration of the truth is really a *lie* and compared it to cases where you have clear intuitions about the wrongness of lying.

This idea that our intuitions are getting at something important that needs to be taken into account is a central part of the predominant methodology in moral theory: wide reflective equilibrium. According to wide reflective equilibrium, we evaluate normative theories by bringing into equilibrium ordinary judgments or intuitions about particular cases, putative normative principles, and background (philosophical and scientific) theories.[1] We may not be able to save all of our intuitive judgments, and some of our principles may need to be modified or thrown out altogether, but the goal is to construct a theory that explains and systematizes as much of this large body of information as possible within the relevant theoretical constraints. We have already used this methodology in other chapters of this book. In Chapters 8 and 9 we talked about *reflective equilibrium* as a method for deciding on the best theory of moral responsibility. And we used this methodology in Chapter 11 when we evaluated different theories of well-being on the basis of how well they capture intuitions about cases and thought experiments (like the experience machine).

Wide reflective equilibrium raises some questions. What are intuitions? Why do they count as evidence for moral truths and under what conditions are they good evidence? There are many different ways of defining what an intuition is, and many different ideas about why intuitions count as evidence. For our purposes, think of a moral intuition as a moral judgment that appears to be fairly obvious to you without argument or inference. When you see someone setting a cat on fire or kicking a child, it seems wrong to you right away, without having to think about it. This rather immediate judgment is a moral intuition. Psychologists tend to define intuitions in terms of emotional or "gut" responses. Notice that because our definition here uses the term *judgment* (which, as we've seen, can have either a rationalist or a sentimentalist interpretation), it is compatible with thinking that intuitions are more like emotional responses or more like beliefs.

Are moral intuitions good evidence? This is a tough question, and the answer depends in large part on why moral intuitions would count as evidence at all. Instead of trying to answer the question in general, we will consider two specific lines of attack on intuitions and see where they lead us. Both lines of attack draw on research that gives us reasons not to trust our moral intuitions as sources of moral knowledge. We'll review this research first, and then we'll turn to discuss in more detail some of the ways in which philosophers have thought intuitions are a source of moral knowledge. At that point we will be able to evaluate the attack on intuitions.

The Attack on Intuitions: Biases and Trolley-ology

What if you were an advisor to the Center for Disease Control and you were asked to decide whether to choose between two treatment plans. You're told that 600 people will die from a disease if no action is taken, but you have some options. If you adopt program A, 200 lives will be saved. On the other hand, if you adopt program B, there is a one-third probability that everyone will be saved and a two-thirds probability that no one will be saved. If you're like most people (72% of the subjects in the original experiment), you'll choose program A, which guarantees that you save 200 people. But what if your options were these instead: If you choose program C, 400 people will die. If you choose program D, there's a one-third probability that no one will die and a two-thirds probability that all 600 will die. If you're like most people (88% of subjects in the original experiment), you'll choose program D, since at least there's a chance you won't cause 400 people to die (Tversky and Kahneman 1981).

But hold on—program A is exactly the same as program C! In both, 200 people live and 400 people die. And program B is exactly the same as program D! In both, there's the same chance of saving everyone. What's going on here is known as a framing effect. When the choice is framed positively in terms of how many people will be saved, we tend to think one way. When it's framed negatively in terms of how many will die, we think another way. We tend to put more weight on negative outcomes (people dying), which makes us think that it's worse to let 400 people die than it is to save 200 out of 600 people. This isn't very logical; it's an example of a kind of bias—negativity bias—that pervades human judgment.[2]

Now you might be thinking that the real problem here is that people are easily confused by probabilities, so that as soon as fractions and chances of this or that are mentioned, rational judgment goes out the window. And, you might think, there are plenty of moral judgments that don't have anything to do with probability. What reason do we have not to trust those? As it turns out, negativity bias and other biases influence our judgments even when probability isn't there to confuse us. For example, in one study, participants were given variants on the now infamous trolley problem, like the one below.[3] (If you haven't heard of it before—don't worry! There will be enough discussion of it in this chapter for you to see why it might have become infamous).

> *Switch.* A trolley is hurtling down the tracks. There are five innocent people on the track ahead of the trolley, and they will be killed if the trolley continues going straight ahead. There is a spur of track leading off to the side. There is one innocent person on that spur of track. The brakes of the trolley have failed and there is a switch that can be activated to cause the trolley to go to the side track.
>
> You are an innocent bystander (that is, not an employee of the railroad, etc.). You can throw the switch, which will result in the five innocent people on the main track being saved, or you can do nothing, which will result in the one innocent person being saved. What would you do?
> (Petrinovich and O'Neill 1996: 149)

Half the subjects in this study got the scenario as above. The other half had to choose between "throwing the switch, which will result in the death of one innocent person, and doing nothing, which will result in the death of five innocent people." The only difference between the descriptions of the two cases is that one emphasizes the positive side (how many were saved) and the other emphasizes the negative side (how many will die). This difference made a difference: when the positive was emphasized, people were likely to think that you should pull the switch, whereas when the negative (death) was emphasized, people on average thought you should do nothing.

Further, it turns out that changing the order in which moral cases get presented to people can also change the judgments they make about them. For example, when people were asked about a case in which someone lied and a very similar case in which a guy named Nick omitted the truth, but didn't tell an outright falsehood, how much worse they thought it was to lie outright than to omit the truth depended on the order in which they heard the two cases. Those who heard "omit the truth" first and "lie outright" second were more likely to judge that lying outright is worse than omitting the truth (Haidt and Baron 1996). Surely, though, the order in which you think about two different actions is not relevant to whether those actions are right or wrong. So something is fishy here.

To anyone who has worked in politics or marketing, these effects are probably familiar. Here's a wonderful example of how the fact that people's moral intuitions or judgments are biased in various ways can be used to help manipulate them. The example comes from a British TV series called *Yes, Prime Minister*. In this dialogue, Bernard Woolley informs Sir Humphrey that the prime minister plans to reintroduce National Service (mandatory government service, usually military service, for young adults). Sir Humphrey is against the plan and demands that another poll be conducted with a different result. But, Bernard wonders, how will simply holding another poll change anyone's mind? Sir Humphrey explains.

SIR HUMPHREY: You know what happens: Nice young lady comes up to you. Obviously you want to create a good impression, you don't want to look a fool, do you? So she starts asking you some questions: Mr. Woolley, are you worried about the number of young people without jobs?
BERNARD WOOLLEY: Yes.
SIR HUMPHREY: Are you worried about the rise in crime among teenagers?
BERNARD WOOLLEY: Yes.
SIR HUMPHREY: Do you think there is a lack of discipline in our comprehensive schools?
BERNARD WOOLLEY: Yes.
SIR HUMPHREY: Do you think young people welcome some authority and leadership in their lives?
BERNARD WOOLLEY: Yes.
SIR HUMPHREY: Do you think they respond to a challenge?
BERNARD WOOLLEY: Yes.
SIR HUMPHREY: Would you be in favour of reintroducing National Service?
BERNARD WOOLLEY: Oh … well, I suppose I might be.
SIR HUMPHREY: Yes or no?
BERNARD WOOLLEY: Yes.
SIR HUMPHREY: Of course you would, Bernard. After all you've told her, you can't say no to that. So they don't mention the first five questions and they publish the last one.
BERNARD WOOLLEY: Is that really what they do?
SIR HUMPHREY: Well, not the reputable ones, no, but there aren't many of those. So alternatively the young lady can get the opposite result.
BERNARD WOOLLEY: How?
SIR HUMPHREY: Mr. Woolley, are you worried about the danger of war?
BERNARD WOOLLEY: Yes.
SIR HUMPHREY: Are you worried about the growth of armaments?
BERNARD WOOLLEY: Yes.

SIR HUMPHREY: Do you think there is a danger in giving young people guns and teaching them how to kill?

BERNARD WOOLLEY: Yes.

SIR HUMPHREY: Do you think it is wrong to force people to take up arms against their will?

BERNARD WOOLLEY: Yes.

SIR HUMPHREY: Would you oppose the reintroduction of National Service?

BERNARD WOOLLEY: Yes.

SIR HUMPHREY: There you are, you see, Bernard. The perfect balanced sample.[4]

Learning about biases and framing effects could be dangerous, when you think about it. Learn how to manipulate your friends with the power of words! I hope that no one will run out to explore this avenue of investigation, but that instead it will provoke thought about the point of this research for our purposes. For our purposes, the point is that we can see how these results would make us a bit queasy about relying on our moral intuitions. Moral intuitions are sometimes heavily influenced by irrelevant factors—factors we would recognize as irrelevant to the moral decision if we acknowledged them.

How queasy should we be, though? Those who think we can rely on our intuitions have some responses. First, not many philosophers think that the intuitions we rely on in arriving at moral knowledge are just unfiltered, immediate gut reactions to situations. Instead, they tend to think that the intuitions we should rely on are "considered judgments."[5] That is, they are the judgments we make about situations after some reflection on what's relevant and what is not relevant. The *considered judgment* of a person thinking about whether to choose a policy that saves 200 or a policy that has a one-third chance that everyone will be saved would be a judgment that's made after thinking about the fact that if you put the same question in terms of the choice between 400 people dying and a two-thirds chance of everyone dying, you feel differently about it. Being reflective about our judgments can eliminate some framing effects and biases, particularly because this reflection can include thinking about our biases.

Second, the defender of intuitions will point out that there are certain basic intuitions that are not subject to framing effects. One such defender suggests this as a genuine moral intuition: "The deliberate humiliation, rape, and torture of a child, for no purpose other than the pleasure of the one inflicting such treatment, is immoral" (Shafer-Landau 2008: 83). The critics of intuitions, according to this line of defense, have focused on tricky situations where it's difficult to know what's right or wrong. If we focus on more basic intuitions, we find that there are some that serve as plausible candidates for the foundation of moral knowledge.

At this point in the dialectic, it's worth considering another line of attack on intuitions as sources of moral knowledge. This line of attack strikes at the causes of intuitions. The basic idea is that some discoveries about how our moral intuitions are caused should make us doubt their reliability. You can see how this attack might work against trusting our senses about the empirical world. If someone could show that most of what we see is caused by hallucinatory drugs in our drinking water, we would have good reason to think that our visual observations are not a trustworthy source of information about the world. Similarly, if someone could show that our moral intuitions are caused by unreliable mental processes, then we would have some reason not to regard them as a good source of moral knowledge.

Josh Greene, a neuroscientist and philosopher, has made just this argument about a *subset* of our intuitions. Greene argues that different moral intuitions are caused in different ways and that, together with some assumptions about when different mental processes are reliable and when not, we have good reason to discount at least some of our moral intuitions.

To understand Greene's argument, we must return to the trolleys. Above we considered a case called *Switch*. Now consider two other cases:

> *Footbridge.* A trolley is hurtling down the tracks. There are five innocent people on the track ahead of the trolley, and they will be killed if the trolley continues going straight ahead. You are an innocent bystander (that is, not an employee of the railroad, etc.) standing next to a large man on a footbridge spanning the tracks. The only way to save the five people is to push this man off the footbridge and into the path of the trolley. What would you do?

> *Footbridge Switch.* A trolley is hurtling down the tracks. There are five innocent people on the track ahead of the trolley, and they will be killed if the trolley continues going straight ahead. You are an innocent bystander (that is, not an employee of the railroad, etc.) standing next to a switch that opens a trap door, which opens onto the tracks. There is a large man on the trap door. The only way to save the five people is to pull the switch, thus dropping the large man into the path of the trolley. What would you do?

The only difference between *Footbridge* and *Footbridge Switch* is that in the first case you have to push a man to his death, whereas in the second case you pull a switch that has the same result. Either way, though, the man falls off the footbridge and is killed by the train. Either way, if you act one will die and five will live, and if you don't act five will die and one will live. Despite the similarity in the numbers, people tend to feel very differently about these cases. Most people (63%) say that it's morally permissible to pull the switch in *Footbridge Switch*, but only thirty-one percent of people think that it is morally permissible to push the large man in *Footbridge* (Greene, Cushman, Stewart, Lowenberg, Nystrom and Cohen 2009). Why this difference?

People's feelings follow the same pattern when we compare *Switch* (the first case we talked about) and *Footbridge*: It's okay to pull the switch to divert the train (thus causing the death of the one innocent person who was stuck on the side track), but not okay to push the large man for the sake of the same results. Much philosophical ink has been spilt trying to articulate a principle that captures why it is okay to pull the switch but not okay to push the large man. In this effort, it has been taken for granted that our intuitions about the two cases (okay to pull switch/not okay to push man) are onto something and worthy of being accommodated. Hence all the ink: the project of explaining these intuitions by appeal to a principle has seemed like an important project.[6] The introduction of *Footbridge Switch* makes things even more difficult to explain because the cases are even more similar to each other: in both cases you cause a man to be dropped onto the tracks into the path of the train and the only difference is how close you are to this man.

Greene thinks that the difference between *Footbridge* and *Footbridge Switch* can't be explained rationally. Think about it: In one case you are right next to the man (close enough to touch him), and in the other case you are a little farther away, but you can still make him fall into the train by pulling a switch. How could this tiny difference of physical distance make the difference between its being morally okay to kill him and its being morally wrong to kill him? On the assumption that this tiny difference cannot make a real moral difference, instead of trying to explain our intuitions rationally, Greene sets about trying to explain them causally. His view is that the different intuitions in *Footbridge Switch* and *Footbridge* are explained by the fact that we have two different cognitive systems in our brains. In short, we have one system that is emotional and automatic; this system is engaged when we respond emotionally to the thought of physically touching the man, and it gives rise to the judgment that we should not push the man into the train. The other system is non-emotional and more reflective; when we read the relatively cold *Switch* cases, our emotions are not engaged, so this system can get to work, and it gives rise to the judgment that we should pull the switch in order to save more people. Let's consider this in a little more detail.

The theory that there are these two systems in the brain is called Dual Process Theory (which was briefly introduced in Chapter 6). The first system (System 1) is automatic, emotional and quick; the second system (System 2) is controlled, deliberate and slow. System 2 is what we normally think of as conscious reasoning or "thinking," but both systems produce judgments. Greene analogizes the two cognitive systems to the automatic and manual modes on a camera. If you put your camera on automatic, you can take pictures very quickly, but you might sacrifice quality. If you put your camera on manual, you have much more flexibility to cope with different lighting conditions and so on, but you won't be able to take pictures very fast because you have to make a conscious effort to set things up (Greene forthcoming). Greene and his colleagues argue that the two processes in Dual Process psychology tend to make different kinds of moral judgments: System 1 produces "characteristically deontological" judgments (judgments naturally defended in terms of rules, rights and duties); System 2 produces "characteristically consequentialist" judgments (judgments naturally defended in terms of the greatest benefit to the greatest number).

With Dual Process Theory in hand, Greene and colleagues hypothesized an explanation for why people tend to make different judgments in *Switch* and *Footbridge Switch* on the one hand and *Footbridge* on the other. The hypothesis is that our automatic, emotional system of judgment will be triggered by the up close and personal nature of the action we have to perform in *Footbridge* (you have to actually touch the man to push him onto the tracks), and this system will cause us to judge that we should not push the man. On the other hand, in the *Switch* cases, without any emotional trigger, our rational, calculative system will determine our judgment, and we will consider the outcomes more rationally, thus leading us to say that it would be right to pull the switch. Psychologists have produced a good deal of evidence in support of this hypothesis. Some of this evidence is neuroscientific: researchers can see from fMRI (functional magnetic resonance imaging) scans that the parts of the brain that are more active when people judge that it would be wrong to push the large man onto the tracks are the parts of the brain that are associated with emotional activity (Shenhav and Greene 2014). More evidence comes from studies of brain-injured patients: in many cases, patients with emotional deficits due to brain injuries are more likely to make consequentialist judgments. (This research gave rise to the fun title: "Consequentialists are Psychopaths" (Schwitzgebel 2011)). Further, consequentialist judgments are associated with controlled cognition, so that when people are given more time to deliberate or encouraged to reflect, they are more likely to make the consequentialist judgment about a case.[7]

Let's say we accept the description of our psychology put forward by this research: we agree, for the sake of argument, that consequentialist judgments are associated with conscious and controlled reasoning processes, while deontological judgments are associated with automatic and emotional cognitive processes. We still haven't reached an illuminating conclusion about *Switch* and *Footbridge*. At this point, Selim Berker (2009), a critic of Greene's work, has argued that there is no bridge from the "is" of Dual Process Theory to the "ought" of ethics. He argues that the scientific evidence about the causes of our moral judgments is irrelevant to any claims about which judgments are right or wrong. According to Berker, to get to any conclusion about which of our intuitions are trustworthy, we would have to rely on moral intuitions about what sorts of features of the world our judgments *ought* to be sensitive to. Only by making such assumptions could we argue that it's *better* to calculate the costs and benefits coldly without being influenced by the "up close and personal" nature of the action.

This is an excellent point: We do need to make some normative assumptions (about what our judgments ought to be sensitive to) in order to get to a normative conclusion (about which judgments we can trust). But Greene does not deny this. Greene's argument is that the scientific evidence *together with* normative assumptions about what counts as good judgment support the conclusion that the consequentialist intuitions are better or more reliable. The argument in favor of trusting consequentialist intuitions depends on the assumption that our judgments *should* (a normative term) not be sensitive to "mere personal force." Judgments that respond to these considerations alone—absent any other consideration that could be related to these things, such as special relationships we might have to those who are close to us—are biased by irrelevant information. The scientific research supports the claim that our non-consequentialist judgments really are just responding to personal contact and proximity. The assumption that these features of a situation are irrelevant is an extra moral premise. The extra moral premise, in terms of our example, is that the mere fact that we are farther away from the large man in *Footbridge Switch* than we are in *Footbridge* cannot be morally relevant.

In this section we have seen two reasons to be skeptical about moral judgments or intuitions. First, the fact that our intuitions can be biased by irrelevant factors gives us some reason to think that they are not reliable sources of knowledge in general. Second, if a particular subset of our intuitions (the deontological ones) are the result of a cognitive process that isn't designed to respond to the facts of an unfamiliar case (because it is fast and automatic), then we have some reason to think that these intuitions in particular are not reliable sources of moral knowledge. Having some reason to be skeptical, however, does not mean we should throw out intuitions altogether. We need to evaluate how strong these reasons are and exactly what philosophical conclusions they support. To do that, we need to know more about what role intuitions are supposed to have in the construction of moral knowledge anyway.

Intuitions, Intuitionism and Reflective Equilibrium

At the beginning of this chapter, I suggested that many philosophers count moral intuitions as evidence for what we should really think about morality. The default method in moral theory, reflective equilibrium, gives intuitions automatic credibility as inputs to our moral deliberations. And even philosophers who do not accept reflective equilibrium as their methodology rely on moral intuitions as evidence. But now we've seen that moral intuitions can be irrational and biased. Why would intuitions be taken as evidence for moral claims? We will consider two basic answers.

First, according to *intuitionism*, moral intuitions have something in common with perception in the realm of scientific discovery. Both intuitions and perceptions purport to track an independent reality. When we see a cat being tortured and we intuit the wrongness of it, we are, in a sense, seeing the wrongness. Intuitions are good evidence insofar as they really track the moral truths they claim to track, just as our visual perception is good evidence about the physical world as long as we are perceiving accurately. Historically, some intuitionists have thought that intuition is a special faculty—something like a sixth sense—that perceives moral truths. Recently, this view has fallen out of favor because the "special faculty" seems very mysterious. Contemporary intuitionists tend to think that our moral intuitions are just beliefs that do not require any special faculty beyond the rational and perceptual capacities we already have. In the previous section we saw an example from Russ Shafer-Landau (the most prominent contemporary defender of intuitionism) of a reliable moral intuition: "The deliberate humiliation, rape, and torture of a child, for no purpose other than the pleasure of the one inflicting such treatment, is immoral" (2008: 83). The important thing about this belief, according to the intuitionists, is that it does not need to be inferred or deduced from other beliefs to be justified; you know it is true just by understanding it. The intuition Shafer-Landau describes is *self-justifying*, and this is why it is supposed to constitute evidence relevant to our moral knowledge. Self-justifying beliefs are a secure foundation for moral knowledge.

Second, some philosophers think moral intuitions are not really like observations; that is, they are not evidence of an independent moral reality or moral properties that exist outside of us. Rather, in this way of thinking, moral intuitions (or considered judgments), are the building blocks with which we cannot but attempt to construct a moral system that works for us. We cannot avoid starting with our own moral intuitions because our goal is to improve what we think for the purpose of getting along in life, and our moral intuitions are just what we think. Moral intuitions are the convictions that it is the business of moral thinking to evaluate. This interpretation of moral inquiry makes the project of finding moral knowledge a project of construction. Moral knowledge is constructed by a method that takes our intuitions or considered judgments about morality and refines them through a reflective process. Hence, this way of thinking about morality is called *constructivism* (Rawls 1980).

Does the psychological research we have been discussing cause problems for intuitionism? If our moral intuitions are systematically biased, then it looks like if we do have a special faculty for discerning a realm of moral truths, it isn't very reliable—it's as if we had evidence that we frequently "see" things that aren't really there. Furthermore, if different people have different intuitions about the same case and it turns out that the explanation for this is that the two groups of people are using different cognitive processes, then again it looks like we don't have a faculty of moral intuition that gives us access to the untainted moral facts. Rather, it looks like we have different faculties, designed for solving different kinds of problems, none of which is the problem of perceiving an independent realm of moral truths.

Of course, contemporary intuitionists do not think we have a special faculty of moral intuition. Rather, they think we discern moral truths using the ordinary mental capacities psychologists agree we have. Does the evidence against intuitions cause problems for this view? If we think again about our example (the intuition about the wrongness of torturing a child for fun), the research we have looked at doesn't give us any reason to doubt *this* intuition. How might the critic of intuitions press her case? First, she could say that genuinely self-evident intuitions are so specific that they can't help us in hard cases, nor do they provide a sufficient foundation for a moral theory. In other words, the critic could say: yes, *that* intuition is reliable, but it doesn't give us enough knowledge to get us to a complete moral theory. Second, the critic could argue that the fact that there is an intuition we have no reason to doubt does not mean that our intuitions are generally reliable and that they should get automatic credence in our moral deliberations. If there is a good argument for thinking that whatever faculties produce our moral intuitions often go awry, it doesn't help if we can find one case where they probably didn't. After all, that one case could just be luck. The problem with luck is that when we confront cases about which we're unsure what it's morally right to do, we won't know if our intuition about that case is trustworthy or not (we won't know if we happened to get lucky). Sure, we know we shouldn't torture children for fun, but what about incest or pushing large men into trolleys?

The contemporary intuitionist might respond to the second criticism that the question of whether a particular moral intuition is reliable or not is answered through the process of reflective equilibrium. Through this process we can think about whether some of our intuitions were produced in ways that make them defective. For example, we can think about whether an intuition was the result of bias, and we can question what it means if it conflicts with another intuition. Just as we might question some of our visual perceptions when we are trying to acquire knowledge of the physical world—"Was the light good?", "Were my eyes tired?"—so too we can ask whether our intuitions are credible moral intuitions on the basis of other knowledge we have.

Constructivists also use reflective equilibrium as a method for acquiring moral knowledge. Constructivists don't think that moral intuitions are like perceptions of an independent reality, but they do think they are the building blocks of moral knowledge. Constructivists disagree with intuitionists, then, about *why* moral intuitions should be taken account of, but they both agree that they have to be taken seriously. For the intuitionists, moral intuitions must be inputs to the search for moral knowledge because they are our access to the independent moral reality. For constructivists, moral intuitions must be inputs to the search for moral knowledge because the point of moral inquiry is to refine the convictions that we start with in a way that can help us get along and thrive. Constructivists don't have to worry in the same way as intuitionists do about the possibility that our mental faculties are not reliably tracking an independent moral reality (because they don't think there is such a thing), but they do need to worry about the reliability of reflective equilibrium, the main method of moral inquiry.

So the important question is this: Does the psychological research we have considered cause problems for reflective equilibrium? I think the answer is: not really. It might, in fact, *inform* reflective equilibrium in an important way. After all, reflective equilibrium requires us to bring together into a coherent whole our considered judgments, our ethical principles *and* any relevant background scientific and philosophical theories. In this way of thinking, psychological theories about biases that affect judgment, or about dual cognitive processes, should be brought into equilibrium with everything else.[8]

Once we see things this way, we can recognize that "trolley-ology" is really about figuring out what we should think. Should we think it's wrong to push a large man into an oncoming train if doing so will save five people? Yes, this is how most of us tend to feel, but is it what we should think after we've reflectively considered all the angles? Should we think that it matters whether you are pushing a large man or flipping a switch when the same number of people will live and die in either case? Certainly, there doesn't seem to be a huge moral difference between flipping a switch that will kill someone and pushing someone to his death. As we have seen, Greene argues partly on this basis that the non-consequentialist intuition isn't to be trusted in the footbridge case. But there is another way to go.

Judith Jarvis Thomson agrees that there is an uncomfortable incongruity between our willingness to flip the switch and our unwillingness to push the large man. We don't have much to draw on to justify this pair of judgments. "Well, in *Switch* I don't have to use both hands!" doesn't seem like much of a moral argument. But instead of concluding that we ought to count both pulling the switch and pushing the large man as the right thing to do (as Greene does), Thomson (2008) argues in a recent paper that we ought to judge both actions to be wrong. She does this by introducing another case in which you are the person on the side track and if you pull the switch you would kill yourself, thereby saving the five innocent people. Sure, it would be nice if you did this, but, Thomson argues, it is not morally required of you to sacrifice yourself to save the five. Sacrificing yourself to save five others would be heroic or supererogatory (beyond the call of duty), but it isn't required. Further, if you aren't required to sacrifice yourself, then the stranger on the track in *Switch* isn't required to sacrifice himself to save five either. By switching the train onto his track, you make him do something that he isn't required to do and something that you yourself would not do. This seems wrong. This new twist on the case makes us think that maybe we ought to make the same judgment in *Switch* and *Footbridge*: in neither case does morality require you to do what you need to do to save the five.

This conclusion is even more anti-consequentialist than the usual intuitions people have about these cases—it says that we should pay even less attention to the cost-benefit analysis of how many would live and how many would die than we originally thought—and it would probably make Greene's head spin. But it is an option. It is also a very interesting illustration about how reflective equilibrium can work. Thomson originally thought, with most people, that we should pull the switch in *Switch* but we should not push the large man in *Footbridge*. But then she changed her mind, in part because she was persuaded that there was no principle that could explain why it's right to pull the switch but wrong to push the man (Thomson 2008). What happened here is that the attempt to reach reflective equilibrium caused her to have to jettison her original intuition about pulling the switch. In contrast, because of the assumption he makes about the reliability of System 1 judgment in novel cases, Greene jettisons the intuition that we should not push the large man.

How will this disagreement be resolved? Unfortunately, reflective equilibrium doesn't give us an easy way out. There's no answer sheet and no simple formula for making the right decision. But, then, no human inquiry is like this. Instead, we have to engage in the messy process of evaluating all the pieces and trying to put them together into something that makes sense. The facts about our psychology are certainly relevant to this process—this is one of the main claims this book has tried to illustrate. Will science replace the messy process of moral reflection? I don't think so. This is the question we turn to in the final chapter.

Summary

- Some moral questions (like whether it's wrong to cheat people out of their retirement savings) are fairly easy, but we do sometimes face moral questions to which we don't know the answers. When this happens we seek moral knowledge, or at least a reasonable position.
- A moral intuition is a moral judgment that seems true without having to engage in reflection or reasoning. Intuitions about cases are often thought to be evidence for moral conclusions.
- Recent studies about the psychology of judgment give us reasons to be skeptical about the value of our intuitions for arriving at moral knowledge.
- One source of skepticism is the fact that our judgments are subject to biases, such as negativity bias.
- Another source of skepticism is the conflicting intuitions we have about trolley cases that differ in morally insignificant ways.
- Dual Process Theory, which says that our moral intuitions are the result of different cognitive systems, is one explanation for why we have these conflicting intuitions. Joshua Greene argues that our quick System 1 processing is not trustworthy in novel situations because it is an automatic system that doesn't pause to consider the new circumstances.

- Intuitionists and constructivists agree that moral intuitions must be taken into account in the search for moral knowledge, though for different reasons.
- The psychological research does not cause problems for reflective equilibrium, a method that could be used by both intuitionists and constructivists. Indeed, psychological research can inform reflective equilibrium by showing us the conditions under which our automatic responses are not necessarily to be trusted.

Study Questions

1. Some have complained that trolley cases are too far from real life for us to learn much from them. Are there more "real life" cases that have the same features as *Switch*, *Footbridge* and *Footbridge Switch*?
2. Think of some moral intuitions that you have. What do you think would be required for you to make these into "considered judgments"? What sort of standards should we apply to our intuitions if we are to trust them?
3. Greene and Thomson resolve the *Switch/Footbridge* quandary in opposite ways. What do you think is the right solution?
4. What might someone who wants to defend the claim that we have a special faculty of moral intuition say in response to objections raised in this chapter? Would analogizing to our other senses help this intuitionist?
5. Think of a moral quandary that you have experienced. How would you proceed to figure out what to do using wide reflective equilibrium? Do you see any pitfalls in this procedure?

Notes

1. Rawls (1951) is the classic defender of reflective equilibrium as a method for defending ethical theories. For more on this method, see Daniels (1979, 2008).
2. For an excellent discussion of this research, see Sinnott-Armstrong (2008). In this book you can also find useful commentaries on Sinnott-Armstrong's argument.
3. The trolley problem was introduced by the philosopher Philippa Foot (2002/1967).
4. *The Ministerial Broadcast, Yes, Prime Minister,* series 1 (first broadcast January 16, 1986). Thanks to Jimmy Lenman for the example.
5. This is what John Rawls (1971), whose worked helped make reflective equilibrium the default method in moral theory, calls the intuitions we should attend to. Intuitions understood this way require clear thinking about the case, though they are still intuitions by our definition because we do not arrive at them by way of argument or inference from a principle.
6. For the papers that started it all, see Foot (2002/1967) and Thomson (1976).

7. See Greene (forthcoming) for an overview of these studies that includes more helpful references.
8. Greene (forthcoming) agrees: "Along with our 'considered judgments' and organizing principles, we must add to the mix a scientific understanding of the psychological and biological processes that have produced them. (Call this *double-wide* reflective equilibrium)."

Further Readings

Berker, S. 2009. "The Normative Insignificance of Neuroscience." *Philosophy & Public Affairs* 37 (4): 293–329.

Foot, P. 2002/1967. "The Problem of Abortion and the Doctrine of Double Effect." Reprinted in *Virtues and Vices and Other Essays in Moral Philosophy.* Oxford University Press: 19–32.

Greene, J. Forthcoming. "Beyond Point-and-Shoot Morality: Why Cognitive (Neuro)Science Matters for Ethics." *Ethics.*

———. 2013. *Moral Tribes: Emotion, Reason, and the Gap Between Us and Them.* Penguin Press.

Greene, J., F. Cushman, L. Stewart, K. Lowenberg, L. Nystrom and J. Cohen. 2009. "Pushing Moral Buttons: The Interaction between Personal Force and Intention in Moral Judgment." *Cognition* 111 (3): 364–371.

Shafer-Landau, R. 2008. "Defending Ethical Intuitionism." In *Moral Psychology*, vol. 2, W. Sinnott-Armstrong (ed), 83–96. MIT Press.

Sinnott-Armstrong, W. 2008. "Framing Moral Intuitions." In *Moral Psychology, Vol. 2: The Cognitive Science of Morality: Intuitions and Diversity.* MIT Press.

Thomson, J. J. 2008. "Turning the Trolley." *Philosophy & Public Affairs* 36 (4): 359–374.

12 Can You Get an Ought from an Is?

- **Is and Ought: A Complex Relationship**
- **Reducing Ought to Is**
- **Summary**
- **Study Questions**
- **Notes**
- **Further Readings**

The topics that we have covered in this book all used to belong to philosophers, but in every chapter we have seen that scientists are beginning to investigate these topics with their methods. One vision of the future is that ethics or moral philosophy will become like physics or biology—these domains of inquiry belong to science now. Moral philosophy might remain a subfield in philosophy, like the philosophy of physics or philosophy of biology, but it would be the philosophy *of* ethics as an empirical science. Is this what's going to happen? Does the changing shape of research in moral psychology mean that ethics will become a science?

What would it even mean for ethics to become a science? From my experience talking to people about moral psychology, I have learned that what many people have in mind when they have this idea is something quite dramatic—for example, that neuroscientists, by looking at people's brains, will be able to tell us what is right and wrong without our having to reflect or deliberate, or that an evolutionary biologist could derive what we ought to do from the scientific theory of evolution. I hope this book has demonstrated the various ways in which scientific methods and research are highly relevant to the deepest questions we have about morality, but there is an obstacle to thinking that ethics will become a science in the dramatic sense just mentioned. The obstacle is the gap between the descriptive and the normative, between fact and value, or between is and ought (which we discussed in the first chapter of this book). In this chapter, I draw on what we have learned so far to consider how is and ought are (and are not) related.

204 Three Big Questions

Is and Ought: A Complex Relationship

How are descriptive claims related to prescriptive or normative claims, facts to values, or is-es to oughts? In each chapter we've seen that there are important relationships between the two, but that relationship has not always been the same one. In this section I'll distinguish four different relationships between the descriptive and the normative. Note that it's tricky to talk about this distinction without begging some questions, since part of what's at issue is whether there are facts about what we ought to do that are similar—or even identical—to the ordinary facts that science discovers. For now, we will proceed with a commonsense distinction and see how it holds up. Here's what I take to be common sense: science uses systematic methods for understanding what is the case about the physical world; science is a descriptive endeavor. Normative philosophy uses systematic methods for understanding what ought to be the case; normative philosophy is a prescriptive or evaluative endeavor.

First, descriptive claims about our intuitions can play a role in the justification of normative theories by the method of reflective equilibrium. We've seen several examples of this. For instance, in Chapter 9, we saw that intuitions about whether a person in a deterministic universe is responsible for his actions play a role in an argument for compatibilism. Of course, the argument is not as simple as "intuitions favor compatibilism, therefore compatibilism is true." Rather, compatibilist intuitions are used against one attack against it, namely, that compatibilism is guilty of changing the subject since it posits such an unintuitive view of responsibility. The fact that people do not in all circumstances find the view unintuitive is just one piece of evidence in favor of compatibilism that must be taken together with all the other relevant information.

We saw another example in Chapter 10 in our discussion of theories of well-being. Nozick's example of the experience machine is an intuition pump designed to make us see the problems with hedonism. This argument against hedonism works (if it does) because the thought experiment brings people to agree that pleasure isn't the only thing worth having in life. If we take this point seriously in reflective equilibrium about the nature of a good human life, we will turn away from hedonism. This example should remind us that what's really relevant to reflective equilibrium are considered judgments or reflective intuitions. Someone who doesn't understand the experience machine example—say, someone who assumes that there couldn't be pleasure without pain and concludes that the experience machine wouldn't be so great after all[1]—doesn't have intuitions that need to be considered in reflective equilibrium. Reflective equilibrium is a method of justification, not a democratic procedure. But the facts about what people would intuit if they understood—facts about people's considered judgments—are still facts that scientific methods could help to uncover. For instance, we could devise tests to see if people understand our thought experiments and focus on the responses of reflective people. If we did this and we discovered that people's considered judgments about cases vary or that people have different intuitions about cases that seem substantially the same, this information is something we should take into account in our ethical theorizing.

Of course, we should also remember, first, that intuitions are not the only things that matter in reflective equilibrium and, second, that even *reflective* intuitions are defeasible (we could end up having to get rid of them). Using reflective equilibrium as our method for constructing normative theories, we do not end up with a simple bridge from is to ought, nor do we end up being able to infer normative claims from descriptive claims without a lot of reflection and theorizing about which intuitions are relevant, and how the intuitions fit together with putative principles, background theories and other considered judgments.

Because wide reflective equilibrium encompasses background theories, we can identify a second relationship between the descriptive and the normative. Normative theories make empirical assumptions, and the empirical facts are relevant to whether these assumptions are true or false. (The first point about intuitions is really just a special case of this second relationship.) We have seen many examples of this. From Chapter 3, recall that many moral theories hold that true moral motivation is other regarding. For Kantians, actions must be motivated by the sense of duty to count as morally worthy, and for virtue ethicists, ethical action is motivated by the emotional states and concerns that are constitutive of the virtues (such as compassion or friendliness). Now, if people are necessarily egoistic and it is psychologically impossible for us to have any motive that is not directed toward some good for ourselves, then these theories are (at least in this one respect) incorrect.[2] Of course, the science of egoism and altruism has not shown that it is impossible for us to be motivated by altruistic desires or passions, but the point here is that this science is relevant to normative theories.

A similar point was made in Chapter 7 on virtue. Virtue ethical theories assume that people can develop virtues. Insofar as virtues are states of our psychology, as Aristotle took them to be, scientific evidence about our psychology is going to be relevant to the assumption that we can develop virtues. As we saw, critics have charged that Aristotelian virtue ethics relies on a picture of virtues that is psychologically implausible because it depicts us as possessing highly stable dispositions to act well in any situation, no matter how much temptation to do otherwise. We also saw some ways in which virtue ethicists have clarified or modified their assumptions in response to this charge. Virtue ethics wasn't killed by the situationist critique, but the facts about what kind of traits we actually have are certainly relevant and will need to be taken into consideration as virtue ethics develops. If a theory doesn't apply to human beings unless they have a certain kind of psychological make-up, it's important to know whether human beings are actually made this way and that is a matter of ordinary empirical fact.

Finally, we have the example from Chapter 10 on well-being and the reasons to be moral. Various moral theories throughout history have assumed that there are self-interested reasons to be moral, and this is an assumption that is open to scientific investigation, once the terms are defined. Once we have answered the philosophical questions of what self-interest is, and what counts as acting morally, it remains to consider whether the one causes the other, and this is a matter of ordinary empirical fact. Testing these assumptions about the link between morality and self-interest will raise a number of other philosophical questions: What kind of reasons do we have to be moral that stem from well-being? Are these reasons overriding reasons? If not, are these the wrong kind of reasons? These are not questions that can be answered by science, but research from positive psychology in this case is certainly important for assessing the normative conclusions of theories that posit a relationship between self-interest and morality.

The third relationship between the descriptive and the normative has to do with empirical assumptions made by metaethical theories. Here the link between is and ought would be indirect: metaethical theories aren't prescriptive on their own, but they are often used to support normative theories. One example of how science is relevant to metaethics comes from discussions of moral realism. As we discussed in Chapter 2, philosophers such as Sharon Street have argued that the facts about evolution would give us reason to be skeptical about the truth of our moral judgments if our moral judgments were about mind-independent moral facts. Recall that Street put the argument in terms of a dilemma. The moral realist who thinks there are moral facts independent of all of our psychological states (our sentiments, desires, rational capacities and so on) is either putting forward an explanatory hypothesis about how our moral judgments came about, or he is not. If he is not, and so he thinks that moral facts are explanatorily inert, then it's not clear why we should think the moral judgments that we tend to make have any relationship to these facts and hence it is unclear what reason we have to think any of these judgments are true. If the facts don't cause anything to happen, then they couldn't cause our judgments to be correct. If, on the other hand, the moral realist is positing an explanation of our judgments in terms of moral facts, then his explanation is in competition with other explanations of our moral judgments. Street argues that there is a much simpler explanation for why we make the moral judgments we do, one that doesn't invoke special, mind-independent moral facts, namely, that cooperating and helping each other was adaptive and that's why we think it's good and right.

You'll also recall from Chapter 2 that this case against moral realism is not a case against moral facts. Facts can be understood differently from the way Street's realist opponent defines them. For instance, we could understand moral facts as facts about our sentimental responses (Prinz), facts about our desires (Railton), facts about what we value or care about (Street), facts about what constitutes our flourishing given our human nature (Kraut), facts about what we would agree to under certain conditions (Scanlon) or facts that are constructed through practical reasoning ending in reflective endorsement (Korsgaard). None of these theories about what moral facts are make morality *mind-independent* in the sense relevant to Street's dilemma. All of them could offer an intelligible, naturalistic explanation for how morality came to be what it is, and science wouldn't undermine the existence of moral facts understood in these ways.

The main example of the way in which empirical research is relevant to metaethics that we have considered is about Kantianism and the role of sentiment or desire in moral judgment and motivation. The sentimentalist theory of moral judgment assumes that there is an intimate connection between moral judgment and sentiment. Evidence for some connection comes from experiments that show that emotions influence our moral judgments in ways that would be surprising if there were no connection between judgment and sentiment. For example, feeling disgusted by our immediate surroundings (because of fart spray, say) makes us judge wrong-doers more harshly. Further, sentimentalism predicts that people with defective sentiments will also have defects in their capacity for moral judgment. We saw some evidence that this is indeed the case. Psychopaths have an emotional deficit, and they also have trouble making the right distinction between moral and conventional norms: they do not seem to understand the gravity of morality.

Notice, though, that the scientific evidence does not carry the day by itself. If we operationalize moral judgment in terms of the content (the specific facts that these judgments pick out, such as facts about harm) rather than in terms of other features of moral judgment (such as seriousness or authority independence), then psychopaths' capacities for judgment do not turn out to be so defective. If we start this way, we will probably conclude that while psychopaths know what is moral and what is immoral, they just don't care. In this way our philosophical assumptions about moral judgment influence how we interpret the empirical evidence. Which is a better starting point depends on the big picture and what we take the point of moral judgment to be. I think it makes more sense to think of the point of moral judgment in terms of its role in helping us live together than to think of it in terms of its role in picking out a particular set of facts. This is not so for judgments about the weather—here we should understand our judgments as responding to facts about rain, temperature and so on. But when it comes to morality, it seems to me correct that the defining feature is its practical role. This inclines me to take seriously the research on psychopaths who do not know how to live in community with others. The fact that they don't understand the practical importance of moral judgment is a profound defect. But these thoughts are preceded by some philosophical reflection on how it makes sense to think about the whole moral enterprise.

Psychological research about psychopaths and the role of sentiments puts pressure on the Kantian to qualify her claims. It does not refute the entire Kantian project, however. We have seen that the Kantian can clarify or modify the picture to preserve the basic insights in light of the research on the role of emotions in moral judgments. In particular, the Kantian can preserve the basic idea that correct moral judgments are justified by rational principles, but reject the idea that moral judgments are typically *caused* by reasoning. As long as we are, at our best and most rational, capable of investigating whether our moral judgments have a principled basis and capable of rejecting the ones that do not, the Kantian could be pretty happy. Greene's evidence about the emotional basis for deontological judgments in trolley cases (discussed in Chapter 11) adds some fuel to the fire, because it makes it seem that emotions are playing a differentially strong role in principled Kantian judgments as opposed to consequentialist judgments. But here again if the Kantian distances herself from claims about the causes of moral judgment and insists that her focus is on justification, she can argue that which moral judgments are justified by rational principles (the real question) is independent of what parts of the brain are activated when "characteristically deontological" judgments are made. The Kantian may even want to reject some "characteristically deontological" judgments on the basis of Greene's research. A Kantian who was sympathetic to Greene's project might say that some of his findings shed light on what courses of action are really justified by the Categorical Imperative by demonstrating that some previous conclusions were the result of irrational, emotional bias rather than objective application of a principle.

Kantians can defend themselves against attacks based on research about the causes of moral judgments, but there is another line of attack, which we considered briefly in Chapter 6 in our discussion of the Kantian challenge to sophisticated sentimentalism. The challenge, in particular as it is formulated by Korsgaard, is that given the kind of reflective creature a human being is, we cannot make do with sentiments when we are looking for reasons: sentiments (or desires, for that matter) do not justify. In other words, reflective creatures like us need to find something at the bottom of the pile of reasons that puts an end to our questions, something like a purely rational principle such as the Categorical Imperative. This argument assumes something about our psychology, namely, that we are reflective creatures of a particular kind: ones whose conviction that we have reasons to do anything at all rests fundamentally on the idea that there are universal principles to support these reasons. But what if instead of being reflective creatures of this kind, the idea that there are no universal principles that underwrite our reasons leaves all of our convictions about having reasons intact? What if we are perfectly capable of acknowledging that if it weren't for our having the desires or the sentiments we have, nothing would seem either moral or immoral, without this thought undermining our moral convictions? This would be a problem for the Kantian argument under consideration. The fact that we don't need rational principles (if it is a fact) would deflate the argument that there must be such principles if there are to be any reasons at all. And this would be a case in which the facts about our psychology are relevant to the assumptions made by a rationalist normative theory.

Things in this case are quite tricky, and I can imagine the Kantian denying that the empirical facts are relevant here. What is relevant, she might say, is what we are like insofar as we are rational and that is not a psychological fact about us. This is a fair point, and the Kantian argument is certainly in part conceptual: the relevant premise is that a consideration cannot count as a *reason* unless it would be sanctioned by a rational law— otherwise it is always sensible to ask whether it really is a reason to do something or not. For example, consider Korsgaard's (1996: 86) case of the lawyer who is trying to decide whether to honor the public will of her deceased client, which gives all his money to medical research, or the most recent valid will (that only she knows about), which gives all his money to someone who will blow it on beer. Korsgaard's point is that when the lawyer considers her sentiments, it always makes sense for her to ask whether they present good reasons. She would disapprove of herself if she destroyed the last (albeit stupid) will of her client. But she would also be pleased if the money went to a good cause. Both courses of action are sanctioned by sentiment. What gives us *reason* to take one course of action rather than the other, on this view, is that one course of action is principled.

True, the Kantian argument is an argument about what a reason must be. But if we cannot recognize ourselves (even our best, most rational selves) in the description of rational agents in this argument, then we don't have any reason to care about reasons as Kantians see them. If we are not at all like the reflective creatures Korsgaard and Kant discuss (creatures who seek principled reasons for action that can put an end to our questioning), then the view of reasons they are discussing is not relevant to us. This by itself would not prove that the Kantian conception of a reason is wrong, exactly, but it would make us question what the point of it is. Or, more radically, we could argue that since we are sure we do things for reasons, and we're sure we're not Kantian agents, there must be something wrong in the Kantian argument; that is, we could decide that achieving reflective equilibrium requires rejecting the Kantian idea about what a reason must be.

For what it's worth, I think we are not so much like the reflective agents portrayed by Kant and Korsgaard. Like Hume, I think we can acknowledge that our reasons would not be reasons for us were it not for what we care about without losing our confidence that these are still good reasons. This is not to say that whatever we care about is the right thing to care about. Figuring out exactly what makes the difference between right and wrong, or between a good reason and a bad reason, when all reasons are ultimately explained by the fact that we have certain sentiments or desires, is one of the most interesting challenges for the Humean. This is a challenge, but not a hopeless task; we have explored the sophisticated sentimentalist answer to the challenge in Chapter 6 and there are other possibilities. With a good answer to this challenge in hand, I think that we do not need more, either psychologically or philosophically. Of course, even if we found that we could do without Kantian rational principles, this would not necessarily impugn the normative recommendations inspired by Kant. The idea that we should treat each other as fundamentally valuable beings who are deserving of respect may be worth keeping whatever metaethics you accept.

We see that when it comes to metaethics, the relationship between philosophical questions and scientific research is complex. Metaethical questions are questions about our moral practice and the normative theories that are part of it—what moral judgments and theories are about, how these judgments and theories may be justified, and so on. The concepts involved in these questions (e.g., REASON, FACT, JUSTIFICATION) are difficult on their own and intertwined in ways that make it even more difficult to know exactly how they should be understood. Answering metaethical questions requires paying attention to science and paying attention to conceptual subtleties until we reach a point at which our concepts help us make the best sense of all the information we have.

I suspect none of the three relationships between the descriptive and the normative that I've described so far is what people typically have in mind when they talk about deriving ought from is. More likely, what people have in mind is a fourth relationship according to which non-normative facts entail normative conclusions about what's morally right and wrong and hence what we ought to do. Here's a simple example of how this might go:

1. In other cultures, people think slavery is morally permissible.
2. Therefore, slavery isn't always wrong; whether it is right or wrong depends on your culture.

Few students of philosophy would put this argument forward seriously, because it is such an obvious example of a bad argument. Without additional premises, nothing follows about what morality is from the fact that people have different beliefs about it. To see this, consider a structurally similar argument: In other cultures, people think the sun revolves around the earth. Therefore, the earth doesn't always revolve around the sun; whether the earth revolves around the sun or vice versa depends on your culture. This isn't right. Different cultures have indeed had different beliefs about planetary motion, but some of their beliefs were just wrong.

This bad argument could be improved by adding a premise or two explaining the connection between the moral code of a culture and what is actually right or wrong. For instance, if we added the premise that culture is the only basis there could possibly be for a moral code, we would have a better argument. It still might not be a sound argument, since we can certainly question whether this new premise is true, but it would be better. To make the argument sound, what we would need to do is to provide a conclusive argument for a *theory* of morality according to which morality is relative to culture. And this, I suggest, is what any argument that attempts to draw normative conclusions from ordinary facts needs to do: it needs to rely on a theory that tells us how these two things are related. Arguments that bridge the is/ought gap by inferring prescriptive conclusions from descriptive facts, then, need to rely on a theory that connects the normative realm to the realm of scientific fact.

Reducing Ought to Is

Looking around at the options, someone who wants to bridge the is/ought gap should be pretty keen on naturalistic, reductive metaethical theories. Such theories "reduce" moral properties to natural properties in the sense that they say that moral properties (such as rightness, wrongness, goodness, badness and so on) can be explained entirely in terms of certain natural properties (such as the satisfaction of desires, pleasure, or being approved of by a person's moral sentiments). With a theory like this in the background, it's easy to see how we might get normative conclusions from descriptive premises. If moral wrongness, for example, is entirely reducible to the production of the greatest happiness for the greatest number, then ordinary facts about what produces happiness will determine what is the right thing to do.

Moreover, theories that reduce normative properties to natural properties have a lot going for them. They locate ethics in the natural world in an ontologically parsimonious way. In other words, they explain how there can be true moral judgments about what we ought to do using just the ordinary stuff that we can observe with our five senses, without positing any supernatural beings or strange substances beyond the grasp of science. There are many different ways of reducing ethical facts to natural facts, far too many to explore them in detail here. Instead, let's consider two basic compelling approaches. According to one, we reduce ethics to facts about human nature. According to the other, we reduce ethics to facts about our desires. In the following discussion of these two basic views, both will be discussed in the most general terms; different thinkers fill out the details in different ways, but these details don't matter to the basic point of this chapter.

What I'll call the *Human Nature Approach* says that there are facts about what is good, bad, right or wrong, and that these facts are facts about our nature as human beings. Typically, the Human Nature Approach holds that, in virtue of being human, there is a particular way that it is good for us to be. (We have seen this theory before in Chapter 7 and again in Chapter 10.) Just as a good oak tree grows toward the sun and produces acorns, a good human being socializes with others and develops his or her human capacities. Human flourishing, in this view, is determined by our nature, and ethical recommendations for how we should live derive from what it is for us to flourish. Notice that for this approach to be genuinely reductive, human flourishing has to be a matter of ordinary natural fact; the idea of flourishing cannot itself be an ethical notion that is infused with value judgments, because then the theory would not reduce ethical facts to natural facts. For instance, this approach would be genuinely reductive if human flourishing were a biological notion (as it is for oak trees).

There is a big problem with the Human Nature Approach.[3] It is very difficult to come up with a definition of human flourishing that is truly non-normative—that does not invoke any value judgments to explain it—and is still a compelling definition of what it is to live a good human life. If you think about it, you can see why this is a problem: if you look at human history and psychology in purely descriptive terms, you'll find quite a bit of ugliness. We are creatures who rape, torture, enslave and kill each other. We are creatures who manipulate and lie to get what we want. We are creatures who sacrifice our loved ones to save our own skins. Of course, we are also creatures who are capable of great self-sacrifice, kindness and generosity. But what is our *nature*? You can't rule out the ugly stuff just because it's ugly—the cold truth might just be that our nature is not a very pretty thing.

If the scientific picture of human nature contains a good deal of ugliness, then it is very unclear why conclusions about what we ought to do follow from our nature, described in purely scientific terms. What if we were to find out with certainty that people are naturally prejudiced against outsiders (a plausible claim already)? Would this mean that we ought to indulge our prejudices? For example, would this information help a CEO think about what hiring practices to adopt in his or her company? One thing it might do is to make the CEO aware of how difficult prejudice can be to get rid of, but the fact that we are naturally inclined to prejudice wouldn't make prejudice okay. Even worse for the Human Nature Approach, if the scientific picture of human nature contains conflicting elements, or if it's just very thin, it's not clear how the science of human nature could answer our pressing moral questions.[4]

So much for the Human Nature Approach to reduction. This is not to say that basing ethics on human flourishing is a bad idea; rather, the point is that basing ethics on the non-evaluative, scientific facts about human nature is not promising. Indeed, many prominent Aristotelians do not think that flourishing is a purely scientific notion (Hursthouse 1999; Kraut 2009; Nussbaum 1995; Nussbaum 2001). Instead, they think that the right conception of flourishing—the one moral philosophers should use as a foundation for their theories—is infused with values. We can't describe what it is to flourish in purely value-neutral terms. If this is the approach to ethics, we avoid the problems discussed above, but we no longer have a reduction and we no longer have an example of how to derive an ought from an is.[5]

The second reductive approach reduces facts about ethics to facts about our desires. This is a more promising metaethical theory. We have already seen (in Chapter 4) one reason for thinking it's a good approach, namely, that according to one very attractive theory about practical reasons (including moral reasons), desires are what explain why we have them. It sure seems obvious that desires sometimes give us reasons to do things. I go to the gym because I want to get some exercise; Jack goes to a bar because he wants a drink; Jill calls Jack because she wants to talk to him; and so on. If Jill didn't want to talk to Jack, she would have no reason to call. If Jack didn't want a drink, he'd have no reason to go to the bar, and so on. That desires seem so intuitively connected to reasons makes a lot of people think desires are essential to practical reasons, or, in other words, that there would be no reasons without desires. Furthermore, if we could explain *all* reasons by appeal to desires, we would have a simple, naturalistic, unified explanation for normativity in general. Moreover, it's not crazy to think that even moral reasons can be explained by desires. We do have plenty of "pro-moral" desires, after all, as we saw in Chapter 10.

A metaethical theory that explains reasons in terms of desires could reduce moral facts to facts about our desires.[6] This kind of theory is promising enough that it's worth considering whether it would allow us to derive an ought from an is. For the remainder of this section, we'll assume that the Desire Approach to reduction is correct, and we'll see how far it can take us in bridging the is/ought gap.

In one sense, in theory, it certainly does bridge the gap. To figure out what we ought to do, we just have to know the facts about our desires, and these are facts that can be investigated scientifically. Perhaps eventually scientists will be able to tell us exactly what we want most at a particular moment in time, and then we would know what we have reason to do without having to think about it!

There are certainly cases in which knowing what you want settles what to do fairly quickly. If you're at a restaurant and you know you want the ravioli, you have a reason to order the ravioli from the waiter. There are cases like this in ethics too: if you know you want to be an honest person, then you know you have a reason not to lie on your resume to get a job (again, we are assuming the Desire Approach is correct here). But there are many other cases—the kinds of cases that preoccupy moral philosophers and that drive ordinary people to ethical reflection—where things are not so obvious. In these kinds of cases, when we think about what we desire, there are lots of reasons for doubt. You might wonder whether what you think you want is what you want most or whether you have other stronger desires that are hidden from you for some reason. You might wonder whether what you want conflicts with your other desires. You might wonder whether getting what you want will really be satisfying, or whether getting what you want will get you what you really, *ultimately* want. You might wonder whether you only want what you want because you're ignorant of some important facts. You might wonder if what you want is what you will want in the long term and whether getting what you want now will frustrate some other, longer term desires. Just knowing what you want now doesn't solve the problem of what to do without answering many other questions.

For example, imagine that you have a friend who is trying to talk you into going vegetarian for moral reasons. Your friend gets you to watch some films about the treatment of animals on factory farms, and she tries to convince you that it's unethical for you to participate in this cruel institution. What would we find if we looked into your head and discovered your desires? If you're like most people, we would find a desire to be a morally decent person, a desire not to appear unethical to your friend, a desire to make your friend happy, a desire to eat bacon, a desire to never have to give up eating bacon and so on. These desires can't all be satisfied at once, so to figure out what you have most reason to do, according to the desire theory, we have to dig a little deeper.

Philosophers who propose desire theories recognize this problem. They recognize that desires can conflict with each other so that they can't all be satisfied at the same time and that desires have different strengths. To solve this problem, most desire theorists say that we should focus on intrinsic or ultimate desires—desires we have for things for their own sakes, rather than as a means to something else. We should also pay attention to the fact that different desires have different weights or degrees of importance depending on their position in the system of desires that we have. If we can derive what we have reason to do from what we desire, we'll have to obey these constraints.

If a scientist could tell us our ultimate desires prioritized by strength, then would we know how to act? If you knew that you had a very strong ultimate desire to help others, would you know what to do? Now we see there is another problem: knowing what our ultimate desires are for does not automatically tell us how to satisfy them. There are probably not that many things that people want intrinsically—pleasure, health, freedom from pain, contentment for oneself and one's loved ones, relationships with other people, self-respect and the respect of others, security, and perhaps a few other basics. Most other things are wanted as a means to these. For example, few people want money for its own sake, but it's very desirable as a means to buying things that will be fun, healthy or nice for someone you love. You can't discern the best means to attaining what you intrinsically desire from the fact that you have an intrinsic desire. What counts as the best means will be constrained by other intrinsic desires you have, your personality, the possibilities open to you and what you predict about how all of this might change. For example, there are many ways to satisfy a strong intrinsic desire to help others. Should you help lots of others, including strangers? Should you focus on your family and friends? Should you help by making large donations to international charities or by doing something more personal like giving out food at a local soup kitchen? Should you help animals as well as people? The intrinsic desire to help isn't enough to guide us here.

For science to answer our moral question, assuming something like a desire theory of reasons in the background, not only do we need to know what our ultimate (as opposed to instrumental) desires are and how strong these desires are relative to each other, we also need to know what particular course of action (out of all the possibilities) will actually satisfy the desire. Could we discover this purely scientifically, without any ethical reflection or deliberation about our desires? Perhaps it is possible in principle, though it's starting to seem extremely unlikely. One problem is that some of our desires are rather vague or unspecific, so that it isn't actually clear what counts as satisfying them. This might be true of the desire to help others, for example. Still, maybe some kind of computer-assisted technology could be developed to discern our ultimate desires and calculate which courses of action have the best probability of satisfying these desires. Let's run with this thought experiment for a moment: Imagine the invention of a small machine we can wear on our wrists—call it "the Oracle"—that can detect exactly what we want most at any moment (without the need for annoying scientists hovering around) and can give us a range of actions that are most likely to satisfy these desires, given various constraints. If you had the Oracle, would you do whatever it told you to do?

The Oracle is supposed to tell us what we have most reason to do, and to know what you have most reason to do is to know *what to do*. In other words, to know what you have reason to do is to have settled on a course of action, to have answered the practical question: What should I do? If the Oracle really did tell us what we have most reason to do, wouldn't it resolve all of our indecision and uncertainty so that we could get busy and do something? The trouble is that knowing what to do, coming to a decision about how you will act, requires reaching some resolution or *conviction*. Would the Oracle give us the conviction we need to act along with its advice? I don't think it would, which is why I would not necessarily do what the Oracle tells me to do.

This is because simply knowing the facts about your intrinsic desires and how to satisfy them will not necessarily produce the kind of justification that will give you the confidence you need to go ahead and do something when you're unsure about what to do. After all, in order to have sufficient confidence in the Oracle's recommendations to act on them, you'd need to have confidence in the Oracle—and where would this confidence come from? You would need to have some grasp of what reasons you have to do this or that in order to have reasons to trust the Oracle in the first place. You could get to the point of doing what the Oracle tells you to do, but this would only happen slowly by way of making the judgment that the Oracle got it right. And this process requires reflection on reasons and values, and even then you'd probably need to check every once in a while to make sure the Oracle is still working as before. To have reasons for action that you can have some confidence in, you'll need to engage in ethical reflection.

To illustrate the point, think again of the friend who is trying to talk you into being a vegetarian. What if the Oracle tells you to stop eating hamburgers because of your intrinsic desire to be kind to animals? For most Americans, this would be a large sacrifice at least in the short term (and if it isn't for you, then think of another example). Wouldn't you want to know how the Oracle arrived at this result? Wouldn't you want to know exactly what the reasons are and what other options there might be? To do something difficult (at least in the short term), you typically need a justification that you can articulate and understand. You need something to say to yourself about why you're forgoing the tasty piece of meat. Your justification can certainly appeal to your desires at some point (and if desires are necessary for explaining reasons, it must do so); the point is that you need to weave the facts about your desires together with other relevant facts (such as the facts about animals suffering, or factory farming) into an account that makes sense of what you do. The issue here is that even if ethics can be reduced to desire metaphysically, there is an epistemological gap between knowing the facts about our desires and knowing what to do.

We have been focused on the basic moral problem of figuring out what to do. In this context, even if reductivism is true, oughts don't follow very easily from is-es, and indeed there is a sense in which the facts discovered by science will never be enough. While there might be a sense in which reduction allows us to derive an ought from an is, it's not the sense that will supplant ethical deliberation and reflection on what we have reason to do (at least not in cases where we are genuinely puzzled). In other words, the method of scientific investigation will not replace the methods used by moral philosophers (and ethical people). This conclusion certainly does not mean that science is irrelevant to moral theory. We have seen all sorts of ways in which the discoveries of science are relevant and important to broadly philosophical thinking about moral questions. But it does mean that ethics is very unlikely to become a pure science.

It is worth noting that there is another context to consider, namely, the political context. Here the moral challenge is deciding what to do *together* or deciding what to do in a way that is acceptable to various stakeholders who have different moral beliefs and values. When we look for political solutions to moral problems (as we do when we debate abortion legislation, capital punishment or animal welfare policy), we are sometimes seeking the morally correct answer, but often we seek a compromise, a workable solution that will allow us to live in harmony together even though we don't all agree about morality. Social science research that allows us to understand each other better and to discover the ways in which different people are willing to compromise could be very helpful to this political enterprise. In using the facts discovered by social science to inform our political deliberations, however, we would not be deriving an ought from an is. We would be deriving an is—"this is the best compromise available to this group of people"—from other is-es about what people are like.

Summary

- In this book we have seen four different relationships between ought and is, between the descriptive and the normative.
- First, facts about people's intuitions are relevant to reflective equilibrium justification of a normative theory that speaks to what such people are interested in (e.g., free will and intuitions about compatibilism; intuitions about happiness and the experience machine).

- Second, scientific facts are relevant to the empirical assumptions made by normative theories (e.g., altruism, virtue, Kantian reflectivism, self-interested reasons to be moral).
- Third, scientific facts are relevant to the empirical assumptions made by metaethical theories (e.g., evolution and moral realism; moral judgment sentimentalism vs. rationalism), which may ultimately have implications for normative theory.
- Fourth, if a reductive metaethical theory is true, then perhaps normative conclusions could be inferred directly from the facts.
- Even if it is true that ethical facts reduce to natural facts (such as facts about our desires), this does not make for easy derivations from is to ought, and ethical reflection will not be replaced by scientific investigation.

Study Questions

1. Can science determine what is human nature? Insofar as it can, what can we conclude about ethics from the study of human nature?
2. What if a brilliant scientist told you that she had developed a program that would tell you what you would think is the morally right way to live your life (what kind of job to take, how much money to donate to charity, and so on) if you were perfectly informed about all the relevant facts. Would you use the program to decide what to do? Would you follow it unthinkingly (assuming you could trust that the program did what it claimed)?
3. Think of a moral dilemma or serious ethical problem you have confronted in your life. What information would have been most useful to help you solve it? Was a lack of correct information part of what made it difficult to solve this problem? If not, what did make it hard to solve?
4. In *The Moral Landscape: How Science Can Determine Human Values*, Sam Harris (2011) argues for a science of morality that takes human well-being to be the foundation for ethics. Does taking human happiness or well-being to be the foundation for ethics make ethics into a science?

Notes

1. This would represent a failure to understand the example, because the experience machine by hypothesis guarantees more pleasure overall. Therefore, if it's true that you need to have some pain in order to have pleasure, the machine would make sure that you have just enough pain so that you can get the most pleasure possible.

2. Or they could be conceptually correct, but completely inapplicable to human beings. This is a possibility some philosophers (such as Kant) acknowledge. Of course, a theory that is conceptually correct but inapplicable to human beings is not really a prescriptive ethical theory anymore.

3. Not everyone agrees that the problem is so big: there are philosophers who favor this approach and who think this problem can be solved. See Foot (2001) and Bloomfield (2014).

4. Jesse Prinz (2012) argues that most of what we are is the result of nurture, not nature. If we don't really even have a nature, ethics can't be reduced to it.

5. For an excellent discussion of the different ways in which human nature might play a role in normative theory that is critical of Nussbaum's approach, see Louise Antony's "Natures and Norms" (2000).

6. Recall from Chapter 4 that the best way to understand desire theories of reasons is that a person's desires *explain* why some consideration counts as a reason for her. To be precise, the theory does not identify reasons with desires; rather, it reduces the explanation of normative reasons to explanations in terms of natural facts, some of which are facts about desires.

Further Readings

Antony, L. M. 2000. "Natures and Norms." *Ethics* 111 (1): 8–36.

Appiah, K. A. 2008. *Experiments in Ethics*. Harvard University Press.

Nussbaum, M. C. 1995. "Aristotle on Human Nature and the Foundations of Ethics." In *World, Mind, and Ethics: Essays on the Ethical Philosophy of Bernard Williams*, J. E. J. Althan and R. Harrison (eds), 86–131. Cambridge University Press.

Prinz, J. J. 2012. *Beyond Human Nature: How Culture and Experience Shape Our Lives*. Penguin.

Schroeder, M. A. 2007. *Slaves of the Passions*. Oxford University Press.

13   Final Thoughts

Maybe you can't derive an ought from an is, but it would be a huge mistake to think that what is—particularly what is true about our psychology—doesn't matter for ethics. I want to conclude with two of the most important things I think we learn from psychological research in moral psychology. These are not the only important lessons from empirical research in psychology, to be sure, but they are two that I think are worth highlighting because they matter to our everyday lives.

First, we are emotional creatures and our emotions are important to ethics in a way philosophers have sometimes failed to notice. I believe psychology is showing us that that David Hume was right at least about one thing: without emotions, we would not have morality at all. We would not care about each other, we would not value anything, and we would not worry about making good, defensible decisions about what to do. If this is true about us, there are some implications for metaethics—for what moral judgments are and whether they are inherently motivating (although, as we've discussed, these implications have sometimes been exaggerated). There are also implications for what is good for us. There has been a tendency in the history of philosophy and religion to think of the emotional self as a beast in need of taming. Life goes best for us when our reason rules the beast and brings it into line. But if emotions are what allow us to have values in the first place, then emotions are not necessarily unruly beasts; they are also sources of information about ourselves and the world. Acknowledging this—elevating the emotions to "partner" status—should make us think differently about what a good human life is. Perhaps the aim should not be to control our emotions, but to live in harmony with them. Living in harmony with our emotional selves does not mean giving up on reflection and thinking, but it does mean that when we are reflecting and thinking, we should listen to what our hearts have to tell us. Not everything that comes from the heart is worth heeding, but then not everything that comes from the head is worth heeding either.

Second, we have less rational control than we thought we have. I believe psychology is showing us that we are often caused to do things by situational factors that bypass our rational capacities. I do not think that this research shows that there are no virtues, because I think there are ways of understanding virtue that are compatible with these facts. Nor do I think the research shows that we are never morally responsible, because I believe that we have enough of a certain kind of control to make sense of attributions of responsibility. We can, for example, make long-term plans and adopt strategies for coping with momentary temptations that will cause us to do things that go against our ultimate desires or our better judgment. But I do think that this fact about us should make us kinder to each other and to ourselves. We are often harsh judges: we get angry at people for slighting us, down on ourselves for slipping up on diets or exercise plans, unforgiving toward those who have done something wrong, deeply ashamed of our own faults. The picture behind all this negative emotion seems to be that there is a pure agent inside each of us who could be perfect if only he or she would exert a little willpower! But this isn't how we are. Insofar as psychology is helping us to see that this isn't how we are, it provides an important lesson, namely, that we should ease up on all the harshness.

At the same time, there is a certain kind of self-criticism that is highly appropriate, given what we know about our psychology. If we are not always under perfect rational control, then some of what we think, want and do is probably not terribly well justified. We would also do well to recognize that we aren't always right about everything. Some of the things we were raised to believe about what's morally right and wrong have nothing else going for them than the fact that we were raised that way. Having a little humility about our own moral perspectives is also a good idea.

Since I'm not a psychologist, it's not quite my place to say what lessons psychologists should derive from moral philosophy. But what I would hope they take away (if any are reading this book) is that throughout human history we have had ethical questions that are not questions about our psychology. We have wanted to know what is worth doing and why, what kinds of people are admirable, and what motivations for acting are good or praiseworthy. These questions can't be answered empirically, though empirical evidence of the right kind is relevant to answer them all.

As research in moral psychology develops, there will be new lessons and new information to absorb. My hope is that, as the field develops, collaboration between psychologists and philosophers will increase and that this will mean that new discoveries and ideas will give us an even better understanding of why we are good when we are good, bad when we are bad, and what it means to make these judgments.

Study Questions

1. Can you think of an example (from your own life, or from a film or novel) in which someone would have been better off listening to their emotions rather than following their reasoning? And an example where it went the other way?
2. Is there anything you have learned about human psychology that has changed how you think about your life (for example, the meaning of your life, how you ought to live your life, or how you ought to treat others)?
3. What do you think is the most important thing psychology has to teach moral philosophers?
4. What do psychologists have to learn from moral philosophy?

Glossary of Theories and Technical Terms

Categorical Reasons: Reasons that apply to us independently of our desires. Moral reasons are often taken to be categorical. Universal reasons, by contrast, are reasons that apply to everyone; they may or may not be contingent on our desires.

Causal Determinism: The thesis that every event is necessitated by antecedent events and conditions together with the laws of nature. Or, to put it another way, the facts of the past, in conjunction with the laws of nature, entail every fact about the future.

Compatibilism and Incompatibilism:
- Compatibilism—if determinism is true, we could have free will.
- Incompatibilism—if determinism is true, we do not have free will.
- Hard incompatibilism—whether or not determinism is true, we do not have free will.
- Libertarianism—determinism is false and we do have free will (a form of incompatibilism).

Construct Validity: In psychology, a measurement tool (such as a survey or a test) has construct validity when it measures what it is supposed to measure (the real, ultimate aim of investigation).

Dual Process Theory: The theory that there are two different cognitive systems that we use for many purposes, such as making a moral judgment: System 1 is fast, automatic and nonconscious; System 2 is slow, controlled and conscious.

Error Theory: In metaethics, the view that all moral judgments are in error (false) because they refer to objective moral properties that do not actually exist.

Eudaimonism: According to Aristotelian eudaimonism, a good life for a person is one in which she fulfills her *human* nature (her nature as a member of the human species). Individualist eudaimonism says that a good life is one in which a person fulfills her individual nature.

Hedonism: Hedonism about well-being is the view that well-being consists in pleasure and the absence of pain.

Humean Theory of Motivation: The theory that desires are necessary for motivating actions; beliefs never motivate by themselves.

Intentional Content: Roughly, "aboutness": a mental state has intentional content if it is directed onto something in the world. Beliefs, desires and emotions have intentional content. Intentional content has nothing to do with a person's intentions.

Internalisms and Externalisms:
- Moral Judgment Internalism—the view that, in making a moral judgment, one is thereby motivated, to some degree, to act on it.

- Moral Judgment Externalism—the view that in making a moral judgment one is not thereby motivated.
- Reasons Existence Internalism (RI)—the view that normative reasons are necessarily motivating, at least under certain conditions.
- Reasons Existence Externalism—the view that normative reasons are not necessarily motivating.

Moral and Conventional Norms: Moral norms are thought to be more serious and have wider applicability than conventional norms. Conventional norms are thought to be contingent on an authority (such as a teacher or the law), and they receive a different kind of justification from moral norms, which are often justified in terms of harm or fairness.

Moral Intuition: A moral judgment that appears to be fairly obvious to you without argument or inference.

Motivating Reasons and Normative Reasons: Motivating reasons explain actions; normative reasons are considerations that count in favor of (and justify) actions.

Practical Reasons and Theoretical Reasons: Practical reasons are reasons for action; theoretical reasons are reasons for belief.

Psychological Egoism: The theory that all voluntary action is selfish or produced by self-interested desires.

Rationalism: Moral Rationalism (in the context of this book) is the view that the truth of a moral judgment is determined by rational principles. Moral judgments are justified and give us normative reasons for action insofar as they conform to these principles.

Reflective Equilibrium: The predominant method for constructing and defending ethical theories, which proceeds by bringing into a coherent whole considered judgments (or intuitions) about cases, putative principles and background theories.

Sentimentalism: The view that moral judgments are expressions of, or reports about, our sentiments. Sentimentalists reject the idea (held by rationalists) that moral judgments are justified by rational principles; they require a different explanation of the fact that we do justify our moral judgments by appeal to reasons. Sophisticated sentimentalists aim to provide this explanation.

Bibliography

Aharoni, E., W. Sinnott-Armstrong and K. A. Kiehl. 2012. "Can Psychopathic Offenders Discern Moral Wrongs? A New Look at the Moral/conventional Distinction." *Journal of Abnormal Psychology* 121 (2): 484–497.

Altham, J. E. J. 1986. "The Legacy of Emotivism." In *Fact, Science and Morality: Essays on A. J. Ayer's Language, Truth and Logic,* G. Macdonald and C. Wright (eds), 275–288. Blackwell.

Anderson, E. 1995. *Value in Ethics and Economics.* Harvard University Press.

Anscombe, G. E. M. 1957. *Intention.* Harvard University Press.

———. 1958. "Modern Moral Philosophy." *Philosophy* 33 (124): 1–19.

Antony, L. M. 2000. "Natures and Norms." *Ethics* 111 (1): 8–36.

Appiah, K. A. 2008. *Experiments in Ethics.* Harvard University Press.

Aristotle, 1985. *Nicomachean Ethics,* T. Irwin (trans). Hackett Publishing Company.

Arpaly, N. 2000. "Hamlet and the Utilitarians." *Philosophical Studies* 99 (1): 45–57.

———. 2002. "Moral Worth." *The Journal of Philosophy.* 99 (5): 223–245.

———. 2003. *Unprincipled Virtue: An Inquiry into Moral Agency.* Oxford University Press.

Arpaly, N., and T. Schroeder. 1999. "Praise, Blame and the Whole Self." *Philosophical Studies* 93 (2): 161–188.

Arpaly, N., and T. Schroeder. 2014. *In Praise of Desire.* Oxford University Press.

Austen, J. 2000. *Emma.* 3rd Edition. W. W. Norton & Company.

Baron, M. 1999. *Kantian Ethics Almost without Apology.* Cornell University Press.

Batson, C. D. 1991. *The Altruism Question: Toward a Social-Psychological Answer.* Lawrence Erlbaum.

Batson, C. D., B. D. Duncan, P. Ackerman, T. Buckley and K. Birch. 1981. "Is Empathic Emotion a Source of Altruistic Motivation?" *Journal of Personality and Social Psychology* 40 (2): 290–302.

Baumeister, R. F., and M. R. Leary. 1995. "The Need to Belong: Desire for Interpersonal Attachments as a Fundamental Human Motivation." *Psychological Bulletin* 117 (3): 497–529.

Berker, S. 2009. "The Normative Insignificance of Neuroscience." *Philosophy & Public Affairs* 37 (4): 293–329.

Berridge, K. C. 2003. "Pleasures of the Brain." *Brain and Cognition* 52 (1): 106–128.

Besser-Jones, L. 2008. "Personal Integrity, Morality and Psychological Well-Being: Justifying the Demands of Morality." *The Journal of Moral Philosophy* 5: 361–383.

———. 2012. "The Role of Practical Reason in an Empirically Informed Moral Theory." *Ethical Theory and Moral Practice* 15 (2): 203–220.

Bjorklund, F., J. Haidt and S. Murphy. 2000. "Moral Dumbfounding: When Intuition Finds No Reason." Unpublished manuscript, University of Virginia.

Blackburn, S. 1984. *Spreading the Word: Groundings in the Philosophy of Language*. Clarendon Press.

_____. 1998. *Ruling Passions: A Theory of Practical Reasoning*. Clarendon Press.

Blair, R. J. R. 1995. "A Cognitive Developmental Approach to Morality: Investigating the Psychopath." *Cognition* 57 (1): 1–29.

Bloomfield, P. 2014. *The Virtues of Happiness: A Theory of the Good Life*. Oxford University Press.

Churchland, P. S. 2011. *Braintrust: What Neuroscience Tells Us about Morality*. Princeton University Press.

Dancy, J. 2000. *Practical Reality*. Oxford University Press.

Daniels, N. 1979. "Wide Reflective Equilibrium and Theory Acceptance in Ethics." *The Journal of Philosophy* 76 (5): 256–282.

_____. 2008. "Reflective Equilibrium." *Stanford Encyclopedia of Philosophy*. www.illc.uva.nl/~seop/archives/fall2008/entries/reflective-equilibrium/.

Darley, J. M., and C. D. Batson. 1973. "'From Jerusalem to Jericho': A Study of Situational and Dispositional Variables in Helping Behavior." *Journal of Personality and Social Psychology* 27 (1): 100–108.

D'Arms, J., and D. Jacobson. 2000. "Sentiment and Value." *Ethics* 110 (4): 722–748.

Deci, E. L., and R. M. Ryan. 2004. *Handbook of Self-Determination Research*. University of Rochester Press.

De Dreu, C. K. W. 2012. "Oxytocin Modulates Cooperation within and Competition between Groups: An Integrative Review and Research Agenda." *Hormones and Behavior* 61 (3): 419–428.

De Dreu, C. K. W., L. L. Greer, M. J. J. Handgraaf, S. Shalvi, G. A. Van Kleef, M. Baas, F. S. Ten Velden, E. Van Dijk and S. W. W. Feith. 2010. "The Neuropeptide Oxytocin Regulates Parochial Altruism in Intergroup Conflict among Humans." *Science* 328 (5984): 1408–1411.

Dennett, D. C. 1984. *Elbow Room: The Varieties of Free Will Worth Wanting*. MIT Press.

_____. 2004. *Freedom Evolves*. Penguin.

Doris, J. M. 1998. "Persons, Situations, and Virtue Ethics." *Nous* 32 (4): 504–530.

_____. 2002. *Lack of Character: Personality and Moral Behavior*. Cambridge University Press.

_____. 2009. "Skepticism About Persons." *Philosophical Issues* 19: 57–91.

Driver, J. 2001. *Uneasy Virtue*. Cambridge University Press.

Dunn, E. W., L. B. Aknin and M. I. Norton. 2008. "Spending Money on Others Promotes Happiness." *Science* 319 (5870): 1687–1688.

Edmonds, G. W., J. J. Jackson, J. V. Fayard and B. W. Roberts. 2008. "Is Character Fate, or Is There Hope to Change My Personality Yet?" *Social and Personality Psychology Compass* 2 (1): 399–413.

Eisenberg, N. 2000. "Emotion, Regulation, and Moral Development." *Annual Review of Psychology* 51 (1): 665–697.

Ekman, P., and W. V. Friesen. 1971. "Constants across Cultures in the Face and Emotion." *Journal of Personality and Social Psychology* 17 (2): 124–129.

Feinberg, J. 2004. "Psychological Egoism." In *Reason and Responsibility*, R. Shafter-Landau and J. Feinberg (eds), 476–488. Wadsworth.

Feldman, F. 2004. *Pleasure and the Good Life: Concerning the Nature, Varieties and Plausibility of Hedonism*. Oxford University Press.

Finlay, S., and M. Schroeder. 2008. "Reasons for Action: Internal vs. External." In *The Stanford Encyclopedia of Philosophy*, E. N. Zalta (ed). http://plato.stanford.edu/archives/fall2008/entries/reasons-internal-external/.

Fischer, J.M. 2007. "Compatibilism." In *Four Views on Free Will,* J.M. Fischer, R. Kane, D. Pereboom and M. Vargas (eds), 44–84. Blackwell.

Fischer, J.M., R. Kane, D. Pereboom and M. Vargas. 2007. *Four Views on Free Will.* Blackwell.

Fischer, J.M., and M. Ravizza. 1998. *Responsibility and Control: A Theory of Moral Responsibility.* Cambridge University Press.

Fleeson, W. 2001. "Toward a Structure-and Process-Integrated View of Personality: Traits as Density Distributions of States." *Journal of Personality and Social Psychology* 80 (6): 1011–1027.

Foot, P. 1972. "Morality as a System of Hypothetical Imperatives." *The Philosophical Review* 81 (3): 305–316.

———. 2001. *Natural Goodness.* Oxford University Press.

———. 2002/1967. "The Problem of Abortion and the Doctrine of Double Effect." Reprinted in *Virtues and Vices and Other Essays in Moral Philosophy.* Oxford University Press: 19–32.

Frankfurt, H.G. 1971. "Freedom of the Will and the Concept of a Person." *The Journal of Philosophy:* 5–20.

———. 1988. *The Importance of What We Care about: Philosophical Essays.* Cambridge University Press.

Frankish, K. 2010. "Dual-Process and Dual-System Theories of Reasoning." *Philosophy Compass* 5 (10): 914–926.

Gauthier, D. P. 1986. *Morals by Agreement.* Oxford University Press.

Gibbard, A. 1992. *Wise Choices, Apt Feelings: A Theory of Normative Judgment.* Oxford University Press.

———. 2006. "Moral Feelings and Moral Concepts." *Oxford Studies in Metaethics* 1: 195–215.

Goldie, P. 2007. "Emotion." *Philosophy Compass* 2 (6): 928–938.

Goldman, A. 2012. "A Liberal Learns To Compete." *The New York Times* magazine, July 27. www.nytimes.com/2012/07/29/magazine/a-liberal-learns-to-compete.html.

Greene, J. Forthcoming. "Beyond Point-and-Shoot Morality: Why Cognitive (Neuro)Science Matters for Ethics." *Ethics.*

———. 2013. *Moral Tribes: Emotion, Reason, and the Gap Between Us and Them.* Penguin Press.

Greene, J., F. Cushman, L. Stewart, K. Lowenberg, L. Nystrom and J. Cohen. 2009. "Pushing Moral Buttons: The Interaction between Personal Force and Intention in Moral Judgment." *Cognition* 111 (3): 364–371.

Haidt, J. 2001. "The Emotional Dog and Its Rational Tail: A Social Intuitionist Approach to Moral Judgment." *Psychological Review* 108 (4): 814–834.

———. 2007. "The new synthesis in moral psychology.? *Science* 316 (5827): 998–1002.

———. 2012. *The Righteous Mind: Why Good People Are Divided by Politics and Religion.* Penguin.

Haidt, J., and J. Baron. 1996. "Social Roles and the Moral Judgement of Acts and Omissions." *European Journal of Social Psychology* 26 (2): 201–218.

Haidt, J., and F. Bjorklund. 2008. "Social Intuitionists Answer Six Questions about Morality." In *Moral Psychology,* vol. 2, W. Sinnott-Armstrong (ed), 181–217. MIT Press.

Halberstadt, J.B., and T. Wilson. 2008. "Reflections on Conscious Reflection: Mechanisms of Impairment by Reasons Analysis." In *Reasoning: Studies of Human Inference and Its Foundations,* J. Adler and L. Rips (eds), 548–565. Cambridge University Press.

Hare, R. D., and H. Vertommen. 2003. *The Hare Psychopathy Checklist-Revised.* Multi-Health Systems.

Harman, G. 1999. "Moral Philosophy Meets Social Psychology: Virtue Ethics and the Fundamental Attribution Error." *Proceedings of the Aristotelian Society* 99: 315–331.

Harris, S. 2011. *The Moral Landscape: How Science Can Determine Human Values.* Simon and Schuster.

Haybron, D. M. 2008. *The Pursuit of Unhappiness: The Elusive Psychology of Well-Being.* Oxford University Press.

Heathwood, C. 2007. "The Reduction of Sensory Pleasure to Desire." *Philosophical Studies* 133 (1): 23–44.

———. 2011. "Preferentism and Self-Sacrifice." *Pacific Philosophical Quarterly* 92 (1): 18–38.

Herman, B. 1981. "On the Value of Acting from the Motive of Duty." *The Philosophical Review* 90 (3): 359–382.

Hill, T. E. 1992. *Dignity and Practical Reason in Kant's Moral Theory.* Cornell University Press.

Hobbes, T. 1994/1651. *Leviathan: With Selected Variants from the Latin Edition of 1668,* Edwin Curley (ed). Hackett Publishing Company.

Hume, D. 2000/1739. *A Treatise of Human Nature.* D. F. Norton and M. J. Norton (eds). Oxford University Press.

Hursthouse, R. 1999. *On Virtue Ethics.* Oxford University Press.

———. 2013. "Virtue Ethics." *The Stanford Encyclopedia of Philosophy*, Fall 2013 ed. http://plato.stanford.edu/archives/win2010/entries/ethics-virtue/.

Isen, A. M., and P. F. Levin. 1972. "Effect of Feeling Good on Helping: Cookies and Kindness." *Journal of Personality and Social Psychology* 21 (3): 384–388.

Jacobson, D. 2011. "Fitting Attitude Theories of Value." In *The Stanford Encyclopedia of Philosophy*, Edward N. Zalta (ed). http://plato.stanford.edu/archives/spr2011/entries/fitting-attitude-theories/.

Jayawickreme, E., Peter Meindl, E. G. Helzer, R. M. Furr and W. Fleeson. 2014. (Invited and under review). "Virtuous States and Virtuous Traits: How the Empirical Evidence Regarding the Existence of Broad Traits Does Not Undermine Virtue Ethics." *Theory and Research in Education* 12 (3).

John, O. P., R. W. Robins and L. A. Pervin. 2008. *Handbook of Personality: Theory and Research.* The Guilford Press.

Johnson, R. N. 1999. "Internal Reasons and the Conditional Fallacy." *The Philosophical Quarterly* 49 (194): 53–72.

Jones, E. E., and V. A. Harris. 1967. "The Attribution of Attitudes." *Journal of Experimental Social Psychology* 3 (1): 1–24.

Jones, K. 2006. "Metaethics and Emotions Research: A Response to Prinz." *Philosophical Explorations* 9 (1): 45–53.

Joyce, R. 2006. *The Evolution of Morality.* MIT Press.

Kamtekar, R. 2004. "Situationism and Virtue Ethics on the Content of Our Character." *Ethics* 114 (3): 458–491.

Kane, R. 2007. "Libertarianism." In *Four Views on Free Will,* J. M. Fischer, R. Kane, D. Pereboom and M. Vargas (eds), 5–43. Blackwell. www.thedivineconspiracy.org/Z5217X.pdf.

Kant, I. 2002/1785. *Groundwork for the Metaphysics of Morals,* A. Zweig (trans), T. E. Hill, Jr. and A. Zweig (eds). Oxford University Press.

Keim, B. 2012. "Brain Scanners Can See Your Decisions Before You Make Them." *WIRED.* www.wired.com/science/discoveries/news/2008/04/mind_decision.

Kelly, D. R. 2011. *Yuck!: The Nature and Moral Significance of Disgust.* MIT Press.

Kennett, J. 2006. "Do Psychopaths Really Threaten Moral Rationalism?" *Philosophical Explorations* 9 (1): 69–82.

Keteyian, A. 2010. "Madoff Victims Vent Their Anger In Print." *CBS News.* March 18. www. cbsnews.com/8301-500690_162-5090670.html.

Kitcher, P. 2011. *The Ethical Project.* Harvard University Press.

Korsgaard, C. M. 1996. *The Sources of Normativity.* Cambridge University Press.

Kraut, R. 2009. *What Is Good and Why: The Ethics of Well-Being.* Harvard University Press.

Latane, B., and J. M. Darley. 1970. *The Unresponsive Bystander: Why Doesn't He Help?* Appleton-Century Crofts.

Lazarus, R. S. 1991. "Cognition and Motivation in Emotion." *American Psychologist* 46 (4): 352–367.

Lerner, J. S., J. H. Goldberg and P. E. Tetlock. 1998. "Sober Second Thought: The Effects of Accountability, Anger, and Authoritarianism on Attributions of Responsibility." *Personality and Social Psychology Bulletin* 24 (6): 563–574.

Libet, B. 1985. "Unconscious Cerebral Initiative and the Role of Conscious Will in Voluntary Action." *Behavioral and Brain Sciences* 8 (4): 529–566.

Little, M. O. 1997. "Virtue as Knowledge: Objections from the Philosophy of Mind." *Nous* 31 (1): 59–79.

Lyubomirsky, S. 2008. *The How of Happiness: A Scientific Approach to Getting the Life You Want.* Penguin.

Machery, E., and R. Mallon. 2010. "Evolution of Morality." In *The Moral Psychology Handbook*, J. Doris and the Moral Psychology Research Group (eds), 3–46. Oxford University Press.

Mackie, J. 1990. *Ethics: Inventing Right and Wrong.* Penguin.

McCann, K. 2012. "Altruistic Donation: 'I Could Save a Life—and That's All That Matters'." *The Telegraph,* November 22.

McDowell, J. 1979. "Virtue and Reason." *Monist* 62 (3): 331–350.

Mele, A. R. 2006. *Free Will and Luck.* Oxford University Press.

Merritt, M. 2000. "Virtue Ethics and Situationist Personality Psychology." *Ethical Theory and Moral Practice* 3 (4): 365–383.

Milgram, S. 1963. "Behavioral Study of Obedience." *The Journal of Abnormal and Social Psychology* 67 (4): 371–378.

———. 1974. *Obedience to Authority: An Experimental View.* HarperCollins.

Miller, C. 2013. *Moral Character: An Empirical Theory.* Oxford University Press.

———. 2014. *Character and Moral Psychology.* Oxford University Press.

Nagel, T. 1970. *The Possibility of Altruism.* Clarendon Press.

Nahmias, E. 2011. "Scientific Challenges to Free Will." In *A Companion to the Philosophy of Action,* T. O'Connor and S. Constantine (eds), 345–356. John Wiley & Sons.

———. 2012a. "The Psychology of Free Will." *The Oxford Handbook on the Philosophy of Psychology.* Oxford University Press. www2.gsu.edu/~phlean/papers/Nahmias_Psychology_of_Free_Will_prepublication.pdf.

———. 2012b. "Free Will and Responsibility." *Wiley Interdisciplinary Reviews: Cognitive Science* 3 (4): 439–449.

Nahmias, E., S. G. Morris, T. Nadelhoffer and J. Turner. 2007. "Is Incompatibilism Intuitive?" *Philosophy and Phenomenological Research* 73 (1): 28–53.

Nichols, S. 2002a. "How Psychopaths Threaten Moral Rationalism." *The Monist* 85 (2): 285–303.

———. 2002b. "Norms with Feeling: Towards a Psychological Account of Moral Judgment." *Cognition* 84: 221–236.

———. 2004. *Sentimental Rules: On the Natural Foundations of Moral Judgment,* vol. 13. Oxford University Press.

Nichols, S., and J. Knobe. 2007. "Moral Responsibility and Determinism: The Cognitive Science of Folk Intuitions." *Nous* 41 (4): 663–685.

Nisbett, R. E., and T. D. Wilson. 1977. "Telling More than We Can Know: Verbal Reports on Mental Processes." *Psychological Review* 84 (3): 231–259.

Nozick, R. 1974. *Anarchy, State, and Utopia.* Basic Books.

Nussbaum, M. C. 1995. "Aristotle on Human Nature and the Foundations of Ethics." In *World, Mind, and Ethics: Essays on the Ethical Philosophy of Bernard Williams,* J. E. J. Althan and R. Harrison (eds), 86–131. Cambridge University Press.

———. 2001. *Women and Human Development: The Capabilities Approach,* Cambridge University Press.

———. 2003. *Upheavals of Thought: The Intelligence of Emotions.* Cambridge University Press.

———. 2009. *Hiding from Humanity: Disgust, Shame, and the Law.* Princeton University Press.

Pereboom, D. 2001. *Living without Free Will.* Cambridge University Press.

Petrinovich, L., and P. O'Neill. 1996. "Influence of Wording and Framing Effects on Moral Intuitions." *Ethology and Sociobiology* 17 (3): 145–171.

Piliavin, J. A. 2003. "Doing Well by Doing Good: Benefits for the Benefactor." In *Flourishing: Positive Psychology and the Life Well-Lived,* C. L. M. Keyes and J. Haidt (eds), 227–247. American Psychological Association.

Prinz, J. 2004a. "Embodied Emotions." In *Thinking about Feeling: Contemporary Philosophers on Emotions,* R. C. Solomon (ed), 44–58. Oxford University Press.

———. 2004b. *Gut Reactions: A Perceptual Theory of Emotion.* Oxford University Press, USA.

———. 2006. "The Emotional Basis of Moral Judgments." *Philosophical Explorations* 9 (1): 29–43.

———. 2007. *The Emotional Construction of Morals.* Oxford University Press.

———. 2012. *Beyond Human Nature: How Culture and Experience Shape Our Lives.* Penguin.

Raibley, J. 2010. "Well-Being and the Priority of Values." *Social Theory and Practice* 36 (4): 593–620.

Railton, P. 1984. "Alienation, Consequentialism, and the Demands of Morality." *Philosophy and Public Affairs* 13 (2): 134–171.

———. 1986. "Moral Realism." *The Philosophical Review* 95 (2): 163–207.

Rawls, J. 1951. "Outline of a Decision Procedure for Ethics." *The Philosophical Review* 60 (2): 177–197.

———. 1971. *A Theory of Justice.* Harvard University Press.

———. 1980. "Kantian Constructivism in Moral Theory." *The Journal of Philosophy* 77 (9): 515–572.

Roberts, R. C. 2003. *Emotions: An Essay in Aid of Moral Psychology.* Cambridge University Press.

Rosati, C. S. 2009. "Self-Interest and Self-Sacrifice." *Proceedings of the Aristotelian Society* 109: 311–325.

———. 2011. "Moral Motivation." In *The Stanford Encyclopedia of Philosophy,* E. N. Zalta (ed). http://plato.stanford.edu/entries/moral-motivation/.

Roskies, A. 2003. "Are Ethical Judgments Intrinsically Motivational? Lessons from 'Acquired Sociopathy'." *Philosophical Psychology* 16 (1): 51–66.

———. 2008. "Neuroimaging and Inferential Distance." *Neuroethics* 1 (1): 19–30.

———. 2010. "Why Libet's Studies Don't Pose a Threat to Free Will." In *Conscious Will and Responsibility: A Tribute to Benjamin Libet,* W. Sinnott-Armstrong and L. Nadel (eds), 11–22. Oxford University Press.

Ross, L. 1977. "The Intuitive Psychologist and His Shortcomings: Distortions in the Attribution Process." *Advances in Experimental Social Psychology* 10: 173–220.

Ryan, R. M., and E. L. Deci. 2001. "On Happiness and Human Potentials: A Review of Research on Hedonic and Eudaimonic Well-Being." *Annual Review of Psychology* 52 (1): 141–166.

Scanlon, T. M. 1982. "Contractualism and Utilitarianism." In *Utilitarianism and Beyond*, A. Sen and B. Williams (eds), 103, 110. Cambridge University Press.

———. 1998. *What We Owe to Each Other.* The Belknap Press of Harvard University Press.

Schachter, S., and J. Singer. 1962. "Cognitive, Social, and Physiological Determinants of Emotional State." *Psychological Review* 69 (5): 379–399.

Scherer, K. R. 2000. "Psychological Models of Emotion." In *The Neuropsychology of Emotion*, Joan C. Borod (ed), 137–162. Oxford University Press.

———. 2005. "What Are Emotions? And How Can They Be Measured?" *Social Science Information* 44 (4): 695–729.

Schnall, S., J. Haidt, G. L. Clore and A. H. Jordan. 2008. "Disgust as Embodied Moral Judgment." *Personality and Social Psychology Bulletin* 34 (8): 1096–1109.

Schroeder, M. A. 2007. *Slaves of the Passions.* Oxford University Press.

Schroeder, T. 2004. *Three Faces of Desire.* Oxford University Press.

———. 2006. "Desire." *Philosophy Compass* 1 (6): 631–639.

Schwitzgebel, E. 2011. "Bartels and Pizarro: Consequentialists Are Psychopaths." *The Splintered Mind.* http://schwitzsplinters.blogspot.com/2011/09/bartels-and-pizarro-consequentialists.html.

Seidel, A., and J. Prinz. 2013. "Sound Morality: Irritating and Icky Noises Amplify Judgments in Divergent Moral Domains." *Cognition* 127 (1): 1–5.

Seligman, M. E. P. 2002. *Authentic Happiness: Using the New Positive Psychology to Realize Your Potential for Lasting Fulfillment.* Simon & Schuster.

Shafer-Landau, R. 2003. *Moral Realism: A Defence.* Oxford University Press.

———. 2008. "Defending Ethical Intuitionism." In *Moral Psychology*, vol. 2, W. Sinnott-Armstrong (ed), 83–96. MIT Press.

———. 2012. "Evolutionary Debunking, Moral Realism and Moral Knowledge." *Journal of Ethics & Social Philosophy* 7: 1–37.

Shenhav, A. and J. Greene. 2014. "Integrative Moral Judgment: Dissociating the Roles of the Amygdala and Ventromedial Prefrontal Cortex." *The Journal of Neuroscience* 34 (13): 4741–4749.

Sin, N. L., and S. Lyubomirsky. 2009. "Enhancing Well-Being and Alleviating Depressive Symptoms with Positive Psychology Interventions: A Practice-Friendly Meta-Analysis." *Journal of Clinical Psychology* 65 (5): 467–487.

Singer, P. 1972. "Famine, Affluence, and Morality." *Philosophy & Public Affairs* 1 (3): 229–243.

Sinnott-Armstrong, W. 2008. "Framing Moral Intuitions." In *Moral Psychology, Vol. 2: The Cognitive Science of Morality: Intuitions and Diversity*, W. Sinott-Armstrong (ed), 47–76. MIT Press.

———, ed. 2014. *Moral Psychology, Vol. 4: Freedom and Responsibility.* MIT Press.

Slater, L. 2004. *Opening Skinner's Box: Great Psychological Experiments of the Twentieth Century.* W. W. Norton & Company.

Smetana, J. G. 1981. "Preschool Children's Conceptions of Moral and Social Rules." *Child Development* 52: 1333–1336.

———. 1993. "Understanding of Social Rules." In *The Development of Social Cognition: The Child as Psychologist*, M. Bennett (ed), 111–141. Guilford Press.

Smith, M. 1987. "The Humean Theory of Motivation." *Mind* 96 (381). New Series (January 1): 36–61.

———. 1995a. "Internal Reasons." *Philosophy and Phenomenological Research* 55 (1) 109–131.

———. 1995b. *The Moral Problem.* Blackwell.

Snow, N. E. 2010. *Virtue as Social Intelligence: An Empirically Grounded Theory.* Routledge.

Sober, E., and D. S. Wilson. 1998. *Unto Others: The Evolution and Psychology of Unselfish Behavior.* Harvard University Press.

Solomon, R. C. 1973. "Emotions and Choice." *The Review of Metaphysics* 27 (1): 20–41.

Sommers, T. 2005. "Interview with Jonathan Haidt." *The Believer.* www.believermag.com/issues/200508/?read=interview_haidt.

Sousa, R. De. 1979. "The Rationality of Emotions." *Dialogue* 18 (1): 41–63.

Steinberg, D. 2003. "Kidneys and the Kindness of Strangers." *Health Affairs* 22 (4): 184–189.

Stich, S. 2007. "Evolution, Altruism and Cognitive Architecture: A Critique of Sober and Wilson's Argument for Psychological Altruism." *Biology & Philosophy* 22 (2): 267–281.

Stich, S., J. M. Doris and E. Roedder. 2010. "Altruism." In *The Moral Psychology Handbook,* J. Doris (ed), 147–206. Oxford University Press.

Stocker, M. 1976. "The Schizophrenia of Modern Ethical Theories." *The Journal of Philosophy* 73 (14): 453–466.

Stocks, E. L., D. A. Lishner and S. K. Decker. 2009. "Altruism or Psychological Escape: Why Does Empathy Promote Prosocial Behavior?" *European Journal of Social Psychology* 39 (5): 649–665.

Strawson, P. F. 2008. *Freedom and Resentment and Other Essays.* Routledge.

Street, S. 2006. "A Darwinian Dilemma for Realist Theories of Value." *Philosophical Studies* 127 (1): 109–166.

———. 2010. "What Is Constructivism in Ethics and Metaethics?" *Philosophy Compass* 5 (5): 363–384.

Sumner, L. 1996. *Welfare, Happiness, and Ethics.* Oxford University Press.

Swartwood, J. D. 2013. "Wisdom as an Expert Skill." *Ethical Theory and Moral Practice* 16 (3): 511–528.

Thoits, P. A., and L. N. Hewitt. 2001. "Volunteer Work and Well-Being." *Journal of Health and Social Behavior* 42 (June): 115–131.

Thomson, J. J. 1976. "Killing, Letting Die, and the Trolley Problem." *The Monist* 59 (2): 204–217.

———. 2008. "Turning the Trolley." *Philosophy & Public Affairs* 36 (4): 359–374.

Tiberius, V. 2008. *The Reflective Life: Living Wisely with Our Limits.* Oxford University Press.

———. 2009. "The Reflective Life: Wisdom and Happiness for Real People." In *Philosophy and Happiness,* L. Bortolotti (ed), 215–232. Palgrave Macmillan.

———. 2013. "In Defense of Reflection." *Philosophical Issues* 23 (1): 223–243.

Tversky, A., and D. Kahneman. 1981. "The Framing of Decisions and the Psychology of Choice." *Science* 211 (4481): 453–458.

Twain, M. 1994/1884. *Adventures of Huckleberry Finn.* Dover Publications.

Wallace, R. J. 1990. "How to Argue about Practical Reason." *Mind* 99: 355–385.

———. 1994. *Responsibility and the Moral Sentiments.* Harvard University Press.

Weinstein, N., and R. M. Ryan. 2010. "When Helping Helps: Autonomous Motivation for Prosocial Behavior and Its Influence on Well-Being for the Helper and Recipient." *Journal of Personality and Social Psychology* 98 (2): 222–244.

Wheatley, T., and J. Haidt. 2005. "Hypnotic Disgust Makes Moral Judgments More Severe." *Psychological Science* 16 (10): 780–784.

Wiggins, D. 1987. *Needs, Values, Truth: Essays in the Philosophy of Value.* Oxford.

Williams, B. 1981. *Moral Luck: Philosophical Papers 1973–1980*. Cambridge University Press.

Wilson, T. D. 2002. *Strangers to Ourselves: Discovering the Adaptive Unconscious*. Harvard University Press.

Wilson, T. D., and D. Kraft. 1993. "Why Do I Love Thee?: Effects of Repeated Introspections about a Dating Relationship on Attitudes toward the Relationship." *Personality and Social Psychology Bulletin* 19 (4): 409–418.

Wilson, T. D., D. Kraft, and D. S. Dunn. 1989. "The Disruptive Effects of Explaining Attitudes: The Moderating Effect of Knowledge about the Attitude Object." *Journal of Experimental Social Psychology* 25 (5): 379–400.

Wilson, T. D., D. J. Lisle, J. W. Schooler, S. D. Hodges, K. J. Klaaren and S. J. LaFleur. 1993. "Introspecting about Reasons Can Reduce Post-Choice Satisfaction." *Personality and Social Psychology Bulletin* 19: 331–331.

Wilson, T. D., and R. E. Nisbett. 1978. "The Accuracy of Verbal Reports about the Effects of Stimuli on Evaluations and Behavior." *Social Psychology*. http://psycnet.apa.org/psycinfo/1980-24471-001.

Wolf, S. 1980. "Asymmetrical Freedom." *The Journal of Philosophy* 77 (3): 151–166.

———. 1981. "The Importance of Free Will." *Mind* 90 (359): 386–405.

———. 1990. *Freedom within Reason*. Oxford University Press.

Index